The Environment, Sustainable Development and Public Policies

The Environment, Sustainable Development and Public Policies

Building Sustainability in Brazil

Edited by

Clóvis Cavalcanti

Director, Instituto de Pesquisas Sociais, Fundação Joaquim Nabuco, Brazil

Edward Elgar
Cheltenham, UK • Northampton, MA, USA

© Clóvis Cavalcanti, 2000

Published by
Edward Elgar Publishing Limited
Glensanda House
Montpellier Parade
Cheltenham
Glos GL50 1UA
UK

Edward Elgar Publishing, Inc.
136 West Street
Suite 202
Northampton
Massachusetts 01060
USA

A catalogue record for this book
is available from the British Library

Library of Congress Cataloguing in Publication Data
The environment, sustainable development, and public policies :
    building sustainability in Brazil / edited by Clóvis Cavalcanti.
        Includes index.
            1. Sustainable development—Brazil. 2. Brazil—Economic policy.
    I. Cavalcanti, Clóvis de Vasconcelos.
    HC190.E5E58 1999
    333.7—dc21   99–12142
                                                                     CIP

ISBN 1 84064 018 9

Printed and bound in Great Britain by Bookcraft (Bath) Ltd.

Contents

Contents

Figures

Tables

Contributors

Alpina Begossi, Brazilian, biologist, senior researcher at NEPAM, University of Campinas (UNICAMP), Brazil. *Areas of interest*: human ecology, bio-sociology.

Hans Christoph Binswanger, Swiss, economist, professor at the Institute for Economy and the Environment, University of St Gallen, Switzerland. *Areas of interest*: economics and ecology, general economics.

Clóvis Cavalcanti, Brazilian, ecological economist, senior social researcher and director of the Institute for Social Research at the Joaquim Nabuco Foundation, Brazil. *Areas of interest*: economics of sustainability, development, public policy.

Herman E. Daly, American, economist, senior research scholar at the School of Public Affairs, University of Maryland, USA. Recipient of 1996 Heinecken Prize (The Netherlands). *Areas of interest*: ecological economics, sustainable development policy.

Salah El Serafy, Egyptian, economist. Formerly at the World Bank. Presently a consultant, USA. *Area of interest*: integrated economic and environmental accounting.

Malte Faber, German, mathematician and economist. Professor of economic theory at the Alfred Weber Institute, University of Heidelberg, Germany. *Areas of interest*: capital theory, ecological economics, thermodynamics, economics and philosophy, political economy.

Philip M. Fearnside, American, ecologist, senior researcher at the National Institute for Research of the Amazon (INPA), Brazil. *Areas of interest*: human carrying capacity, climate changes, impacts of deforestation, sustainability of Amazonia.

Frank Jöst, German, economist, professor at the University of Heidelberg, Germany. *Areas of interest*: ecological economics, population growth and sustainability.

Héctor Ricardo Leis, Brazilian, political scientist, professor at the Federal University of Santa Catarina, Brazil. *Areas of interest*: environmental policy, political theory, environmentalism.

Reiner Manstetten, German, philosopher and philologist, assistant at the Department of Economics, University of Heidelberg, Germany. *Areas of interest*: philosophical foundations of ecology and economics, philosophy of mysticism.

Peter H. May, American, economist, professor at the Federal Rural University of Rio de Janeiro, Brazil. *Areas of interest*: economics of natural resources, agroecology, property rights, eco-efficiency.

Richard B. Norgaard, American, economist, professor at the University of California-Berkeley, USA. President of the International Society for Ecological Economics (ISEE). *Areas of interest*: evolutionary economics, values.

Darrell A. Posey, American, anthropologist, researcher at the Goeldi Museum, Belém, Brazil. Now at the University of Oxford, UK. *Areas of interest*: ethnoscience, traditional resources rights.

John L. R. Proops, British, physicist and mathematician, doctorate on the application of concepts from modern thermodynamics to the structural evolution of economic systems. Professor of ecological economics at Keele University. *Areas of interest*: energy modelling, application of concepts from thermodynamics in economic analysis.

Sérgio C. Trindade, Brazilian, chemical engineer. Former UN assistant secretary-general for science and technology. Presently a consultant at SE^2T International in New York, USA. *Areas of interest*: management of change, energy, sustainable technology and development.

Acknowledgements

Financial support for the work leading to the publication of this book was provided by Brazil's Ministry of the Environment, Water Resources, and the Legal Amazon (MMA), through the Brazilian Institute for the Environment and Renewable Natural Resources (IBAMA), and by the Joaquim Nabuco Foundation. Thanks are due especially to minister Gustavo Krause, to the then president of IBAMA, and now minister for the Agrarian Reform, Raul Jungmann, and to Fernando de Mello Freyre, president of the Nabuco Foundation, for their incentive.

Inside the Institute for Social Research of the Joaquim Nabuco Foundation where this book was produced, Cláudia Braga deserves especial thanks for her professional support and expertise along the different stages of preparation of the manuscript.

Recife, October 1999.

Clóvis Cavalcanti, Editor

1. Government Policy for Sustainable Development: Building Sustainability in Brazil

Clóvis Cavalcanti

1. AN INTRODUCTION TO THE THEME AND TO THIS BOOK

This book assembles papers written for the workshop on 'The Environment, Development and Government Policy: Basis for Building a Sustainable Society in Brazil (Taking Nature into Account)', organised and directed by the editor in Olinda, Brazil, in April 1996. This meeting, which took place under the aegis of the Institute for Social Research of the Joaquim Nabuco Foundation, was made possible thanks to financial support provided by Brazil's Ministry of the Environment, Water Resources and the Legal Amazon (MMA) and the Brazilian Institute for the Environment and Renewable Natural Resources (IBAMA). Its origins can be traced to a conversation I had in July 1995 with minister Gustavo Krause (of MMA) about the subject of sustainability, when I made an exposition of the (thermodynamic) view of ecological economics regarding the issue of sustainable development. Minister Krause then asked me to set up a workshop with distinguished people doing research on the subject, so that an exchange of information and of distinct perspectives about sustainability could take place with a view to policymaking for building a sustainable society in Brazil (taking nature into account). A number of people accepted the invitation I made for them to come to the workshop (following minister Krause's proposal) and to write a paper according to some guidelines which I gave them (especially concerning the preoccupation with formulating public policies committed to the goal of sustainable development).[1]

The present volume includes, besides this first chapter, eleven papers written in accordance with the rules set by the editor. They were selected for being more in line with the workshop's general orientation and its emphasis on Brazil. This by no means diminishes the relevance of the content of the papers which were excluded from the book (see references at the end of this chapter). Their exclusion is also due to the fact that many required significant further work for completion according to the needs of the book.

Behind the ample diversity of disciplines and theoretical perspectives of the workshop texts and of those which figure in this book there exists, thus, a common ground that somehow unifies them; namely, the *concern with the formulation of public policies for sustainable development in Brazil.* It is not a question of listing rules or providing recipes for reaching sustainability – this, after all, is an impossibility in the complex world of human societies, where each situation, from the one of an indigenous group living remotely in the Amazon to the model of the US modern lifestyle, has its own, peculiar challenges which it is necessary to understand before anything is proposed. However, this does not impede thinking about principles, searching for references, or building a framework of orientations to the process of decision-making in the real world taking nature into account (an activity that is not by necessity restricted only to the governmental sphere). It was precisely this search for references concerning sustainability that constituted the workshop's *leitmotiv*. It also directed the preparation of this book.

It is a general perception in many areas of human endeavour that the world faces today a critical crossroads. Modes of economic organisation which destroy natural resources are becoming ever more unsustainable, since in the context of biophysical reality – on which the economy crucially depends – only those processes which behave according to the principles of the functioning of the biosphere (among which frugality is a paramount one) can last indefinitely. Observing the landscape of the real world, in which a finite ecosystem encompasses a growing economy and shelters exponentially expanding numbers of people, it is inescapable that a reflection be made about the theme of sustainability, about the type of development which the French call '*durable*'. Sustainable development is generally alluded to in everybody's current discourse, chiefly as a by-product of the Earth Summit (Rio-92). The subject is treated, though, on several occasions, with a meaning which contradicts its own essence, transforming it to an authentic oxymoron. It is here that science should be called on to explain the significance of this idea and to indicate the serious implications that result from it. It was with such a compass, turned to the construction of a sustainable society in Brazil which takes Mother Nature duly into account, that the Olinda workshop was convened.

In the remainder of this chapter, a comprehensive view of the topics covered in the discussions of the workshop is offered as a general introduction to this volume. It begins with the basic motivations of the requirements of sustainability (section 2). Then, in section 3, the co-ordinates of public policies for sustainability are outlined. Section 4 indicates possible lines of action to reach sustainable development. A final section follows with some conclusions. Obviously, the panorama which this chapter exhibits reflects how the author (and book's editor) understands the subject. It is not intended to represent either an impossible unanimity among the workshop participants or even a dominant tendency among them in relation to the topics under discussion. Maybe this is why several notions of sustainability can be found in the book.

2. BASIC WORRIES

As a developing country (or 'emerging market', in present day jargon), it is obvious that Brazil has to pay more attention to principles of an adequate husbandry of its natural resources. More than that, it has to devise ways to promote human welfare without accepting that its natural capital is used or degraded as if it were almost nothing.

In fact, Brazil faces up to the challenge of fighting poverty with due consideration to the environmental costs involved as part of development policies. Up to now, however, and in spite of a rhetoric (in more recent times) of sustainability on the part of the government, what has prevailed are initiatives that do not take nature properly into account. In the past, natural resources in the country have traditionally been exploited to exhaustion (Cavalcanti, 1991). A case in point is a 42-million ton reserve of manganese in the Amazon state of Amapá which, from 1957 to the mid-1990s, was completely emptied (Brito, 1994). Each year, over less than four decades, around 1 million tons of manganese ore, on average, were mined, generating annual export earnings of US 40 million dollars or so, of which only 4 percent represented royalty payments on the reserve (US 1.6 million dollars yearly). Clearly, a strategy of development cannot be based on such a predatory approach without any sizeable compensation for the loss of natural capital that is incurred.

As a matter of fact, the environmental question that has to be dealt with in relation to development initiatives does not boil down to merely exploiting non-renewable resources parsimoniously. A *distinct* view of the economic process is required, taking into account the *biophysical dimension*, the laws and principles of nature. The elaboration of rules for sustainable development has to come to grips with the fact that conventional economics does not take the ecological base of the economic system into account within its analytical framework, which has led to a belief in unbounded growth. Sustainability, in turn, implies a definite limitation in growth possibilities. It is on this foundation that it is indispensable that ecological (or eco-social) concerns be attached to public policies in Brazil. It is necessary to show that the economic process cannot go unpunished if it violates the rules that guide nature to maximum efficiency (as to the use of matter and energy), minimum stress and losses, to frugality and ecological prudence. The irreversible loss of natural capital – as in the case of the manganese from Amapá – constitutes a cost passed on to future generations, aggravated by the way the consumption of assets is considered as income in the prevailing systems of national accounts (see on the subject, in this book, Chapter 6 by Daly, and Chapter 7 by El Serafy). For 40 years Brazil was being deprived forever of an ore which is not so easily found around the world, and this counted positively in terms of GDP. The same happens with respect to other source and sink functions of the ecosystem. It is with this perception in mind that a set of new policies for development must be devised.

But what sort of policies are those and how should they be formulated? Of course, there is no finished recipe with which to provide an answer to this question. What can be said tentatively is that the true environmental problem consists precisely of raising the productivity of nature's capital, using its stocks soundly, without overcharging the *source* and *sink* functions of the ecosystem. This is a general, rather vague orientation. But it is also a starting point for the consideration of the *ecological limitation* imposed by nature on the economic process. Restrictions and constraints are, in effect, what one finds when trying to understand how development can be promoted within the framing of the ecosphere, chiefly if one considers the inexorable laws of conservation of matter and energy, and of entropy. It is here that the great challenge of sustainable development must be faced up to by intelligent policies – policies that may lead to an actual improvement in the living conditions of poor people without disturbing basic ecosystem functions. In sum, development policy cannot neglect the relationships between man and nature that dictate what is *possible* ahead of what is *desirable*.

3. PRINCIPLES BEHIND POLICIES FOR SUSTAINABILITY

The first principle to be stressed in the context of policies for sustainable development is that, since growth always means some environmental degradation (Georgescu-Roegen, 1974), the economic process has to use nature on a more enduring, sounder basis than has been the practice up to now. Although, rigorously, one should not confuse growth (expansion) with development (realisation of potential) – as some people have stressed (Daly, 1991) – it is undeniable that the talk about development in a country like Brazil always means increasing *per capita* income indefinitely, and this is perceived as growth. It would be nice if the latter actually implied reducing (or, even better, eliminating) poverty permanently. This is not, unfortunately, what has happened on the scale both of Brazil and the world at large.[2]

Furthermore, one witnesses nowadays, all over the world, the phenomenon of 'jobless growth' (Sheng, 1996) with increasing inequality and squalor almost everywhere. The search for sustainable development mirrors the incompetence of the modern economy to allow masses of people to overcome what I have called elsewhere 'the blockade of poverty' (Cavalcanti, 1988), as well as the need to consider 'finitude, entropy, and ecological dependence' (Daly and Cobb, 1994: 199).

Scale of the economy is the second reference that has to be alluded to in relation to principles for sustainability. If, rightly, the economic system is to be seen as a subsystem of the ecosystem, and if the latter is a nongrowing entity, there is an absolute scale of natural resource flows that has to be considered in the expansion of the economy. This may suggest insensitivity concerning the fate of the poor (who, presumably, need economic growth to escape from poverty). However, instead of condemning them to remain so, the issue of scale should be interpreted as a challenge to the rich to face up to the moral obligation of *division* of the pie (Fearnside, Chapter 11 in this book). The world situation shows that there are countries and social groups whose 'environmental space' exceeds, in some cases greatly so, their territory (Martínez-Alier, 1996).[3] This is an instance of excessive scale being appropriated by given countries and social groups at the expense of some other countries and social groups (unequal distribution), thus requiring that a principle be established concerning the optimal scale of the economy that can be adopted and shared more equally. Of course, the Earth has only one optimal scale that is conceivable at any one time – given the technology, consumer preferences, and so on – as the choice that can be made by the economic system. Social groups and countries may negotiate their environmental space, selling or buying part of it, but there are limits and trade-offs which cannot be disregarded for both the present and future generations. The use of nature cannot disrespect the scale of the ecological functions and the ecocycles. This surely must be a guiding principle for the sake of sustainable development.

The issue of scale is intimately related to the concept of the carrying capacity of the ecosphere (see Begossi, Chapter 3). The latter, and resilience, limits and sustainability, are ecological categories with an enormous significance in terms of the relationships between the economic process and the ecosystem. Government policy toward sustainable development cannot ignore them. Much to the contrary, it has to link public initiatives with the co-ordinates set by the natural functions and processes which indicate the limits of the possible. It is thus a cause for concern that the neo-classical framework of economics – which forms the basis in general of economists' reasoning, and therefore presides over the adoption of development proposals everywhere – does not pay attention to the environmental foundations for the achievement of human well-being, ruling out limits. Such a neglect leads to the acceptance of infinite growth unhindered by ecological limitations, arousing unfounded expectations in common people. It makes it possible, too, to treat nature as simply another factor of production, which the aggregate production function, in turn, normally leaves aside (Binswanger, Chapter 2 in this book). Not only must nature – or matter and energy – be treated as the primordial factor of production, but the human-induced material turnover has to be set in correspondence with the natural cycles. Material flows which are not subject to control represent a permanent risk, implying that one has to think about putting restrictions on society's exchange with nature, on throughput (Eriksson, 1996). In other words, the carrying capacity of the ecosystem cannot be ignored.

The question becomes more acute when one empirically verifies that increasing amounts of natural capital are required to deliver a given unit of resource to society, as several studies on the biophysical manifestation of scarcity are showing (Cleveland and Ruth, 1996). On the other hand, an expanding economy provokes changes that cause imbalances to the environment. Market prices, nevertheless, do not consider such changes, leaving them out of the economic calculus, thus reinforcing the imbalances they have generated. In fact, there are presently many incentives in the institutional order of the market set by the state for exploiting and destroying the environment. In Brazil, an illustration is offered by the energy which is supplied by the big Tucuruí dam in the Amazon state of Pará at very low prices to two aluminium plants which use it intensively (see Chapter 11 of this book). This is natural capital that is provided almost free to make Brazilian aluminium competitive in world markets, and promote consumption in industrialised countries (who, supposedly, do not need such a bounty). Obviously, an intervention is needed to offset the way natural capital is treated and valued by the market. The principle to be adopted here is not to leave out of the economic calculus the 'ecological footprint' caused by an expanding economy. Environmental losses make up real, physical damages which are very often irreversible. The costs they shape cannot be treated as purely external.

To opt for sustainability means setting aside more natural capital for future generations. This implies the acceptance of a philosophy of finitude and self-restriction (which is not easy to reconcile with globalised consumer attitudes) (Brüseke, 1996). In connection with this, the choice society will make is based on ethical grounds, for it involves distribution on a time perspective. To say that sustainable development for a number of people tending to infinity is an impossibility or that to be sustainable society must have a stable biophysical foundation, is a statement of fact. A very different question is the decision to follow the path to sustainability, for here efficiency is not involved. But to insist on a model whose unsustainability – measured by the loss of nature's assets – compromises the ability of future generations to meet their own needs is also an ethical choice. Policymakers (and the economists who give them advice) usually overlook this feature of their decisions. Government policies for sustainable development must be designed in the context of ethical principles concerning the well-being of present and future generations. To admit continuous growth may be desirable, even charming, but it merely represents a 'postponement of restraining the offtake of products to within the bounds that limit their sustainable production' (Fearnside, Chapter 11).

An important principle for policymaking for the sake of sustainability is to have a sound system for measuring a country's economic performance. In a sustainable society, progress should be grasped by the quality of life (health, longevity, psychological maturity, education, a clean environment, community spirit, leisure enjoyed in an intelligent fashion, and so forth), and not by pure material consumption (Viola, 1996). *Per capita* national income and GDP refer to material progress. But it is on the basis of their values (obtained by means of a faulty system of national accounts that has existed for fifty years) that development policies are usually conceived and evaluated. The result is policies and institutions that promote economic growth to the neglect both of social progress and maintenance or improvement of the environmental conditions. As is well known, the procedures of national accounting treat the consumption of natural capital as income, besides creating strong incentives for the destruction of the environment to the extent that depletion (for example the case of Amapá manganese) and degradation are considered as positive contributions to GDP and national income. A frugal, concerned use of resources adds less to economic aggregates than immoderation or dissipation.

On the other hand, even within the framework of the methodology of 'green' accounting – which is being introduced to correct the national accounting methodology for environmental losses – a great difficulty remains regarding the measurement of ecological impacts in *money* terms (Fearnside, Chapter 11). Evidently, government policies for sustainable development have to rely on a different, more relevant approach to the calculation of the true GDP (that is, deducting losses) and other macroeconomic variables. The productivity of nature has to be measured in physical terms (production per unit of used natural resources and waste and emissions) and presented together with the estimates of the money flows of production and consumption (El Serafy, Chapter 7).[4] This means the rejection of the frequent utilisation of GDP figures (in their conventional form) as a measure of welfare or an indicator of the quality of life. A system of national income accounting which does not count the consumption of natural capital as income, and which internalises depletion and degradation as costs constitutes a key element for policymaking aimed at sustainable development (van Dam, 1996).

4. GOVERNMENT POLICY FOR SUSTAINABILITY

Government policy aimed at sustainable development means an orientation of public actions motivated by the acknowledgement of the fundamental ecological limitation of resources (matter and energy, ultimately), without which no human activity can be undertaken. This imposes the need for both a sparing utilisation of the biophysical, environmental basis of the economy, and a reorientation in the manner in which the resources of nature are employed and the correspondent benefits shared. The strategic problem here is to find a sustainable metabolic flow, or throughput, which can boost the welfare of society without impairing environmental functions and services. In other words, the level of the social product must be warranted, as well as the quality of the natural environment and the quality of life. Sustainable development, in effect, means *qualifying* (or restricting) growth, reconciling economic progress with preservation of the natural basis of society (Binswanger, Chapter 2). To sustain the metabolic flow of low-entropy resources into high-entropy matter and energy which is the essence of the economic process (Georgescu-Roegen, 1971) means investing in raising the productivity of natural capital, preventing the ruinous exploitation of natural resources and maintaining their capacity for regeneration and absorption. It means that the ecosystem must have a stable biomass. To be sustainable, the development process has to imitate the processes of nature as much as possible, incorporating the co-ordinates of homeostasis, sobriety, and maximum yields with ecological efficiency within its framework – adopting, in a word, the principles of a 'conservative economy' (Branco, 1989: 90).

A policy committed to sustainability has to discourage all that threatens the long-term health of the ecosystem and the economy's biophysical basis, such as inefficiency, waste, pollution, throughput, overuse or mining of renewable resources, and dissipation of exhaustible resources. In contrast, it has to further all that is desirable, such as real income, employment, welfare, a clean environment, a beautiful landscape, personal security, and a balanced use of natural resources (including air and water). This can be done through the tax system, by shifting away the burden of taxation from the more desirable to the less desirable things (Binswanger, Chapter 2; Daly, Chapter 6 of this book; Goodland, 1996). This can also be done by introducing devices into the market mechanism (like full-cost pricing) that protect the environment and promote its use on a more prudent basis. Severance taxes could likewise be collected on non-renewable resources (compensating for their disappearance), as for example in the case of Amapá manganese, to make society pay for the loss of natural capital. All those measures, obviously, amount to an interference in the way the market operates. They are justified by the fact that the price mechanism is biased against the environment and does not reflect the scarcities and the ensuing values in the very distant future (Georgescu-

Roegen, 1974), thus requiring that the state lead the market rather than follow it as at present (Jöst et al., Chapter 5 in this book). In some cases, in fact, the market can be made more realistic by the removal of subsidies which encourage the overuse of natural capital. The example of aluminium produced with artificially cheap electricity from Tucuruí (Pará, Brazil) is certainly an instance of the need for more realism in dealing with natural resources. Another instance is the official stimulus to beef cattle-raising in the Brazilian Amazon which some time ago promoted that activity at the cost of the destruction of the rainforest (Fearnside, Chapter 11).

One aspect of government policies committed to the goal of sustainable development which deserves special attention is the treatment given to consumption and lifestyle habits. On the one hand, excessive consumption levels of goods and services (by the rich, of course) must be curtailed. On the other hand, the inducement to consume more and more of everything which is nourished by the mass media (mainly, television) has to be revised and put within the parameters of ecological prudence that are indispensable for sustainability. This depends on the very difficult task of influencing the demand side so that consumption may drop – which in any case is a measure that has to be contemplated on a long-run perspective (after all, sustainability implies lifestyle changes to assure the maintenance of natural capital). To achieve a sustainable world, the demand side cannot be left untouched. A system of penalties and incentives has to be devised (Goodland, 1996) so that people (a) walk, bike or use mass transportation rather than the individual automobile (which concentrates resources and is much more polluting); (b) open windows and adopt appropriate architecture rather than use air conditioners (which are very inefficient converters of energy)[5]; (c) recycle rather than pile up trash (re-using envelopes, for example); (d) seek durability rather than obsolescence; (e) opt for grain-based diets rather than for meat-based ones (which raise energy inefficiency and are less equitable); (f) cultivate land with agroforestry food plots instead of the less productive agribusiness food; (g) avoid pollution and waste damages first, instead of relying on treating them; (h) prefer labour-intensive growth which costs environmentally less than the capital-intensive variety; (i) resort more and more to renewable energies; and (j) further the use of renewable resources on a sustainable basis.

It must be stressed here that sustainability must not overlook its social and economic dimensions, in spite of the fact that it is governed by biophysical principles, thus having an unavoidably strong ecological significance.[6] That is mainly relevant in relation to the issue of social exclusion, caused by structural factors which tend to make it even more crystallised (Neder, 1996). However, the mere attempt to overcome social exclusion through traditional development policies seems to be inappropriate, in the sense that a process of development which cannot be healthily sustained is not a reliable way of defeating the very exclusion it purports to beat. The latter has to be traced to socio-economic structures (supported by a socio-political layer that institutionalises them) which make the economy dysfunction in terms of social harmony. This is a situation requiring an intervention at the economic, social and political foundations of social exclusion as a component of the strategy for sustainability. Therefore, environmental considerations are to be mixed with the prospects for social equity (measures for generating income and jobs are indispensable in this connection), economic efficiency and political feasibility. In any event, the formulation of policies for sustainability in all sectors of government action must rely first on basic biophysical criteria for the sustainable use of nature, combined with instruments for the correction of socio-economic imbalances and the promotion of the well-being of the population. In Brazil, the reference to the ecological frame of sustainability has been more rhetorical up to now; the government is still dominated at its core by a classical view of development which gives supreme importance, for instance, to the economics, planning, transportation and energy ministries, following traditional recommendations of economic advisers.

The internalisation of environmental costs can be made by both taxation and the elimination of subsidies that induce the utilisation of natural resources. Shifting the base of taxation from value added to that to which value is added corresponds to raising the effective price of the natural resource flow yielded by natural capital (Daly, Chapter 6). This in turn will lead to a more prudent use of nature. The same can be said concerning the price of energy, which can be raised by a tax leading both to energy conservation and more efficiency in energy transformations (Binswanger, Chapter 2). To make the use of matter and energy in general more expensive may have a positive effect on recycling, thus counterbalancing the tendency to discard which characterises modern industrial society, whose addiction to the disposable product – of which the microprocessor is a very close relative – is so great that Branco (1989: 94), a biologist, judges that, for many people, '*an industrial product's greatest virtue is its being thrown away*' (his emphasis). From the perspective of sustainable development, discarding – which means piling up waste ever more – has to be reduced as much as possible. By taxing the generation of trash or providing another form of disincentive, a revenue could simultaneously be raised for the purpose of social promotion and environmental protection.

Since the capital of nature is the factor which limits the economic process (the economy is sustained physically, after all, by the ecosystem), the primary preoccupation of sustainable policies should be to maximise the productivity of natural capital in the short run and increase its supply in the long haul (Daly, Chapter 6). To invest in natural capital, in fact, is the surest way to make the economy function and develop in a durable way. This is not exactly what actual globalisation and free trade tend to engender, for competition in world markets tends to lower the standards of environmental protection and the prices of natural resources, which in turn produces more dissipation and wastage. Brazilian aluminium (processed with energy from Tucuruí, as mentioned before) is a case in point. Free trade, on the other hand, tends to leave outside the economic calculus the 'external' factors associated with depletion and degradation. Environmental costs, in effect, do not enter into the prices of traded commodities, which depend solely on the quantities exchanged in the markets,[7] thus having a very short-term bias against nature.

The same happens to policies of structural adjustment, which are frequently implemented without consideration for their ecological impacts and environmental losses. The environment is even treated in some cases as an impediment to accelerated growth in trade. A policy of liberalisation with a lax framework of environmental regulation can be an instrument to ecological dumping and the 'overgrazing' of the commons (May, Chapter 10 of this book), which are incompatible with public policies for sustainability. A country like Brazil has to possess instruments capable of directing trade, foreign private finance, and integration into global markets toward the goals of sustainable development and the preservation of natural capital. It is true that the quest for globalisation dominates the international arena nowadays; but this may be a fad, if one thinks of the hidden ecological costs of globalisation (Daly, Chapter 6). Certainly, the environment – by providing life-support functions – is the factor which in the very long run has to dictate what can be done. Integration into the global market should be evaluated, therefore, in terms of its ecological implications, of the costs associated with the ecological footprint left by the way natural resources are exploited now. This in no way denies the fact that national economies are today increasingly interdependent and may benefit from that integration. The question is that increasingly broad and severe environmental problems may be accumulating in coming years as a result of practices that do not internalise certain actual costs. Sustainability is harmed to the extent that price signals from world markets do not internalise environmental costs. In other words, nature cannot be left alone under the control of the market. Government intervention is required here to include extraction, production, depletion, and environmental costs (full-cost pricing) in the prices of tradables, as well as to establish a market-based system of environmental incentives (Reed, 1996).

Government policy for sustainability has to contain measures to stimulate those sectors which effectively add value, contributing less to depletion and degradation. True, the identification of such sectors requires further investigation, but one possibility lies, for example, in ecotourism (which also generates employment), provided that appropriate care is taken with the environment (and local culture) to avoid situations like that found, for instance, in the region of Victoria Falls (Zambeze river, between Zaire and Zimbabwe),[8] and in many parts of Brazil itself. A step should also be taken by government policy to establish a framework for monitoring and certification of compliance with norms for environmental protection and adequate exploitation of natural resources (May, Chapter 10). Environmentally friendly technologies likewise should be rewarded somehow. And initiatives giving priority to mass transport and the use of biomass as fuel are fundamental in the scope of sustainable development.

The fuel alcohol program in Brazil should be contemplated from that perspective, and not solely by a cold comparison of sugar-cane alcohol with oil – although the former depends to a large degree on the latter for its production (Sevá Filho et al., 1995). Brazil has pioneered in the field of biofuels, and has gained expertise in dealing with the replacement of gasoline by alcohol. But it requires more research to advance the technology of biomass use as combustible. Even if it is foolish to insist that the use of petrol should be discontinued, it is at least necessary to consider alternatives for its substitution at some moment. And the commitment to sustainability points inevitably toward *renewable sources*, like solar radiation and its product, the biomass. In the case of sugar cane, it is necessary to consider the ecological impacts associated with its production and transformation into alcohol, but this is a challenge that can be dealt with properly through research and development. It is absurd, anyhow, to evaluate economic costs and benefits of fuel alcohol simply on the basis of the present, unsustainable oil prices (which, anyway, have shown recently some upward tendency).

Sustainability of development depends on the preservation of environmental services. In the case of Brazil, certain environmental services (conservation of biodiversity, carbon storage, water cycling) of the rainforest could be transformed into an income stream by being sold to beneficiaries around the world who might be willing to pay for them (Fearnside, Chapter 11). This should be part of government policy and of Brazil's agenda for international negotiations. 'Whether or not one believes that biodiversity is worth spending money to protect, it is sufficient to know that many people in the world do believe it is important' (Fearnside, idem), thus allowing ways to be devised for converting it – and other environmental services – into a source of income that could be used for purposes of sustainable development in the Amazon and in the rest of the country. This is a much better solution to demands for exploiting the forest than selling hardwood at depressed prices or felling the trees for the expansion of cattle ranches or slash-and-burn agriculture. To be sure, there remains the question of valuing nature and its services. But the alternative is treating the forest as an instrument of immediate private profit-making. It is worth noticing here that the Amazon is the last big existing rainforest in the world. To the extent that the benefits of biodiversity and other ecological services are global rather than local, this could be an opportunity for Brazil to enjoy a monopoly power for making a deal regarding the preservation of this resource.

An important aspect of the search for sustainability is the treatment to be given to the population problem. Certainly, policies should be conceived for preventing explosive growth in the number of people or for stabilising population. But in Brazil, the problem is not so much the quantity of inhabitants (the rhythm of population growth has diminished sensibly in the last two decades), but the fact that the non-solution of the agrarian question and internal migration cause very serious stress in large urban and metropolitan areas. It is the urban environment, with its host of ills (polluted water, untreated sewage, inadequate disposal of waste, miserable housing, violence), that causes special concern in terms of the quality of life of poor people (Hogan, 1996; Jacobi, 1996). Violence is serious in the cities' low-income sections, and people live there in squalor. This demands social policies which can be adjusted to the general framework of sustainability. The population as such does not represent a serious threat to sustainability. And the deceleration of its expansion should be counted as a favourable factor for facilitating attempts to stem and to reverse the degradation of Brazilian cities (which, it must be said, will not occur automatically, but only as a result of deliberate policies cutting deep into the structures of society).

A final word on policies for sustainability has to do with institutional reform. In fact, existing social institutions which favour the ephemeral against the lasting, the homogenising tendencies of globalisation instead of diversity (both biological and cultural, which are basic for evolution), a *laissez-faire* attitude concerning the environment as opposed to the setting-up of biophysical limits, and so on, must be adjusted to the requisites of sustainability. New institutions are needed to conserve natural assets, to encourage the regeneration of renewable resources, to protect biodiversity, to generate more ecologically friendly technologies, to promote less energy- and material-intensive lifestyles, to keep constant the capital of nature to the benefit of future generations (Norgaard, Chapter 4) and to protect the knowledge of indigenous and traditional peoples, including their intellectual property rights (Posey, Chapter 12). New forms of democratic regulation and a new mixed economy (different from the neoliberal version) are possibilities to be considered.

Certainly, to engage all sectors of society in the pursuit of a sustainable, equitable, economically efficient, and politically feasible type of development, at least three parameters should be considered for institutional reform: (1) education (Jacobi, 1996; Leonardi, 1996), (2) participatory management (Sekiguchi, 1996), and (3) stakeholders' dialogue (Leis, Chapter 8; Trindade, Chapter 9). Ecologically correct choices can be made through an informed, science-based process of dialogue between the relevant actors (stakeholders). Participation will enhance the involvement of the population, creating not only consistent expectations but a sense of responsibility regarding the choices made. And the decision concerning the rights of the present generations in front of the future ones can thus be taken within a better system of co-ordinates (Goulet, 1996) and a framework of value judgements clearly presented. In Brazil, the lack of stakeholders' dialogue is conspicuous, as illustrated by the way the process of environmental negotiation is still conducted in the country with token environmental impact assessments undertaken merely to justify choices already made (Leis, Chapter 8). In sum, institutional reform has to be part of government policy toward sustainability, as a means to promoting durable, genuine wealth (Goulet, 1996).

5. CONCLUDING REMARKS

Sustainability means recognising biophysical limits imposed on the economic process by the ecosystem. This is a perception which underlines the fact that the latter sustains the economy, thus requiring the economic process to be attuned to the principles of nature. The official discourse, however, hovers around the idea that sustainable development can be accomplished with endless growth, provided that certain clauses for environmental protection are observed. This notion differs greatly from the understanding (can it be distinct?) that the environment must be seen as the ultimate source of certain functions without which the economy cannot exist or operate, and whose rhythms dictate the pace of what can be done. In order to be sustainable, in fact, the economic system must have a stable basis of support. This requires that regeneration rates and absorption capacities must be respected. Otherwise, the economic process will become irremediably unsustainable. A strategy for sustainable development is thus required for policymaking, taking nature into account as a limiting factor whose productivity must be maximised in the short run, whose availability must be preserved into the long-distant future, and whose integrity cannot be defaced.

To be relevant, government policies for sustainability have to be able to redirect the course of economic events in such a way that activities which destroy natural capital or dissipate renewable resources, upsetting the corresponding ecocycles, be checked. On the other hand, those activities that preserve or cause little disturbance to vital life-support functions of the ecosystem are to be maintained or promoted. Sustainable development must assure that such functions are transferred unimpaired to future generations. Sustainability will not be achieved if natural capital is ruined, making the ecosystem incapable of generating those services that allow humans to meet their needs. The notion of sustainable development represents a sound alternative to the concept of economic growth, indicating that without nature nothing can actually be produced. It shows what is *possible* from the very material point of view, which should be compared with the longing for more and more wealth that, in today's modern society, constitutes what is *desirable*. Possibilities are determined by production frontiers. Nature must be the reference for the choice of the optimal scale of economic activities that is contained within those frontiers. Evidently, the precise point where the economy will be located depends on moral considerations concerning the interests of present and future generations (Norgaard, Chapter 4). It is the duty of government to evaluate society's preferences in such a context, and act to bring the fulfilment of the aspirations of the present generations into harmony with the aspirations of our descendants.

In the remaining chapters of this book, an attempt is made at showing an itinerary for the attainment of the goal of a sustainable, durable, ecologically responsible society. This is a permanent duty of all present generations, which need to be committed to bestowing on future generations a biophysical basis for the undertaking of the relevant human activities of any time, assuring the preservation of the ecosystem's carrying capacity and of natural capital, in connection with a non-decreasing quality of life.

NOTES

1. The participants of the workshop were (in alphabetical order): Alpina Begossi, Hans Binswanger, Franz Josef Brüseke, Marcel Claude, Cutler Cleveland, Herman Daly, Karl-Erik Eriksson, Philip Fearnside, Robert Goodland, Denis Goulet, Daniel Hogan, Pedro Jacobi, Frank Jöst, Maria Lúcia Leonardi, Héctor Leis, Joan Martínez-Alier, Peter May, Ricardo Toledo Neder, Richard Norgaard, Darrell A. Posey, Guillermo Scarlato, Celso Sekiguchi, Salah El Serafi, Fulai Sheng, Sérgio Trindade, Erik van Dam and Eduardo Viola.
2. In 1940 Brazil had 41.2 million inhabitants (IBGE, 1982). In 1990, the number of those living in the country below the 'poverty line' reached 42 million people (PNUD-IPEA, 1996: 22). Fifty years of rapid, unlimited 'progress', with GDP growth rates of over 5 percent a year (see Baer, 1995), then led simply to the situation that those in extreme poverty at the end of the period more than corresponded to the total population at the beginning. The world population in 1900 was 1.5 billion people. In 1996 those living under the poverty line in the planet amounted to 1.6 billion (UNDP, 1996). This situation may have worsened following the 1997 Asian debacle. Where in heaven is poverty being reduced in global terms? This problem has led James Gustave Speth, administrator of UNDP, elaborating on the above report, to affirm: 'If present trends continue, economic disparities [...] will move from inequitable to inhuman' (apud *Time*, **148** (5) 29 July 1996: 7).
3. According to an evaluation of the Intergovernmental Panel on Climate Change (IPCC), quoted by Eriksson (1996), one life in an industrial country corresponds to fifteen lives in a developing one.
4. An attempt to estimate in physical terms part of the environmental impact of the charcoal-based steel industry in the state of Minas Gerais, Brazil, indicates that the 'true' value of its product should be almost halved in money terms compared to the official figures (Medeiros, 1995). Young and Serôa da Motta (1995) provide estimates of mineral depletion in Brazil with implications for the measurement of sustainable income in the mineral sector between 1970–88. These are illustrations of the sort of initiatives that are necessary for offering a suitable numerical background to the benefit of sound policymaking for sustainability.

5.   Although air-conditioning is (seemingly) a desirable thing in the tropics, its inefficient conversion of energy (see Commoner, 1976) makes its widespread use almost an impossibility.
6.   'Environmental sustainability is a rigorous, universal and non-negotiable concept and is not at all subjective' (Goodland, 1996).
7.   It is illustrative of this picture to recall the fall of 16 percent in the world price of copper in June 1996 due simply to criminal activities of an important trader of the Japanese Sumitomo Group (*The Economist*, 339 (7971), 22–28 June 1996: 69–70), whereas the fact that copper is a resource which is slowly becoming scarce does not weigh in as to its prices.
8.   See *Time* magazine, **148** (1) 1 July 1996: 36–7.

REFERENCES

Baer, Werner (1995), *The Brazilian Economy,* New York: Praeger, 4th ed.

Branco, Samuel Murgel (1989), *Ecossistêmica: uma abordagem integrada dos problemas do meio ambiente* [*Ecosystemics: an integrated approach to the problems of the environment*], São Paulo: Editora Edgar Blücher.

Brito, Daniel (1994), 'Extração mineral na Amazônia: a experiência da exploração de manganês da Serra do Navio no Amapá' [Mining in the Amazon: The experience of the exploitation of manganese from the Navio Sierra in Amapá], MA Dissertation. Belém: Universidade Federal do Pará.

Brüseke, Franz Josef (1996), 'Pressão modernizante, estado territorial e sustentabilidade [Modernizing pressure, territorial state and sustainability], Workshop paper (see Claude).

Cavalcanti, Clóvis (1988), 'O bloqueio da pobreza: estudo de caso de uma cooperativa de teceloas em Pedro II, Piauí' [The blockade of poverty: a case study of a cooperative of women weavers at Pedro II, Piauí], in Clóvis Cavalcanti (ed.), *No interior da economia oculta* [*Inside the hidden economy*], Recife: Editora Massangana, pp. 241–294.

Cavalcanti, Clóvis (1991), 'Government policy and ecological concerns: some lessons from the Brazilian experience', in Robert Costanza (ed.), *Ecological economics: the science and management of sustainability,* New York: Columbia University Press, pp. 474–485.

Claude, Marcel (1996), 'The Chilean environmental accounts project: theoretical framework and results', paper for the workshop on 'The Environment, Development and Government Policy: Basis for Building a Sustainable Society in Brazil (Taking Nature into Account)', Olinda: Fundação Joaquim Nabuco, Apr., xerox.

Cleveland, Cutler and Mathias Ruth (1996), 'When, where, and by how much do biophysical limits constrain the economic process? The contribution of Nicholas Georgescu-Roegen to ecological economics', Workshop paper (see Claude).

Commoner, Barry (1976), *The poverty of power. Energy and the economic crisis,* New York: A. Knopf.

Daly, Herman (1991), 'Ecological economics and sustainable development: from concept to policy', World Bank Environment Department, Divisional Working Paper no. 1991–24, Washington, DC: World Bank.

Daly, Herman and John Cobb Jr (1994), *For the common good: redirecting the economy toward community, the environment, and a sustainable future,* Boston: Beacon Press, 2nd ed .

Eriksson, Karl-Erik (1996), 'Science for sustainable development', Workshop paper (see Claude).

Georgescu-Roegen, Nicholas (1971), *The entropy law and the economic process*, Cambridge: Harvard University Press.

Georgescu-Roegen, Nicholas (1974), 'Energy and economic myths', in W. Burch and F.H. Borman (eds), *Limits to growth: The equilibrium state and human society*, San Francisco: W.H. Freeman.

Goodland, Robert (1996), 'Environmental sustainability: eat better and kill less', Workshop paper (see Claude).

Goulet, Denis (1996), 'Authentic development: making it sustainable', Workshop paper (see Claude).

Hogan, Daniel (1996), 'Environmental change and the new demographic regime', Workshop paper (see Claude).

IBGE (Brazilian Institute of Geography and Statistics), *Anuário Estatístico do Brasil 1982* [*Brazil's Statistical Yearbook 1982*], Rio: IBGE.

Jacobi, Pedro (1996), 'Meio ambiente urbano e sustentabilidade: alguns elementos para reflexão' [Urban environment and sustainability: some elements for reflection], Workshop paper (see Claude).

Leonardi, Maria Lúcia (1996), 'A educação ambiental como um dos instrumentos de superação da insustentabilidade da sociedade atual' [Environmental education as an instrument for overcoming the unsustainability of present-day society], Workshop paper (see Claude).

Martínez-Alier, Joan (1996), '"Environmental Justice" (local and global)', Workshop paper (see Claude).

Medeiros, Josemar (1995), 'Aspectos econômico-ecológicos da produção e utilização do carvão vegetal na siderurgia brasileira' [Economic-ecological aspects of the production and utilization of charcoal in the Brazilian steel industry], in Clóvis Cavalcanti (ed.), *Desenvolvimento e natureza: estudos para uma sociedade sustentável* [*Development and nature: studies for a sustainable society*], São Paulo: Cortez Editora, pp. 366–398.

Neder, Ricardo Toledo (1996), 'Para uma regulação pública ambiental pós-desenvolvimentista no Brasil' [For a post-developmentist environmental public regulation in Brazil], Workshop paper (see Claude).

PNUD (United Nations Development Program)-IPEA (Institute of Applied Economic Research) (1996), *Relatório sobre o Desenvolvimento Humano no Brasil 1996* [*Brazil's Human Development Report 1996*], Brasília: PNUD-IPEA.

Reed, David (ed.) (1996), *Structural adjustment, the environment, and sustainable development*. London: Earthscan Publications.

Scarlato, Guillermo (1996), 'Dinámica agrícola en zonas subtropicales de Sudamérica: sistemas productivos, uso del territorio y políticas públicas' [Agricultural dynamics in subtropical zones of South America: productive systems, use of territory and public policies], Workshop paper (see Claude).

Sekiguchi, Celso (1996), 'Por uma política de governo compatível com as sustentabilidades ética, sociocultural, política, econômica e ambiental: o caso do Vale do Ribeira, no Estado de São Paulo' [For a government policy compatible with the ethical, socio-cultural, political, economic and environmental sustainabilities: the case of the Ribeira Valley, São Paulo State, Brazil], Workshop paper (see Claude).

Sevá Filho, Oswaldo, Josemar Medeiros, Guilerme Mamma and Regina Diniz (1995), 'Renovação e sustentação da produção energética' [Renewal and sustenance of energy production], in Clóvis Cavalcanti (ed.), *Desenvolvimento e natureza:*

estudos para uma sociedade sustentável [*Development and nature: studies for a sustainable society*]. São Paulo, Cortez, pp. 345–365.

Sheng, Fulai (1996), 'A conceptual framework for building a sustainable society', Workshop paper (see Claude).

UNDP (United Nations Development Program) (1996), *The Human Development Report 1996*. Vienna: UNDP.

Van Dam, Erik (1996), 'Taking nature into account: a plea for the inclusion of social aspects and natural capital in our information system', Workshop paper (see Claude).

Viola, Eduardo (1996), 'Reflexões sobre os dilemas do Brasil na segunda metade da década de 1990 e sobre uma agenda de políticas públicas baseada na democracia, na eqüidade, na eficiência e na sustentabilidade' [A reflection on Brazil's dilemmas in the second half of the 1990s and on an agenda of public policies based on democracy, equity, efficiency and sustainability], Workshop paper (see Claude).

Young, Carlos Eduardo and Serôa da Motta, Ronaldo (1995), 'Measuring sustainable income from mineral extraction in Brazil', *Resources Policy*, **21** (2): 113–125.

2. Towards Sustainable Development

Hans Christoph Binswanger

The concept of sustainable development should be seen as an alternative to the concept of economic growth, which today is commonly associated with the quantitative, material growth of the economy. To show this I am now going to discuss three points.

I.

First, we have to undertake a re-orientation of economic theory that is used as a guideline of practical and political decisions. The point is to integrate again nature and environment into the economy.

Usually economic theory assumes that society's national product (Y) that stands as a synonym for human welfare as a whole is the result of combining labour (L) and capital (K), which are taken as the sole factors of production. Therefore the economy can be described by formula (relation) (1).

$$Y = f(L, K) \tag{1}$$

What exactly does this function mean? At first sight simply that the national product (Y) is a function of labour (L) and capital (K). But saying this is the same as saying – and now we are reading the above function from the right to the left – take X units of labour and Y units of capital and you will get Z units of social product. In arguing like this we totally neglect nature and all the natural services which are essential for every material production and the welfare derived from it. It is as if one would try to make a cake by using the simple recipe: First, take a pot and a spoon (capital) and then start to stir (labour) for a prescribed while. When you have finished the result will be called a cake. Obviously this is far from reality. What will happen then? In fact, nothing! Without flour, water, eggs and sugar nobody will be able to make a cake. The same is true for the economy as a whole. Without nature – or more exactly, without matter taken from natural resources – nothing can be produced. And from this it follows in turn that during the process of consumption nothing but the use value of the consumed goods is destroyed. Matter incorporated in consumed goods is always returned into nature as waste and emissions. Therefore we can state: Nothing results from nothing. And vice versa: Nothing is returned to nothing.

In essence, the economic activity of production and consumption is nothing but a transformation of natural substances. In the course of this transformation a certain use value is added to these substances or respectively subtracted from them. But the material amount of the natural inputs will neither be increased nor diminished. This seems rather obvious. But if so, why has economic theory for long argued, and still continues to argue, that producing and creating welfare was possible by combining *only* labour and capital? Why does it construct a production function that totally neglects the role of nature, especially regarding the fact that natural substances may exhibit utility (as intact nature) or disutility (as waste) outside the economic process? The reasons are the following.

The point of reference of common economic theory still is the – long foregone – economy of pre-industrial times, that was *solely* based on the use of renewable resources. Renewable resources basically maintain a form of production close to nature like agriculture, forestry or fisheries. Of course, the waste which such a traditional economy produces will be renewed by the circular flows of ecology and converted into new productive resources that can be used again as inputs to the production processes.

Figure 2.1 underlines this fact: waste materials brought back into the circular flows of ecology will be renewed to become soil, water, air and nutrients again. In short: they will become new resources. Even more, this is accomplished by natural forces alone. No human help is needed. Nature – and this is the basic point – works free of charge. Without hesitation this regeneration service that goes on as long as the speed and cycles of regeneration are respected can be taken as a gift. But gifts are not part of the economy. Only acts where goods and services are exchanged for a – real or monetary – price are classified as being economic and generating utility. Therefore, as long as the natural regeneration process went on without disturbance and as long as mainly renewable resources were used there had been *no* necessity to integrate nature and natural services into the production and welfare function of economic theory. One was allowed to say: the regeneration gift of nature is not part of the economy although natural services are essential and indispensable elements of production.

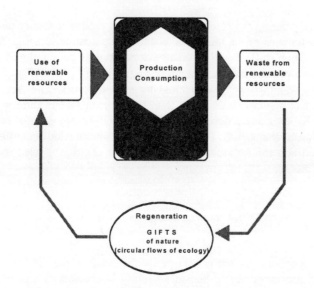

Figure 2.1 Scheme of the traditional economy based on renewable resources

In such a traditional economy we don't need to bother about natural processes, but may concentrate on production and consumption which indeed are the only economic activities. But then, the simple production function (1) reveals its contents when read from the left to the right. It now is a statement on how the social product shall be distributed between the factors of production and not a statement on how the social product is actually produced. Only those factors which could not be employed in production if they are not compensated, at least to the extent of their necessary reproduction costs, can claim a share of the social product. And these factors are labour and capital. It follows that everything that is produced in the traditional economy can fully be handed out to labour and capital, respectively to the social partners behind them: the group of employees and the group of employers. Nature itself does not demand reproduction compensation. Therefore its 'value-added' to the social product can be given to the other factors, labour and capital. This has been incorporated in:

$$Y = f \ (L, K) \tag{1'}$$

Unfortunately during the further development of economic theory the simple production function of the traditional economy has been misleading. In an act of generalisation of (1) it was assumed that nature was not employed at all in the economic process and that therefore the growth of production or – more generally – welfare was never caused by natural forces. The fact that the social product regularly rises faster than the input of labour and capital was explained by inventing a new factor of production, for the sake of simplicity called technical change (A). The original production function accordingly was transformed into the orthodox form of equation (2), that is used in today's economic theory:

$$Y = f(L, K) \longrightarrow Y = f(L, K, A) \tag{2}$$

However, economic growth is only partly the result of the efficiency rise in production processes due to human ingenuity in research and development. Another part must be accounted to an ever increasing use of nature made possible not only by extracting matter from natural resources but also by extracting energy that in turn is used to extract more matter and energy. The rapid growth of energy inputs to the economic system that we witness for more than 150 years of industrialisation, especially since World War II, illustrates very well the enormous intensification in the use of nature which has taken place.

Now, moving into the direction of sustainability makes it necessary to see that not only the reproduction of labour and capital is relevant to the economy, but also the reproduction of the natural factors of production. Nature (N) in all its manifestations is to be treated as a third factor of production and must be granted equal rights as a third social partner. This means that maintaining the manifold functions of nature supporting economic and social development and the creation of wealth and welfare must be taken as a genuine economic task. Accordingly, an aggregate production function compatible with the idea of sustainability must allow for the fact that the economic process not only brings about the goods and services of the social product and rise in material welfare but very often – as the omnipresent threats of pollution and environmental degradation show – also negatively influences the state and the quality of the environment (E), thereby diminishing the human quality of life. The enlarged aggregate production function that should replace the one of (2) deriving from this argument is given in (3).

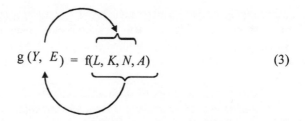

$$g\,(Y,\ E) \;=\; f(L,\,K,\,N,\,A) \tag{3}$$

This function states that only the growth surplus resulting from technical change alone can be returned to the two factors labour and capital, but not the surplus due to the ruinous depletion of natural capital. Consequently, this has somehow to be returned to nature. We can decide between two alternatives of compensation. Either a share of the social product is given back to nature, which means that we must spend money for certain economic activities aimed at maintaining natural services, or we try to preserve the substance of nature by sacrificing part of the possibilities to use natural resources. And this is the essence of the concept of sustainability: in today's modern economy the services of nature have to be paid for according to their scarcity – and the value they add to production, either by real expenditures or by abandoning certain production possibilities.

Figure 2.2 shows the scheme of a modern, sustainable economy where nature has been incorporated as the third factor of production establishing a social partnership in the way described above. Notice that the whole process running from the input of natural resources via the economic transformation process of production and consumption to the output of waste and emissions as well as those activities which are not investment into consumption possibilities or into new machinery or buildings but are needed for the reproduction of natural services are integral parts of the economy. Therefore, economy and economic policy are being assigned a much higher social responsibility. Not only the level of the social product must be guaranteed but also the quality of the natural environment or respectively the quality of life has to be preserved or reproduced.

II.

With the background sketched above, I am now turning to my *second point*. My postulate is that to make sustainability work, we must develop detailed guidelines for a sustainable economy. Especially we have to find a reasonable balance between the contradictory objectives inherent to the concept of sustainability.

Following the work of Herman Daly I will attempt to somewhat extend his rules of sustainability and try to subordinate them under two targets: 1. Maintaining the basis of economic activity (N), 2. Maintaining the basis of the quality of life (E).

1. Maintaining the basis of economic activity: This comprises at first the management of renewable resources including land – regarding the fertility of soil – to prevent their ruinous use and to safeguard their regeneration capacities. In addition, resource-management must be directed to a sparing use of non-renewable resources so that the rates of extraction are slowed down as far as possible. This again includes land-management, now in regard to its function as location for production and living.
2. Maintaining the basis of the quality of life: This comprises the prevention of pollution, the reduction of waste and emissions, that is to diminish the threat of a climatic collapse, and the avoidance of technologically induced risks. Also, measures have to be taken to secure the habitats of man, animals and plants. This demands the protection of biodiversity and the conservation of a living space, where man can experience physical as well as mental well-being.

Obviously, these general targets have to be explained further; each in detail and in connection to each other. There is already an extensive discussion going on around this issue. However, one question is – in my opinion – not being dealt with adequately and not taken seriously enough. This is the question of how the use of non-renewables can be managed in a way that is in line with the ideas of sustainability. Concentrating on this point here is not to claim that the management of non-renewable resources is the only aspect relevant to a policy of sustainability. As will be clear from above the maintenance of natural sinks or the avoidance of environmental hazards are equally important tasks. But I believe that without solving the problem of the adequate treatment of non-renewable resources any concept of sustainable development may be doomed to fail.

It is obvious that extracting part of a non-renewable resource will irreversibly diminish the given stock of the resource. Eventually it is used up totally. This means, strictly speaking, that the use of non-renewables can never be sustainable. Now a seemingly promising alternative to compensate the loss of non-renewable resources by substituting renewable resources for them imposes itself. Regarding, for example, fossil energy sources this would

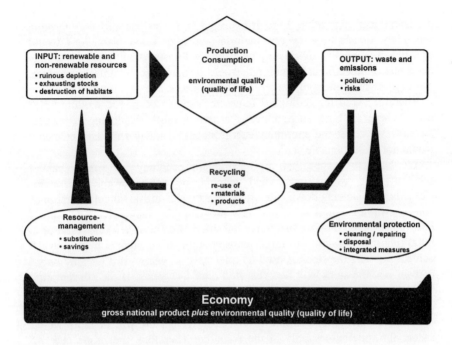

Figure 2.2 Scheme of a modern, sustainable economy

imply the massive employment of all forms of solar energy, for example through photovoltaic, hydroelectric or wind power generation, or by using alcoholic fuels or wood. Without doubt this presents an attractive vision on how to overcome the dilemma of a sustainable use of non-renewable resources. However, we often forget that in a modern economy the substitution of renewable for non-renewable resources alone does not yet guarantee sustainability because the renewable resources themselves must be employed in a sustainable manner that secures the integrity of the basic fundamentals of life. If we started to cover today's energy consumption to full or only to half extent by renewable resources this would lead *inevitably* to a ruinous exploitation of natural capital that would by far exceed the degree of destruction that would result from further using non-renewable resources. Because the amount of renewable resources, is absolutely constrained in time by the speed of the ecological regeneration processes and in space by the land available to grow renewable resources, they are even more scarce than non-renewables are! An extensive use of photovoltaic, hydroelectric or wind power-generation would bring about the threat of enormous spatial stress and of destroyed landscapes. Mass-production of alcoholic fuels may make barren the land under cultivation. Even if managed in a sustainable manner farming secondary forests to grow raw materials in huge wood plantations would sacrifice biodiversity by destroying primary forests. Additionally, we may need lots of material from non-renewable resources to be able to produce, transport or store energy from renewable resources.

Therefore, also for ecological issues the famous economic wisdom holds true: 'There ain't no such thing as a free lunch!' Employing renewable resources to cover the enormous energy needs of today's modern economy would not be sustainable at all.

We have to accept that in our modern economy we simply cannot substitute the whole range and amount of non-renewable resources. Nevertheless, slowing down extraction rates by slowing down consumption of non-renewables would be remarkable progress. An easy calculation shows how remarkable. Suppose that today the stock of a non-renewable resource is 1,000 times the amount of current consumption. If consumption rises by 10 percent per year the stock is used up after only 48 years.[1] If it rises by only 1 percent p.a. the stock will be exhausted after 241 years. If the consumption rate remains at today's level the resource will last for 1,000 years. But if we could manage to reduce the consumption rate it would be available for an even longer period. A constant decrease of 0.1 percent p.a. or more would ensure the indefinite supply of the resource. Therefore, the prime task we have to accomplish today is not to substitute renewable for non-renewable resources but to reduce the consumption of matter and energy. This will be achieved by consequently exploiting the given potential to save natural inputs, which may mean to use given inputs more efficiently or in the last – and presumably unavoidable – instance to change personal and societal patterns in the consumption of goods and services.

III.

Last but not least, as my third point, let me now explain some concrete steps to realise sustainable development.

In my opinion, it is being overlooked too often that the performance of the market is to a high degree influenced by the institutional order set by the state. In the first instance this refers to the effects caused by state regulations concerning the definition and distribution of property rights, the fiscal order and the tax system, or the order of the monetary and banking system. We must re-arrange the institutional order that defines the basic rules of the market economy so that it may function in an environmentally friendly manner.

In regard of property laws this could be accomplished by (re-) introducing the concept of patrimonium (from Latin *pater* = father) instead of the current concept of dominium (from Latin *dominus* = master). The latter comprises the unlimited right of the private owner to use and to abuse, even to destroy his property. In contrast, the former definition limits private property by only granting to the owner the right of usufruct. The things owned may be used but their substance must be preserved, just as the heir ought to preserve the heritage for his own children.

The problematic relationship between sustainability and property rights is very well exemplified by the manner in which property is created in the Brazilian rain-forest region.[2] The case of Brazil is especially instructive because here we can still witness how private ownership of land is born. In general, in Brazil private property is created by two acts: at first, a certain part of land is occupied, then after the squatter has effectively made use of it – that is, has deforested the land – a formal title to possess the land is granted to the occupier. The property right normally includes not only the right to possess the land but also to extract and to use the natural resources found on or in the ground and to sell the goods produced with the help of these resources. The situation is aggravated by the fact that Amazonia is steadily developed by building roads which make it possible to increasingly extend property claims into untouched frontier areas. Since it is allowed to build roads on private initiative, land corporations and large ranches are favoured because they command the capital needed to build roads. To make things worse, deforestation is accelerated by the system of land tax. Because a farm containing forests is taxed at higher rates than one containing pastures or crop land, unused land – which essentially means forest area – carries a higher tax burden than the land that is in use.

Therefore, one possibility to ensure sustainability and to protect rain-forests would be to make property titles in rain-forest regions conditional on the provision to preserve a certain amount of primeval forest on the land in question. It should be laid down, too, that secondary forests must be used sustainably, that is through securing biodiversity and preventing erosion. Additionally, forest land including primeval rain-forest should be taxed in the same way as land used for agriculture.

The same conclusions can be drawn for similar situations in many other countries, especially with regard to agriculture. Of course, in principle the same is true for the use of any natural resource.

Coming back to the general discussion and regarding the fiscal order of the economy, a great change may be to levy taxes on the consumption of natural goods, for example a tax on the use of energy. Two positive effects could be combined. At first, the higher price for energy will slow down energy consumption, which will contribute to environmental protection. Second, the earnings of the tax could be used to lower indirect labour costs by, for example, financing old-age pensions schemes, thereby giving incentives to increase employment. Often it is objected that an energy tax would erode its own base of taxation. However, this concern should not be overrated because normally the elasticities of demand in the field of energy are very low. In Germany for example the elasticity of demand for primary energy has been estimated to be around −0.3. Based on this it can been calculated that an energy tax in ten years amounting to 50 percent of the average price of all energy sources used will reduce energy consumption by 10–15 percent. This however implies that still 85–90 percent of the amount of energy initially consumed will remain for taxation. Generally this shows that by introducing an energy tax it is undoubtedly possible to generate a constant flow of revenues even over longer periods of time and that it is possible to earn the shared dividend of reduced pollution and increased employment mentioned above. How much employment will increase is difficult to predict. But one cannot deny that there will be an increase, if one does not question the basic law of the market economy: that demand is high when the price is low, and it is low when the price is high.

To adapt the system of money and credit to the concept of sustainability will be a similar task. Generally, central bank policy concerning interest rates should be targeted on the rate of consumption of natural capital, that is energy consumption. That means interest rates should be set high and money and credit be made expensive if energy consumption rises, and easy money and low interest may prevail if energy consumption goes down. In practice such a monetary policy would be placed between a Keynesian growth policy and a monetaristic policy of price stabilisation, but would in addition promote a tendency towards an ecologically qualified growth.

I am aware of the fact that all the suggestions above to bring the modern economy in line with environmental protection and nature conservation may not be sufficient to reach all the aims of sustainability. Nevertheless, I do believe that they constitute an important and necessary step towards the realisation of sustainable development.

NOTES

1.   This is calculated from:

$$S_T = S_0 - C_0 \left[1 - (1+\tfrac{r}{100}) - (1+\tfrac{r}{100})^2 - \ldots - (1+\tfrac{r}{100})^{T-1} - (1+\tfrac{r}{100})^T\right] = 0$$

with $C_0 = \dfrac{S_c}{10000}$

2. The following remarks draw on a work of Hans P. Binswanger: 'Brazilian policies that encourage deforestation in the Amazon', *World Development*, **19**, 1991: 821–829.

3. Scale, Ecological Economics and the Conservation of Biodiversity

Alpina Begossi

INTRODUCTION

This study, after describing aspects of the ecosystem, considers patterns of scale as a useful approach to management. A hierarchical approach in ecology, and a parallel of such an approach to ecological economics, are shown using concepts such as resilience, capital, and carrying capacity. Applications for conservation are considered at different scales, and in terms of local management of resources (*res communes*). Finally, suggestions for Brazilian environmental policies are drawn, along with some evaluation on sustainability.

1. ECOSYSTEM CONCEPT

Ecology probably originated in Europe, when the German E. Haeckel defined it, in 1866, as 'the body of knowledge concerning the economy of nature'. Nevertheless, the development of ecology and of the concept of ecosystem is considered as an 'American tale' (Golley, 1993). The term ecosystem was introduced in 1935 by A.G. Tansley, in a study on plant community, published in *Ecology*. According to Golley (1993), in about fifteen years, the ecosystem concept became established and described as 'an ecological machine constructed of trophic levels that were coupled through flows of energy' (p. 104).

Ecological resources and services are produced and sustained by ecosystems. An ecosystem is a functional term for the continuous interactions between organisms, populations, communities and the physical/chemical environment (Barbier et al., 1994). Thus, the conservation of species has a key role in supporting the ecosystem.

According to Holling et al. (1993) there are some key features of the structure and function of ecosystems, as follows: (a) change is not continuous and gradual, but the result of episodic events; (b) spatial attributes are not uniform: there are different ranges of scales with different patches; and (c) ecosystems have multiple equilibria: instead of functions controlled remaining near a single equilibrium, the different states and movements define ecosystem structure and diversity. Therefore, uncertainty and surprises are an integral part of adaptive responses (Holling, 1994). Due to these features, policies and management using single rules have a great probability of failure. Contemporary literature in ecology has revised at least four points, with consequences for management (Holling, 1992): (a) invasion of persistent species after disturbance and during succession are probabilistic; (b) early-and-late successional species can be present continuously; (c) large and internal disturbances (fire, wind, herbivores) are part of internal ecosystem dynamics; and (d) some disturbances can carry the ecosystem into different stability domains.

The ecosystem is placed by Odum (1959) within a hierarchy of biological systems, as follows:

Protoplasm – cell – tissue – organ – organ system – organism – population – community – ecosystem – biosphere

The hierarchy, the level of analysis or simply the 'scale' of ecological systems is an important point in ecology, not only for its theoretical aspects, but also for determining priorities for studies concerning biodiversity conservation.

2. SCALE AND ECOLOGY: HIERARCHICAL PATTERNS

Scale is thus a fundamental point in ecology because different questions may be drawn according to the level of analysis (if populations or landscapes, for example) and also different information is obtained from those approaches. Misunderstandings among ecologists may have occurred under different scale approaches. For example, those who study long-term changes at a single site may reach different conclusions from those reached by short-term studies of similar communities at different sites (Wiens et al., 1986: 145).

Solbrig (1992) showed different levels of analysis on biodiversity fundamental for management: from the biodiversity of the genes to the species (the ultimate source of biodiversity), to the community (patterns of species richness), and to biogeographical (spatial scale, immigrations and extinctions) and ecosystem (the biosphere and global change) levels. The importance of scale is emphasised in the words of Solbrig (1992: 133):

All biological processes are the product of evolution, and genetic diversity is the basis of the evolutionary process. Therefore genetic diversity is of fundamental importance for the maintenance of biodiversity at other levels.

Neilson (1993) observed that ecological systems can be viewed as hierarchies of demographic organisation, such as individual, association, community and formation or of functional organisation, such as species, group, ecosystem and biome. Holling (1992: 479) exemplifies hierarchical levels in a boreal forested landscape, taking into consideration structuring variables and processes (Table 3.1). The author argues that there are relatively few ecosystems structuring processes, expressed at relatively few scales. Tracy and Brussard (1994) pointed out that conservation biologists have recognised the importance of scale in terms of climate change on the presence of some species and in terms of understanding demographic and genetic aspects to environmental changes.

Table 3.1: 'Natural capital': hierarchical levels, structuring variables and processes in the boreal forested landscape (partially taken from Holling, 1992: 479)

Level	Categories of structuring processes	Structuring variables	Structuring processes
needle	physiological	leaves, herbs grass, detritus nutrients	photosynthesis, respiration, decomposition
crown	autoecological	volume, density soil structure, herbivory, nutrients, seeds	plant growth, seed production, population dynamics, decomposition
patch/gap	plant competition	dominant trees, bush sizes, soil structure	tree growth, competition, mortality, soil, vegetation/microclimate
tree stand	disturbances dispersion	insects/diseases tree/plant age/ density	disturbance dynamics tree harvesting seed dispersal
landscape	watershed processes	topography forest aquatic ecosystems	erosion hydrology mesoclimatic interaction
boreal zone	planetary evolutionary processes	precipitation temperature	evolution geomorphology

On the other hand, some authors (Franklin, 1993) have overemphasised a focus on large-scale approaches, such as on landscapes and ecosystems as the *only* (stressed by the author) way to conserve biodiversity. Levin (1992) stresses that there is no 'correct' scale on which to study populations or ecosystems; otherwise, we should understand how information is transferred from fine scales (a leaf) to broad scales (ecosystems or landscapes). A hierarchical approach seems a more appropriate way to address environmental research because it organises the different levels of questions, analysis and information.

3. SCALE AND ECOLOGICAL ECONOMICS

Ecology borrowed many concepts from economy to use in analytical models concerning reproduction and foraging behaviour (Rapport and Turner, 1977). Patterns of scale in ecology have some parallels with economy: population studies tend to use and adopt microeconomics concepts whereas ecosystem, or higher levels of analysis, tend to adopt a macroeconomic reasoning.

At the population level, for example, many ecological studies use models to estimate trade-offs, such as the costs and benefits of decisions that an organism faces. In such an estimation, concepts such as utility are important, because optimal levels of resource use are expected (as predictions). Such 'optimal models' are based on evolutionary concepts of adaptation and fitness and are widely employed in biology (Maynard Smith, 1978). Optimal foraging theory is one example: this model is used to predict 'optimal behaviour' of organisms while foraging, such as optimal diet, optimal places to feed on and optimal time to spend feeding, among others (Stephens and Krebs, 1986).

In human ecology optimal foraging models help to analyse the cost and benefit of activities such as hunting or fishing. For example, the model predicts that fishermen should bring back a higher catch from far fishing grounds, compared to close grounds, and that a long time spent fishing in a ground should also represent a higher catch (Begossi, 1992a). An optimal diet is analysed comparing the cost and benefit of search and consumption of different food items, using indifference curves and utility functions. The model predicts that food is not consumed according to its availability but following trade-offs that place each item at different rankings.

At the ecosystem level biological concepts such as resilience and economic concepts such as capital are important.

Resilience is the magnitude of disturbance that can be absorbed before a system changes. Contrary to definitions that concentrate on stability (equilibrium-centred view), the contemporary view emphasises disturbances that flip a system from one equilibrium to another (Berkes and Folke, 1994). Ives (1995) considered resilience in stochastic systems by taking into account the variability in population growth rates (the more resilient system has lower variabilities in population densities). Holling (1992) stated that cycles are organised by four functions: exploitation, conservation, release (or 'creative destruction', a term borrowed from Schumpeter –(Holling et al.(1993)), and organisation. Resilience is thus determined by release and reorganisation sequence. As part of the processes which link organisms in an ecosystem, the concept of resilience is connected to the contemporary view that ecosystems have multiple equilibria. For example, there is more than one possible climax state, each being controlled by different species assemblages (Holling et al. 1993).

The concept of capital, in ecological economics, covers natural, human-made and cultural capital. Natural capital includes the non-renewable resources (such as oil and minerals), renewable resources (such as plants, animals water), and environmental services (such as the hydrological cycle, waste assimilation, recycling of nutrients, and pollination of crops); human-made capital is capital generated via economic activity, and cultural capital refers to factors that provide human societies with the means and adaptations to interact and to modify the environment (Berkes and Folke, 1992). Cultural capital has included other terms, given by other authors, such as 'adaptive capital' (evolutionary sense), 'social capital' (social organisation), and 'institutional capital' (supply of organisational abilities and structures of a society) (Berkes and Folke, 1994).

Other ecological concepts, such as that of carrying capacity, may be employed in different ecological scales and economic scales (micro/macro).

Carrying capacity (K) is defined as 'the maximum population size of a given species that an area can support without reducing its ability to support the same species in the future' (Roughgarden, 1979 cited in Ehrlich, 1994: 42). It is a difficult measure to obtain, especially when applied to our species, because it is a function of both population and organism: it includes a *biophysical K* (maximum number of people supported at a given technology), and a *social K* (the biophysical K and the social organisation of the population, including patterns of consumption and trade) (Ehrlich, 1994).

The concept of carrying capacity when applied to human populations may also be viewed under different scales of analysis. For example, on a global scale, we may wonder how useful and realistic is this concept. One example is the so called 'IPAT model', where: I = environmental impact, P = population, A = per capita economic activity and T = impact per unit of economic activity, referred to as technology. The IPAT model in a stochastic form is formulated as $I = Ap^b A^c T^d e$, where a, b and c are parameters and e the residual term (Dietz and Rosa, 1994). This model and other so-called 'neo-Malthusian approaches' are a subject of debate in human ecology (for such a debate, see Harrison, 1993 and *Human Ecology Review*, **1**, 1994). Still at a global scale, Hardin (1993) approached the classic 'cowboy economics' versus 'spaceship ecology': the first representing the exploitation of the open earth of the past, and the second, the earth without limitless reserves (a spaceship). In a spaceship ecology, maximisation must be substituted for minimisation concerning resource exploitation. Other terms for this figure are 'empty world' and 'full world' (Daly, 1994), or 'expansionist worldview' and 'ecological worldview' (Rees and Wackernagel, 1994), respectively.

On a local scale, Fearnside (1986) used the concept of carrying capacity studying trans-Amazon settlers and proposed a method to calculate K and the probability of success of settlers. According to this author, the concept of carrying capacity includes the instantaneous and sustainable carrying capacity. The first is based in the classical logistic equation derived – according to Fearnside (1986) – by Verhulst in 1838 (and independently by Pearl and Reed in 1920). It represents an instantaneous value of the population's ability to survive and reproduce at given levels of resource consumption. The second is defined as the maximum number of persons supported in perpetuity in an area, with a given technology and set of consumptive habits, without causing environmental degradation (similar to that defined by Roughgarden, 1979 cited in Ehrlich, 1994). Rees and Wackernagel (1994) use the idea of 'ecological footprints', showing that the ecological impact of populations is usually bigger than the sites used by them, introducing the concepts of appropriated carrying capacity, and including, for example, the 'importing' of carrying capacity by wealthy countries from low income countries.

4. APPLICATIONS FOR CONSERVATION IN BRAZIL

Scale analyses in ecology have led to a contemporary approach, which takes into account both the systems (ecosystems) and the evolutionary aspects included in population and community ecology. Holling (1992) stressed how important is the relation between ecosystem and community ecology, recognising that animals shape their ecosystems.

On a local scale, 'indicator tax', or 'target assemblages of organisms' are suggestions that have been useful in helping to obtain information on habitat, niche breadth and ecological function, and on other groups (predators and prey, for example). Tracking patterns of distribution and abundance of target species may help in evaluating rare species and habitat richness (hot spot diversity). Examples of such approaches, specially with invertebrates (butterflies), are available in Debinsky and Brussard (1994) and Kremen (1992).

Fearnside (1986) suggested that human carrying capacity should be central for development policies. Contemporary management, including native populations in conservation areas, such as tropical forests, must include measures of carrying capacity. It is impossible today to deal with the local management of natural resources without an analysis of carrying capacity.

The current literature on local management (*res communes*) (Begossi, 1995c; Berkes and Farvar, 1989) has stressed the importance of local institutions on rules for management. Ecological activities and management employed by natives are also usually emphasised, as local people are expected to be more familiar with an area than are outsiders (Table 3.2). Examples of traditional system management show that native populations maintain special refugia, minimising the harvest; others use forest succession; keep crop diversity; enhance diversity and resilience; consider the environment 'as a whole'; use the waste from one system as food for another; and manage landscape encoding environmental ideals in traditions (Berkes et al., 1993; Gadgil et al., 1993). Berkes and Folke (1994) stressed analogies between the field of common property resources and ecological economics, both leading to the search for self-regulatory systems towards sustainable policies.

In Brazil, efforts to associate local management, from local populations such as Indians, Caboclos (Amazon) or Caiçaras (Atlantic Forest), to local policies have usually been ignored by the Federal (IBAMA) or State Environmental Governmental Agencies. Conflicts among local populations and those Agencies are frequent (Begossi, 1995a; Cunha and Rougelle, 1989), in spite of the contributions local populations can give to the maintenance of biodiversity (Table 3.2) and in spite of international environmental policies for integrating local economies with conservation objectives in protected areas. Such policies include Unesco's Man and the Biosphere Programme, IUCN programmes (Berkes et al., 1993), and during the past decade, the ICDPs (Integrated Conservation and Development Projects) (Alpert, 1995).

Actually, in many cases we observe a failure of the State (*res publica*) in dealing with the management and conservation of resources. In the particular case of Brazil, policies lack scientific support and local co-operation and there is no technical competence and infrastructure in the Brazilian governmental agencies to sustain policies. Conflicts between Federal and State governmental agencies and researchers are also frequent, concerning research projects and priorities.

The best examples, in Brazil, of associating local knowledge, institutions, and scientific sound proposals are the Extractive Reserves, created after long political battles by rubber-tappers (the first is the Extractive Reserve of the Upper Juruá, 1990 – Begossi, 1995a). In this example, the conservation of natural capital, cultural capital (local and scientific knowledge) and human-made capital (including economy and trade) are associated. Extractive reserves are also an example of close co-operation between researchers and local populations (Cunha et al., 1993).

Some suggestions for management are listed below, taking into consideration that research is important for conservation at *any scale*. I hope scale analysis will help representatives of governmental environmental agencies to stop 'judging', 'selecting' or avoiding the environmental research that comes from the universities and research institutes. Researchers must be free to do any research at conservation sites. We know very little about species and their function in the ecosystem. Even tiny, or apparently 'irrelevant' species may be discovered to be keystone species someday.

Table 3.2: 'Cultural capital': some examples of local knowledge, institutions and management

Reference	Country/Area	System
Begossi (1992b)	Brazil/Búzios Island	food taboos*/conservation of medicinal animals
Begossi and Braga (1992)	Brazil/Tocantins river	food taboos*/conservation of medicinal animals
Begossi (1995a)	Brazil/Atlantic Forest	fishing territories: from families to communities
Berkes (1985)	Bermuda, Borneo, Brazil, Canada, Mexico, Japan, Oceania, USA	fishery-resource tenure systems: individual parcels, 'harbour gangs', kinship groups, villages, and communities
Berkes et al. (1993)	a) Java	*kebun-talun*: increasing productivity in agriculture (crops/trees), and *pekarangan*: a home-garden with annual and perennial crops
	b) Indonesia	*subak:* integrated rice-fish culture, and *tambak*: inshore polyculture pond management
Clay (1990)	Latin America	Bora (Peru) management of agriculture; *conucos*: the Swidden gardens of the Waika Indians (Venezuela); The *chinampa* system of irrigation (Mexico), among others
Gadgil et al. (1993)	a) India	sacred trees, sacred groves
	b) Hawaii	*ahupua'a* system: fish ponds integrated with agriculture
McGrath et al. (1993)	Brazil: Lower Amazon	fisheries: community managed lakes
Posey (1985)	Brazil: Kayapó	*apête*: creation of forest islands with high diversity

Note:

* Reviews on the significance of food taboos are found in Colding (1995) and Ross (1978).

A.   **Lower (Local) Scale (Population/Microeconomy)**

1.   **Knowledge on species and on population dynamics:** Knowledge on 'target species', including their habitat, abundance, distribution and relation to other species. Knowledge on consequences of habitat fragmentation concerning species and probabilities of extinction (Aizen and Feisinger, 1994; Sinclair et al., 1995).

   Solbrig (1992: 133–137) analysed the body of knowledge necessary for such a enterprise, suggesting research on the following; the items b, c and d are also applied at larger scales (see list B, below):

---

a. Biodiversity from the gene to species
   i.   Consequences of intraspecific genetic diversity
   ii.   Consequences of spatial fragmentation
   iii. Speciation (micro/macro evolution)
   iv.   Biodiversity and life-history
b. Species diversity at the community level
   i.   Functional redundancy, species diversity and stability
   ii.   Regional biogeography
   iii. Disturbance, human impacts, and community structure
c. Biodiversity and ecosystem attributes
   i.   Controlled experiments (species added or subtracted)
   ii.   Inadvertent experiments (result of human activities)
   iii. Natural experiments (result of natural events)
d. Monitoring and inventoring biodiversity
   i.   Taxonomy
   ii.   Network of systematists and institutions

---

2.   **Knowledge on resource uses and users:** (type, abundance, diversity, technology).

3.   **Knowledge on strategies of resource use:** (local resource perception and knowledge, decisions of foraging, taboos, sacred habitats, territories); for example, fishing (Begossi, 1992a) and hunting (Bodmer, 1995).

4.   **Knowledge on the value of natural resources:** methods for valuation of non-timber products and ecological and economical models concerning habitat diversity and forest product values are in the literature (Godoy et al., 1993; Hansen et al., 1995).

B.   **Higher Scale (Ecosystem/Macroeconomy)**

1.   **Local management (*res communes*). *Example in Brazil:* Extractive Reserves** – knowledge on carrying capacity, economic feasibility,

local management, and on the role of local institutions in management. Such aspects also include alternative sources for natural products, sources for local cash income, local facilities, and links between resource availability and conservation, with active local participation (Alpert, 1995).

2.   **Landscape ecology:** interprets disturbances and ecological processes on the landscape; for example, human disturbances can increase or decrease landscape heterogeneity (Mladenoff et al., 1993). The use of GIS is very useful to link ecological information and cultural practices. For examples, see Cunha et al. (1993), Brondisio et al. (1994) and Lewis (1995).

3.   **Macro level:** the biosphere, macroeconomics, political ecology.

C.   Sustainability: 'How to Get It?'

Several definitions of sustainability are shown in the literature (Goldman, 1995). Gatto (1995) pointed out at least three definitions for sustainability: (a) from the 'applied biologist' as synonymous with sustained yield; (b) from the 'ecologist' as sustained abundance and genotypic diversity of species; and (c) from the 'economist' as sustained development, without compromising the resources for future generations. The same author pointed out that, besides the mentioned flawed definitions, the uncertainty and dynamic aspects of natural resources (natural capital) make the discussion on sustainability unfruitful. It is better is to analyse specific, well-defined issues. Goodland (1995) defines social, economic and environmental sustainabilities: environmental sustainability is much more than sustainable yield, because, on one side, it includes constraints in the use of resources; and, on the other side, on pollution and waste assimilation.

The Brundtland Report (WCED, 1987 in Ludwig et al., 1993) has plenty of references to sustainability to be achieved in ways not specified; it assumes that global economic activity could be safely increased in order to face the necessity of resources in quantitative and qualitative terms. Ehrlich (1994) showed this important restriction and the challenges of ecological economics: (a) to identify the 'premiums' worth paying to achieve environmental insurance; and (b) to develop 'robust strategies', which are insensitive to uncertainties. One strategy suggested is birth control associated with the empowerment of women. In spite of the continuous population increases, documents approaching sustainability have not directly addressed such a problem (Ludwig, 1993). Turner et al. (1994) define different levels of sustainability from 'weak' to 'strong'; the last includes interactions of natural capital, with cultural and human capital with the emphasis on equity.

The notion of a sustained climax is a static and incomplete equilibrium view (Holling, 1992) because natural resources are uncertain and subject to fluctuations. Policies that apply single rules to obtain constant yields, such as fixed carrying capacity of cattle or fixed sustainable yield for fish, lead to systems with increasing lack of resilience, which are systems that break up in the face of disturbances (Holling et al., 1993). For example, the consequences of the use of maximum sustained yield in fisheries (MSY) has contributed to the elimination of fish stocks, such as herring, cod, ocean perch, salmon, and lake trout (Ludwig et al., 1993).

On the one hand, we know very little about nature. On the other hand, there is no time to wait for detailed knowledge of 'spaceship ecology'. Conservation biologists make guesses in the face of uncertainties and even incomplete data can be used for testing (Brussard and Ehrlich, 1992). Ehrlich (1994) calls attention to the *rigour trap* characteristic of academia, in which methods are sometimes more important than results. Actually, information contained in basic ecological research is useful to the policymaker, but it has to be 'translated' from academic language to practical propositions or information. To reach this point, environmental governmental agencies should be interested in academic research and working more closely with universities and research institutes.

ACKNOWLEDGMENTS

I thank Clóvis Cavalcanti for the invitation and for kind support in order to participate in the workshop 'Meio Ambiente, Desenvolvimento e Política'; CNPq for research scholarships and grants, and Fapesp for grants (1995–8).

REFERENCES

Aizen, M.A. and Feisinger, P. (1994), 'Habitat fragmentation, native insect pollinators and feral honey bees in Argentina "Chaco Serrano"', *Ecological Applications*, **4** (2), 378–392.

Alpert, P. (1995), 'Applying ecological research at integrated conservation and development projects', *Ecological Applications*, **5** (4), 857–860.

Barbier, E.B., Burgess, J.C. and Folke, C. (1994), *Paradise lost? The ecological economics of biodiversity*, London: Earthscan Pub. Ltd., for the Beijer Institute of Ecological Economics.

Begossi, A. (1992a), 'The use of optimal foraging theory to understand fishing strategies: a case from Sepetiba Bay (Rio de Janeiro)', *Human Ecology*, **20** (4), 463–475.

Begossi, A. (1992b), 'Food taboos at Búzios island (Brazil): their significance and relation to folk medicine', *Journal of Ethnobiology*, **12** (1), 117–139.

Begossi, A. (1995a), 'Resilience and neotraditional populations: Caiçaras of the Atlantic Forest and Caboclos of the Amazon', in F. Berkes and C. Folke (eds.), *Linking social and ecological systems for resilience and sustainability*, Cambridge: Cambridge University Press, Chapter 2.

Begossi, A. (1995b), 'Fishing spots and sea tenure: incipient forms of management in the Atlantic Forest coast', *Human Ecology*, **23** (3): 387–406.

Begossi, A. (1995c), 'Aspectos de economia ecológica: modelos evolutivos, manejo comum e aplicações', Trabalho apresentado no I Seminário de Economia do Meio Ambiente da Unicamp, 21–23 November 1995, Campinas.

Begossi, A. and Braga, F.M. de S. (1992), 'Food taboos and folk medicine from the Tocantins river (Brazil)', *Amazoniana*, **12**: 101–118.

Berkes, F. (1985), 'Fishermen and the "tragedy of the commons"', *Environmental Conservation*, **12** (3), 199–206.

Berkes, F. and Farvar, M.T. (1989), 'Introduction and overview', in F. Berkes (ed.), *Common property resources*, London: Belhaven Press, pp. 1–17

Berkes, F. and Folke, C. (1992), 'A system perspective on the interrelations between natural, human-made and cultural capital', *Ecological Economics*, **5**: 1–8.

Berkes, F. and Folke, C. (1994), *Linking social and ecological systems for resilience and sustainability, Program Research Rights and the Performance of Natural Resource Systems*, Stockholm: The Beijer International Institute of Ecological Economics.

Berkes, F., Folke, C. and Gadgil, M. (1993), 'Traditional ecological knowledge, biodiversity, resilience and sustainability', Beijer Discussion Paper Series no. 31, The Beijer Institute of Ecological Economics, Stockholm.

Bodmer, R. E. (1995), 'Managing Amazonian wildlife: biological correlates of game choice by detribalized hunters', *Ecological Applications*, **5** (4), 872–877.

Brondisio, E.S., Moran, E.F., Mausel, P. and Wu, Y. (1994), 'Land use change in the Amazon Estuary: patterns of Caboclo settlement and landscape management', *Human Ecology*, **22** (3), 249–278.

Brussard, P.F. and Erhlich, P.R. (1992), 'The challenges of conservation biology', *Ecological Applications*, **2** (1), 1–2.

Clay, J.W. (1990), *Indigenous peoples and tropical forests*, Cambridge: Cultural Survival Inc.

Colding, J. (1995), "Taboos and the conservation of natural resources, species and ecosystems', Masters thesis, Systems Ecology, Stockholm University, Sweden.

Cunha, L.H.O. and Rougelle, M.D. (1989), *Comunidades litorâneas e unidades de proteção ambiental*. Série Estudos de Caso, São Paulo: UICN/F, Ford/USP.

Cunha, M.C, Brown, K.S. Jr. and Almeida, M.W.B. (1993), *Can traditional forest-dwellers self-manage conservation areas? A probing experiment in the Juruá Extractive reserve*, Annual Report, MacArthur Foundation (grant # 92-21848).

Daly, H.E. (1994), 'Operationalizing sustainable development by investing in natural capital', in A. Janson, M. Hammer, C. Folke and R. Costanza (eds), *Investing in natural capital*, Covelo, CA: Island Press, 22–37.

Debinsky, D.M. and Brussard, P.F. (1994), 'Using biodiversity data to access species–habitat relationships in Glacier National Park, Montana', *Ecological Applications*, **4** (4), 833–843.

Dietz, T. and Rosa, E.A. (1994), 'Rethinking the environmental impacts of population, affluence and technology', *Human Ecology Review*, **1**, 277–300.

Ehrlich, P. (1994), 'Ecological economics and the carrying capacity of earth', in A. Jansson, M. Hammer, C. Folke and R. Costanza (eds), *Investing in natural capital*, Covelo, CA: Island Press, 38–56.

Fearnside, P. (1986), *Human carrying capacity in the Brazilian rainforest*, New York: Columbia University Press.

Franklin, J.F. (1992), 'Preserving biodiversity: species, ecosystems, or landscapes?', *Ecological Applications*, 3 (2), 202–205.

Gadgil, M., Berkes, F. and Folke, C. (1993), 'Indigenous knowledge for biodiversity conservation', *Ambio*, 22, 151–156.

Gatto, M. (1995), 'Sustainability: is it a well defined concept?', *Ecological Applications*, 5 (4), 1181–1183.

Godoy, R., Lubowski, R. and Markandya, A. (1993), 'A method for the economic valuation of non-timber tropical forest products', *Economic Botany*, 47 (3), 220–233.

Goldman, A. (1995), 'Threats to sustainability in African agriculture: searching for appropriate paradigms', *Human Ecology*, 23 (3), 291–334.

Golley, F.B. (1993), *A history of the ecosystem concept in ecology*, New Haven: Yale University Press.

Goodland, R. (1995), 'The concept of environmental sustainability', *Annual Review of Ecology and Systematics*, 26 (1), 1–24.

Hansen, A.J., German, S.L., Weigand, J.F., Urban, D.L., McComb, W.C. and Raphael, M.G. (1995), 'Alternative silvicultural regimes in the Pacific Northwest: simulations of ecological and economics effects', *Ecological Applications*, 5 (3), 535–554.

Hardin, G. (1993), *Living within limits: ecology, economics and population taboos*, Oxford: Oxford University Press.

Harrison, P. (1993), *The Third Revolution; population, environment and a sustainable world*, New York: Penguin Books.

Holling, C.S. (1992), 'Cross-scale morphology, geometry, and dynamics of ecosystems', *Ecological Monographs*, 62 (4), 447–502.

Holling, C.S. (1994), 'New science and new investments for a sustainable biosphere', in A. Jansson, M. Hammer, C. Folke and R. Costanza (eds), *Investing in natural capital*, Covelo, CA: Island Press, pp. 57–73.

Holling, C.S., Gunderson, L. and Peterson, G. (1993), *Comparing ecological and social systems*, Beijer Discussion Paper no. 36, Stockholm: The Beijer International Institute of Ecological Economics.

Ives, A.R. (1995), 'Measuring resilience in stochastic systems', *Ecological Monographs*, 65 (2), 217–233.

Kremen, C. (1992), 'Assessing the indicator properties of species assemblages for natural areas monitoring', *Ecological Applications*, (2), 203–217.

Levin, S.A. (1992), 'The problem of pattern and scale in ecology', *Ecology*, 73 (6): 1943–1967.

Lewis, D.M. (1995), 'Importance of GIS to community-based management of wildlife: lessons from Zambia', *Ecological Applications*, 5 (4), 861–871.

Ludwig, D. (1993), 'Environmental sustainability: magic, science, and religion in natural resource management', *Ecological Applications*, 3 (4), 555–558.

Ludwig, D., Hilborn, R. and Walters, C. (1993), 'Uncertainty, resource exploitation, and conservation: lessons from history', *Ecological Applications*, 3 (4), 547–549.

McGrath, D., Castro, F., Amaral, B.D. and Calabria, M. (1993), 'Fisheries and the evolution of resource management on the Lower Amazon floodplain', *Human Ecology*, 21, 167–195.

Maynard-Smith, J. (1978), 'Optimization theory in evolution', *Annual Review of Ecology and Systematics*, 9: 31–56.

Mladenoff, D.J., White, M.A., Pastor, J. and Crow, T.R. (1993), 'Comparing spatial pattern in unaltered old-growth and disturbed forest landscapes', *Ecological Applications*, **3** (2), 294–306.

Neilson, R.P. (1993), 'Transient ecotone response to climatic change: some conceptual and modelling approaches', *Ecological Applications*, **3** (3), 385–395.

Odum, E.P. (1959), *Fundamentals of ecology*, 2nd. edn, Philadelphia: W.B. Saunders.

Posey, D.A. (1985), 'Indigenous management of tropical forest ecosystems', *Agroforestry Systems*, **3**, 139–158.

Rapport, D.J. and Turner, J.E. (1977), 'Economic models in ecology', *Science*, 195: 367–373.

Rees, W.E. and Wackernagel, M. (1994), 'Ecological footprints and appropriated carrying capacity: measuring the natural capital requirements of the human economy', in A. Jansson, M. Hammer, C. Folke and R. Costanza (eds), *Investing in natural capital*, Covelo, CA: Island Press, pp. 362–390.

Ross, E.B. (1978), 'Food taboos, diet, and hunting strategy: the adaptation to animals in Amazon cultural ecology', *Current Anthropology*, **19**: 1–36.

Sinclair, A.R.E., Hik, O.J., Scudder, G.G.E., Turpin, D.H. and Larter, N.C. (1995), 'Biodiversity and the need for habitat renewal', *Ecological Applications*, **5** (3), 579–587.

Solbrig, O.T. (1992), 'The IUBS-SCOPE-UNESCO program of research in bio-diversity', *Ecological Applications*, **2** (2), 131–138.

Stephens, D.W. and Krebs, J.R. (1986), *Foraging theory*, Princeton: Princeton University Press.

Tracy, C.R. and Brussard, P.F. (1994), 'Preserving biodiversity: species in landscapes', *Ecological Applications*, **4** (2), 205–207.

Turner, R.K, Doktor, P. and Adger, N. (1994), 'Sea-level rise and coastal wetlands in the U.K.: mitigation strategies for sustainable management', in A. Jansson, M. Hammer, C. Folke and R. Costanza (eds), *Investing in natural capital*, Covelo, CA: Island Press, pp. 266–290.

Wiens, J., Addicott, J.F., Case, T.J. and Diamond, J. (1986), 'Overview: the importance of spatial and temporal scale in ecological investigations', in J. Diamond and T.J. Case (eds), *Community ecology*, New York: Harper & Row, pp. 145–153.

4. Environmental Valuation in the Quest for a Sustainable Future

Richard B. Norgaard

There is considerable agreement with respect to the directions we need to go in order to attain economic, environmental, and social sustainability. New institutions are needed to conserve natural assets and pass them on to our children, to encourage the regeneration of renewable resources and the maintenance of biological diversity, to develop new technologies which use renewable resources, and to facilitate less energy- and material-intensive lifestyles. These institutions will take many forms. We will need new social mores about consumption, the education of youth, and saving for the future. Corrections in market incentives will certainly help. Green measures of aggregate economic performance are needed. The creation of research facilities to redirect the growth of scientific knowledge and development of technological options will be essential. No single approach will do all that is needed because reality is complex; a multiplicity of approaches will be necessary. Taking such a pragmatic approach saves us from having to pick one solution over another, yet eventually, we will have to select the balance of approaches. Furthermore, many who espouse other goals are challenging us to justify the pace of change in the search for sustainability.

Thus, even while we seem to be far from economic, environmental, and social sustainability, ecological and environmental economists are being asked to systematically weigh the pros and cons of alternative approaches and to value the gains of sustainability relative to other objectives, or simply business as usual. The values used in any such balancing need to reflect how our actions work out in environmental terms. And so environmental valuation must be critical to the rational, informed choice process that is being demanded. By greening the system of national accounts, we will be in a better position to compare alternative development paths. By including environmental benefits and costs in project analysis, we will be able to choose between appropriate and inappropriate technologies. There is some concern as to whether our approaches to environmental valuation are adequate to the task, but nearly all accept the inevitability of valuation. From a utilitarian perspective, every time we make a choice, values are implied.

Thus both neo-classical environmental economists and ecological economists are finding common ground in their efforts to develop methods of environmental valuation.

I document in this paper that rational economic valuation cannot exist apart from moral choices and political decision-making. I do not argue against environmental valuation or generally against developing systemic approaches to understanding complex issues. But the search for a strictly rational approach to making social decisions is a search for an epistemological Eldorado, for a place about which we know from the imaginings of 19th century social philosophers and physicists dreaming of a world of scientist-kings (Norgaard, 1994). Rather, this paper shows how environmental valuation, to be consistent with the neo-classical rationality in which it is rooted, must work with moral discourse and politics. I also show that existing environmental valuation techniques that attempt to work without moral discourse and politics are probably biased against sustainability.

1. INTERGENERATIONAL EQUITY

Economists have developed the techniques of environmental valuation thus far almost solely from within a partial equilibrium neo-classical economic framework. The general equilibrium framework of economics provides a much richer understanding of the nature of valuation in the context of social goals.

Let's consider valuation in light of the goal of sustainability. A possibility frontier illustrating the maximum utility the current generation can experience given the level of utility possible for each future generation is presented in Figure 4.1. Each point on this frontier is efficient because the current generation cannot be made better off without making each future generation worse off and vice versa. Different points on the possibility frontier are attained by redistributing rights to natural and other assets or otherwise changing how the current generation respects future generations (Bator, 1957; Howarth and Norgaard, 1992, 1995). At each point on the utility frontier, factor and product prices, including those for environmental services, are different. Furthermore, at every point on the graph, the rate of interest is different. The economic value of an environmental service external to the market differs with respect to whether one is trying to move from Point A to Point B or from Point A to Point C (Howarth and Norgaard, 1992).

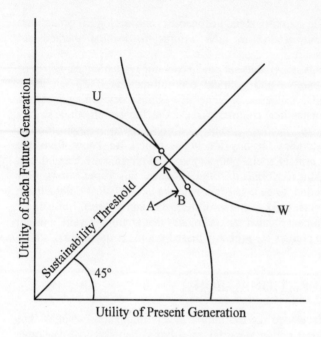

Utility of Present Generation

Note: Utility frontier U shows the maximum amount of utility the current generation can enjoy without diminishing the utility of each future generation, and a sustainability threshold above which the utility of each future generation is equal to or greater than that of the current generation.

Figure 4.1 Frontiers of Utility

Where an economy operates on Figure 4.1 depends on the moral choices it chooses to make with respect to the rights of current versus future generations. Such moral choices entail value judgements, but these values are not economic values. Rather, moral values set the operating conditions of the economy within which economic values arise.

The current consensus that development should be sustainable is such a moral value judgement. If we are operating at an unsustainable position such as Point A, current environmental valuation techniques could move us to a more efficient, but still unsustainable, position represented by Point B. To implement sustainability, we would have to make moral choices with respect to transferring assets to future generations to move to a position such as Point C above the 45° line.

In the general equilibrium framework, it is clear that prices are simply equilibrating mechanisms which bring the economy to different points on the frontier depending on moral choices with respect to intergenerational equity.

Economic values as expressed through markets are determined in conjunction with moral values expressed through politics. Simply by shifting to a general equilibrium framework, we see that the initial expectation of environmental economists that the determination of environmental values could resolve policy disputes is naïve. Economic values do not simply exist. Moral values with respect to equity between generations, which can only be expressed politically, are interactive with the economic values we can express individually through our behaviour and expressions of individual preference.

Now, for the second part of the argument with respect to the probable bias of existing environmental valuation techniques. Overlapping generation models of economic sustainability have been developed to provide an elaborate version of what is summarised in Figure 4.1. These models indicate that environmental values are higher when sustainability is an objective compared to when it is not (Howarth and Norgaard, 1992, 1995). The values are higher for two reasons. First, since environmental services are essential to achieving sustainability, environmental services have greater economic value when sustainability is given greater moral value. Second, when the rights of future generations are protected or augmented in order to achieve sustainability, the rate of interest goes down. This would make the present value of environmental services greater even if their current values remained the same.

2. INTRAGENERATIONAL EQUITY

Questions surrounding the equity between generations illustrated in Figure 4.1 are rather abstract in the glaring reality of the inequities we face today within current generations and between rich and poor nations. Many of the theoretical issues, however, are the same. The techniques for environmental valuation developed to date take existing income inequalities as given. Thus Lawrence Summers, as Chief Economist at the World Bank, rationally argued that poor nations should accept the polluting industries of the world because the value of life is lower in poor countries because wages are lower than in rich countries (*The Economist*, 1992). Many are arguing that ecotourism will help save wild animals and tropical rainforests in developing countries (Lindberg, 1991). But the environmental values that justify saving these environments by this rationality are derived from the resources expended by the rich people in order to travel to poor, but environmentally rich, countries. With less inequality, there would be fewer rich able to travel and fewer poor to serve them cheaply in tropical countries.

In the United States, an environmental justice movement has arisen to address the inequities of environmental decisions. The evidence is fairly strong that people of colour and people in lower economic classes are more likely to live near a toxic waste dump or breathe air of poor quality. Associated with this social movement, there is a growing academic literature documenting how these inequities arise through 'rational' decision-making and through a willingness by the more powerful to impose environmental costs on the weak (Robinson, 1991; Gelobter, 1992) as well as the macro-structure of the US economy (Wolcott, Drayton and Kadri, 1995).

As in the case of intergenerational equity, the environmental values we presently calculate are unlikely to guide us to a sustainable future. Current techniques perpetuate intragenerational inequities by giving too little 'value' to the lives of poor people, hence perpetuating them in this state by justifying sending them the world's pollution. There is good reason to believe that intragenerational inequity itself is a major cause of environmental problems (Boyce, 1994; Norgaard, 1995). Inequity aggravates sustainability in several ways. When the poor are so poor that they must think only of their immediate needs, they cannot worry about conserving the land they work in order to pass on environmental assets to the next generation. Similarly, many rich are so rich that even when they pass on half of their assets to their children, their children will still be very rich. If intragenerational inequity works against intergenerational equity and current environmental valuation techniques perpetuate intragenerational inequity, then clearly the current techniques perpetuate unsustainability.

The general relationship between intragenerational equity and sustainability is summarised in Figure 4.2. Sustainability is possible in region A on the graph, representing reasonable equality between groups. It is only possible in this region because intragenerational equity alone does not assure that assets are transferred to subsequent generations. In the B regions, sustainability is highly improbable even with institutions in place to facilitate transfers of assets to future generations because the current distribution makes it difficult to make such transfers effectively. In regions C, sustainability is impossible. Figure 4.2, of course, is a gross abstraction, but even with a more detailed representation, we know little about the nature of the gradient from possible to impossible as inequity increases at this time.

3. DISTRIBUTION AND VALUATION

Environmental economists have long known that environmental services have different values depending on how rights to environmental services are assigned. For example, economic theory indicates that different efficient solutions are reached when an externality is internalised depending on how pollution rights are assigned. Assigning the rights to the polluters results in a less clean environment and lower environmental values than when the right is assigned to the pollutees (Randall, 1972; Norgaard and Hall, 1974).

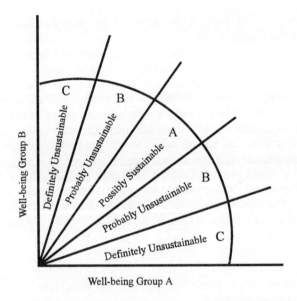

Figure 4.2 The relationship between intragenerational equity and sustainability

Empirically, this has resulted in two terms: willingness-to-pay or 'WTP' presumes polluters have the right to pollute and pollutees must pay them not to do so. Willingness-to-accept or 'WTA' presumes pollutees have the right to a clean environment and have to be paid by polluters for the right to pollute. Empirical work shows that WTA is always larger, typically about three times larger, than WTP.

Here is a clear case where environmental economists have been well aware for several decades of the importance of how the assignment of rights affects valuation and justifies different outcomes, of how moral choices interact with economics. We would justify more environmental protection using WTA measures than WTP measures. Curiously, however, the profession has down-played the difference and argued that willingness-to-pay is a superior measure because there has been greater variation in the estimates of willingness-to-accept. Thus, even though there has not been any political decision rooted in moral discourse giving those who desecrate the environment the right to do so, environmental economists have accepted a measure of environmental value supported by such an ethical choice on the grounds that it is empirically easier to get consistent results (Hanley and Spash, 1993, Chapters 3 and 7). The desire for a single objective valuation apart from moral discourse and politics no doubt drives this illogical, atheoretical behaviour among economists.

Rather than trying to avoid the difficulties generated by WTP and WTA, we need to learn from them and develop better approaches for understanding valuation in the context of distribution. This well explored case raises some questions already. The large difference in the empirical estimates between WTP and WTA is difficult to explain by an income effect that is either small or, if large, is probably not factored into the calculation of the respondents, given the way they currently are asked to respond to the question. Are there ways to instigate the appropriate response? Are there ways to simulate how the economy would behave under different distributional rules and then ask people to respond to questions of value from different hypothetical conditions? The point is simply that if economists truly want to participate in a process of change they will have to develop techniques that are not rooted in the status quo.

4. ENVIRONMENTAL VALUATION WITHIN A LARGER MORAL PROCESS

The foregoing theoretical arguments have very direct practical implications. Ecological economists must resist the temptation to think that objective valuation is possible; neo-classical environmental economists must reconsider the econocratic position they have assumed in light of how it has encouraged them to misuse their own theory. Again, this is not to say that environmental valuation is a wasted effort. Rather, valuation must be seen as a phase in an iterative process with moral discourse and political decision-making.

To start, valuation should be undertaken in the context of current distributional goals, not in the context of current inequities. Environmental legislation in the United States over the past quarter of a century has shifted rights away from polluters and toward pollutees. Where this is the case, WTA is the correct measure, though as indicated above, it is not clear that we have developed appropriate empirical techniques. Where environmental rights have not been assigned to either the pollutees or the polluters, both WTP and WTA are 'correct' answers implying very different environmental outcomes. Economists should not take it upon themselves to presume which of these is correct. Rather, we should be alerting the public to the implications of the different results. Similarly economists should work with the political process to determine whether the lives of rich and poor should be valued at some median, or how we want the ratio of the values of lives of the rich and poor to approach one over time. If economists continue to base environmental values on existing disparities, the disparities will persist. Similarly, we must be explicit about the rights of future generations. It is not enough to presume that progress will take care of our progeny. We must be more explicit as to our social goals.

Here we have a difficulty from the start, for most societies have avoided engaging in moral discourses and developing explicit policies. A quarter of a century ago, when public discussion came to such a point, the metaphor of an expanding pie where all can have more was developed. The 'pie metaphor' is now rarely invoked because the greened evidence indicates that growth has been insignificant if even positive for several decades while the rich clearly have been getting bigger slices. Now, we do not even have a metaphor to invoke when it comes to equity discussions.

Nevertheless, some broad directions of change are commonly held to be ethically superior. For example, the publicly-stated goal of development has been to improve the well-being of the poorest peoples. Certainly specific interest groups have had other goals. The goal of dam building corporations, for example, has been to build dams, not to help the poor. These specific interests have influenced the particulars of development policy immensely. The ability of these interests to do so, however, has been facilitated by the lack of broader public moral discourse and oversight. In any case, the World Bank has had the stated policy for several decades that the poor should be helped most directly. It is in this context that Chief Economist Summer's argument about moving the dirty industries to the poorest countries so contradicts the larger moral frame in which the World Bank claims to be grounded.

5. CONCLUSIONS

Environmental economic valuation must be undertaken with distributional goals in mind. If it is not, environmental valuation will reinforce existing inequities. This is especially critical to achieving sustainable development, for sustainability is ultimately a distributional issue, not a matter of increasing efficiency. To achieve sustainability, more assets must be transferred to future generations. To make such a transfer feasible, existing inequities within generations need to be reduced. While valuation itself cannot solve the problems of distributional equity, it at least should not contribute to the maintenance of such inequities. If it does, sustainability will be more difficult to achieve. New techniques need to be developed within environmental and ecological economics to avoid being a part of the problem of unsustainability.

REFERENCES

Bator, Francis (1957), 'The simple analytics of welfare maximization', *American Economic Review*, **57** (1): 22–59.

Boyce, James K. (1994), 'Inequality as a cause of environmental degradation', *Ecological Economics*, **11**: 169–178.

The Economist (1992), 'Let them eat pollution', 8–14 February: 66.

Gelobter, Michael (1992), 'Toward a model of "environmental discrimination"', in Bunyan Bryant and Paul Mohai (eds), *Race and the incidence of environmental hazards: a time for discourse*, Boulder, Co: Westview Press.

Hanley, Nick and Spash, Clive L., (1993), *Cost-benefit analysis and the environment*, Cheltenham: Edward Elgar.

Howarth, Richard B. and Norgaard, Richard B., (1992), 'Environmental valuation under sustainable development', *American Economic Review*, **82** (2): 473–477.

Howarth, Richard B. and Norgaard, Richard B., (1995), 'Intergenerational choices under global environmental change', in Daniel W. Bromley (ed.), *Handbook of environmental economics*, Oxford: Basil Blackwell.

Lindberg, Kreg (1991), *Policies for maximizing nature tourism's ecological and economic benefits*, Washington, DC: World Resources Institute.

Norgaard, Richard B. (1994), *Development betrayed: the end of progress and a coevolutionary revisioning of the future*, London: Routledge.

Norgaard, Richard B. (1995), 'Biodiversity: processes of loss', in *Encyclopedia of environmental biology*, Vol 1, New York: Academic Press.

Norgaard, Richard B. and Hall, Darwin C. (1974), 'Environmental amenity rights, transactions costs, and technological change', *Journal of Environmental Economics and Management*, **1**:251–267.

Randall, Alan (1972), 'Market solutions to externality problems: theory and practice', *American Journal of Agricultural Economics*, **54**: 175–183.

Robinson, James C. (1991), *Toil and toxics: workplace struggles and political strategies for occupational health*, Berkeley, CA: University of California.

Wolcott, Robert M., Drayton, William and Kadri, Jamal (1995), 'Environmental equity and economic policy: expanding the agenda of reform', in Bunyant Bryant (ed.), *Environmental justice: issues, policies, and solutions*, Washington DC: Island Press.

5. Achieving a Sustainable World[1]

John L.R. Proops, Malte Faber, Reiner Manstetten and Frank Jöst

1. OUR POSITION

Viederman (1993) rightly emphasised that sustainability is an ethical issue (see also Faber, Jöst and Manstetten, 1995). In particular, he gave five principles on '[H]ow a sustainable society will differ from our society today'. In this note we take up Viederman's theme and offer an outline of policy formulation for sustainability.

Sustainability is often looked upon as a scientific problem, for which technical and economic solutions have to be sought. While this is a necessary step, the limits of this approach are now apparent. More than scientific knowledge, in its narrow sense, we need wisdom and ethics to formulate the goals, the social will to achieve these goals, and the maturity of judgement to realise the goals.[2] In summary, 'there are many ways in which society may formulate its goals, and many means towards sustainable development' (Faber, Jöst and Manstetten, 1995: 247).

With regard to the political processes that would be necessary for sustainability, our view is that the role of the state is to 'lead' the market (with all its imperfections), rather than to 'follow' it as at present. While the market will surely be the nexus of economic interaction, the framework within which it operates will need to be established by consensus, through the state. Although even in democratic systems the state is susceptible to interests of powerful interest groups, we believe that only the state, as an institution, can potentially offer the long-run time scale necessary for sustainability, and has the potential authority and means to act as a balancing agent to powerful special interest groups.

Before proceeding, it is worth noting that Immanuel Kant maintained that the greatest form of despotism is if politicians treat their subjects like children, who are not able to distinguish what is useful or harmful to them. We think that this insight holds for the topic of sustainability. Therefore, we emphasise not only the necessity of political leadership, but also the roles of freedom and consensus.

2. DIAGNOSIS

There exist two tendencies concerning sustainability in Western societies:

(i) Concerning the supply side, there is a beneficial tendency to use more 'soft' technologies and products.[3]
(ii) Concerning the demand side, there is a harmful tendency always to consume more and more.[4]

In general, there is a considerable asymmetry between the policy use of these two tendencies; environmental policy is mainly restricted to action on the supply side. This is so because change on the demand side is considered to be a threat to social harmony. However, we believe that policies targeting the supply side are not sufficient on their own. A major issue for an effective policy for sustainability is therefore to influence the demand side. To this end, the consensus of the people is necessary.

3. PRESENT STEPS TOWARDS SUSTAINABILITY

Present work into sustainability seems to be of two types:

(i) conceptual analysis, which seeks to illuminate what the term 'sustainability' could mean (for example, de Graaf, Musters and ter Keurs, 1996);
(ii) work on economic and physical indicators, seeking to test to what extent present and prospective behaviour is sustainable (for example, Azar, Holmberg and Lindgren, 1996).

In our view, neither current approach is sufficient, alone nor together, for formulating policies for economic and social development that is environmentally sustainable.

Sustainability is not a thing to be achieved but a constant process. Nevertheless, a prerequisite for formulating a policy concerning sustainability is a vision of the state of the world towards which we wish to progress. However, a great number of possible sustainable states of the world can be envisioned, and many more will become feasible, even though they are currently beyond imagining.

Therefore, policy formulation for sustainability requires the use of imagination to formulate a state of the world in the (quite distant) future, which we can take as a goal or *telos*. To make progress towards sustainable development, one needs creative policies concerned with the longrun (for example, over a century).[5]

The goal for a sustainable future is in three parts:

(i) The Overall Goal of Sustainability; this is the vision that sustainability should be achieved. This is necessary to allow the building of an ethical consensus.

(ii) The Operational Goal of Sustainability; this expresses a particular target sustainable state for the rather distant future.

(iii) The Goal Towards the Intermediate Target; this is a state on a chosen path towards the Operational Goal of Sustainability, but within a short time, and is used for detailed policy formulation.

Using the Overall Goal of Sustainability, one needs to formulate an Operational Goal of Sustainability. One then needs to recognise how the differences in structure and relationships to nature between what the economy and the social system is now, and what it is in our Operational Goal. The difference between the current state and the Operational Goal indicates that policy steps are necessary. It is important that policy will derive from participation, because the way to sustainability requires a consensus in society as a fundamental prerequisite.

The first step in formulating policy is to examine in detail the differences between the technology, capital structure, final demand and state of nature at present and for the Operational Goal. The role of policy will be:

(i) to ensure the appropriate restructuring of the capital stock, to move away from old techniques towards new ones;

(ii) to bring about the 'renewal' of nature from its present often degraded state, so that the services of nature allow sustainable economic activity;

(iii) and through education and institutional change, to move consumption patterns towards those compatible with the technology and the state of nature at our sustainable Operational Goal.

We need to achieve a three-stage consensus. First, especially in the developed world, we need the consensus to take the ethical stance to allow the building of the Overall Goal of Sustainability. This will give a framework for the establishment of the Operational Goal and the Goal Towards the Intermediate Target.

Second, we need to develop a consensus concerning the nature of the Operational Goal regarding the provisional long-run future sustainable state.

For technical and social reasons, one is unlikely to achieve the same degree of consensus as for the Overall Goal of Sustainability. However, the Operational Goal does not need to have such a high degree of consensus to serve its purpose.

Third, the Goal Towards the Intermediate Target must also command a reasonable degree of consensus, as it is this which will guide policy formulation.

The achievement of these consensuses has to be seen as an evolutionary process, mediated by education and persuasion, but without coercion and always open to reasoned objection. Hence as well as exercising responsible leadership, the political establishment and the civil administration must maintain an attitude of openness concerning constructive criticism. In the process of policy formulation and implementation, it will be necessary to take up new information and insights, on what is technically feasible, and ways of life that become socially acceptable. Of course, this latter will itself coevolve with the consensus-forming debate about the sustainability project.

The movement from the current state towards the Operational Goal will constitute a path of economic restructuring. Analysts have to check that there is at least one feasible path of capital restructuring and renewal of nature which will achieve the Operational Goal. There can be no simple feasibility check on whether consumption patterns can also be restructured; this must be a matter for faith in the good sense of humankind and the effectiveness of education.

If feasible paths to our Operational Goal are available, we need to select a path which is most socially acceptable. For example, one might approach sustainability while minimally disrupting patterns of employment. This step requires not only the process of identifying a path towards the agreed Operational Goal; it also requires the social will to follow that path towards a long-run goal, derived from the maintenance of the Overall Goal of Sustainability. The difficulty of this over an extended period should not be underestimated, as it is likely to require a high degree of stamina by the political and administrative leadership. This will must be supported by the consensus of the people on the Overall Goal of Sustainability. The relationship between this goal and its supporting will is recursive and mutually reinforcing.

The chosen path towards the Operational Goal will not be immutable; much will be learned simply by attempting to follow such a path, and this new information must be used periodically to re-assess both the nature of the Operational Goal and the path that policy seeks to follow. Recognising the contingent nature of the Operational Goal, we should take as our immediate task for policy the achievement of a state on the path to our Operational Goal, which lies only a short time in the future, for example, ten years. To this end, we need to specify our third goal, the Goal Towards the Intermediate Target.

Therefore, our path to our Operational Goal should be considered to be a series of steps of restructuring the economy and social system.

Having established the Goal Towards the Intermediate Target, one needs to implement this target, by identifying policies and instruments (for example, taxes, subsidies, regulations) which are consistent with this Goal. Given policies to implement the Goal Towards the Intermediate Target, progress must be monitored, by the use of various quantitative and qualitative economic and natural indicators, to check whether one is following the target path.

One needs to recognise that any decision making concerning the longrun is liable to be invalidated by one's state of ignorance and the emergence of novel techniques of production and modes of social relationship. Such technical and social novelty will arise from the exercise of human creativity. Therefore, the path and associated policies being followed must be open to periodic revision, although this revision must be within the Overall Goal of Sustainability. Strenuous efforts must be made to insulate the sustainability policy from short-run political expediency.

4. CONCLUSIONS

We have developed a framework which allows us to distinguish between three steps towards a sustainable future: Overall Goal, the Operational Goal and the Goal Towards the Intermediate Target. Our exposition above shows that the state plays a crucial role towards a sustainable future, because only the state, as an institution, can offer the long-run time scale necessary for sustainable development.

However, the state might be susceptible to the concerns of powerful interest groups. Therefore the political system should allow the participation of the society in the decision-making process. This requires not only a democratic constitution. An unequal income distribution and large differences between urban and rural areas, such as we observe in Brazil, are restrictions for the participation of the whole society, which make it more difficult to achieve sustainable development.

NOTES

1. This article was first published in *Ecological Economics*, **17** (3): 133–6. We thank Elsevier Publishing for the permission to reprint this article. We are grateful to Stephen Viederman for helpful and encouraging comments.
2. For further discussion of these epistemological issues, see Faber, Manstetten and Proops (1996a, Chapter 12).
3. One example for such a development is the chemical industry in Germany; see Faber et al.

(1996b).
4.   The public debate about the environmental problems of private traffic, for example in Germany, illustrates this.
5.   For a fuller discussion of teleological principles in ecological economics, see Faber, Manstetten and Proops, 1995.

REFERENCES

Azar, C., Holmberg, J. and Lindgren L. (1996), 'Socio-ecological indicators for sustainability', *Ecological Economics*, **18**: 89–112.

De Graaf, H.J., Musters, C.J.M. and ter Keurs, W.J. (1996), 'Sustainable development: looking for new strategies', *Ecological Economics*, **16**: 205–216.

Faber, M., Jöst, F. and Manstetten, R. (1995), 'Limits and perspectives of sustainable development', *Economie Appliquée*, 48: 231–249.

Faber, M., Manstetten, R. and Proops, J.L.R. (1995), 'On the conceptual foundations of ecological economics: a teleological approach', *Ecological Economics*, **12**: 41–54.

Faber, M., Manstetten, R. and Proops, J.L.R. (1996a), *Ecological Economics*, Aldershot: Edward Elgar.

Faber, M., Manstetten, R., Proops, J.L.R., Jöst, F. and Müller-Fürstenberger, G. (1996b), 'Linking ecology and economy: joint production in the chemical industry', in M. Faber, R. Manstetten and J.L.R. Proops, *Ecological Economics*, Aldershot: Edward Elgar.

Viederman, S. (1993), 'A dream of sustainability', *Ecological Economics*, 8: 177–179.

6. Policies for Sustainable Development

Herman E. Daly

1. INTRODUCTION

The main thrust of this chapter is to present four interrelated policies for sustainable development. The policies should apply to any country in principle, including Brazil. Before getting to the specific policies, I discuss a basic point of view within which the policies appear most sensible and urgent, even though I think they are also defensible to a degree within the standard neo-classical framework. The four policies are then presented in order of increasing radicalism. The first two are fairly conservative, fundamentally neo-classical, and should be relatively noncontroversial, although often they are not. The third will be hotly debated by many, and the fourth will be considered outrageous by most economists. It would be politic to omit the fourth, but I really cannot, since it is the complementary external policy that is logically required if the first three internal policies are not to be undercut by economic globalisation – that is, by free trade and free capital mobility.

2. POINT OF VIEW

Much depends on which paradigm one accepts – the economy as subsystem versus the economy as total system. For those who, understandably, have become allergic to the word 'paradigm', I suggest Joseph Schumpeter's earlier and more descriptive term, 'preanalytic vision'. Since I think preanalytic visions are fundamental, I will take the time to illustrate their importance for the issue at hand with a story about the evolution of the World

Bank's 1992 World Development Report (WDR), *Development and the Environment.*

An early draft of the 1992 WDR had a diagram entitled 'The relationship between the economy and the environment'. It consisted of a square labelled 'economy', with an arrow coming in labelled 'inputs' and an arrow going out labelled 'outputs' – nothing more. I worked in the Environment Department of the World Bank at that time, and was asked to review and comment on the draft. I suggested that the picture was a good idea, but failed to show the environment, and that it would help to have a larger box containing the one depicted, and that the large box would represent the environment. Then the relation between the environment and the economy would be clear – specifically that the economy is a subsystem of the environment and depends on the environment both as a source of raw material inputs and as a sink for waste outputs. The text accompanying the diagram should explain that the environment physically sustains the economy by regenerating the low-entropy inputs that it requires, and by absorbing the high-entropy wastes that it cannot avoid generating, as well as by supplying other systemic ecological services. Environmentally sustainable development could then be defined as development which does not destroy these natural support functions.

The second draft had the same diagram, but with an unlabelled box drawn around the economy, like a picture frame, with no change in the text. I commented that the larger box had to be labelled 'environment' or else it was merely decorative, and that the text had to explain that the economy was related to the environment in the ways just described.

The third draft omitted the diagram altogether. There was no further effort to draw a picture of the relation of the economy and the environment. I thought that was very odd.

By coincidence, a few months later the Chief Economist of the World Bank, Lawrence Summers, under whom the 1992 WDR was being written, happened to be on a review panel at the Smithsonian Institution discussing the book by Donella Meadows et al., *Beyond the Limits*, which he considered worthless. In that book there was a diagram showing the relation of the economy to the ecosystem as subsystem to total system, identical to what I had suggested. In the question-and-answer time I asked the Chief Economist if, looking at that diagram, he felt that the issue of the physical size of the economic subsystem relative to the total ecosystem was important, and if he thought economists should be asking the question, 'What is the optimal scale of the macro economy relative to the environment that supports it?' His reply was immediate and definite, 'That's not the right way to look at it', he said.

Reflecting on these two experiences has strengthened my belief that the difference truly lies in our 'preanalytic visions'. My preanalytic vision of the economy as subsystem leads immediately to the questions: How big is the subsystem relative to the total system? How big *can it be* without disrupting the functioning of the total system? How big *should it be*, what is its optimal scale, beyond which further growth in scale would be anti-economic – would it increase environmental costs more than it increased production benefits? The Chief Economist had no intention of being sucked into these subversive questions – that is not the right way to look at it, and any questions arising from that way of looking at it are simply not the right questions.

That attitude sounds rather unreasonable and peremptory, but in a way that had also been my response to the diagram in the first draft of *Development and the Environment*, showing the economy receiving raw material inputs from nowhere and exporting waste outputs to nowhere. That is not the right way to look at it, I basically said, and any questions arising from that picture, say, how to make the economy grow as fast as possible by speeding up throughput from an infinite source to an infinite sink, were not the right questions. Unless one has in mind the preanalytic vision of the economy as subsystem, the whole idea of sustainable development – of an economic subsystem being sustained by a larger ecosystem whose carrying capacity it must respect – makes no sense whatsoever. It was not surprising therefore that the 1992 WDR was incoherent on the subject of sustainable development, placing it in solitary confinement in a half-page box where it was implicitly defined as nothing other than good development policy. It is the preanalytic vision of the economy as a box floating in infinite space that allows people to speak of sustainable *growth* (quantitative expansion) as opposed to *development* (qualitative improvement). The former term is a clear oxymoron to those who see the economy as a subsystem of a finite and nongrowing ecosystem. The difference could not be more fundamental, more elementary, or more irreconcilable.

It is interesting that so much should be at stake in such a simple picture. Once you draw the boundary of the environment around the economy, you have implicitly admitted that the economy cannot expand forever. You have said that John Stuart Mill was right, that populations of human bodies and populations of capital goods cannot grow forever. At some point quantitative growth must give way to qualitative development as the path of progress, and we must come to terms with Mill's vision of the classical stationary state.

But the World Bank cannot say that – at least not yet and not publicly – because growth is the official solution to poverty. If growth is physically limited, or if it begins to cost more than it is worth at the margin and thereby becomes uneconomic, then how will we lift poor people out of poverty? We pretend there is no answer, but the answer is painfully obvious: by population control; by redistribution; and by improvements in resource productivity. The last comes from both technical advance and ethical clarification of priorities. But population control and redistribution are considered politically impossible. Increasing resource productivity is considered a good idea only until it conflicts with capital and labour productivity – until we realise that historically we have bought high productivity and high incomes for capital and labour by using resources lavishly, thereby sacrificing resource productivity in exchange for a reduction in class conflict between capital and labour. Yet resources are the limiting factor in the long run – the very factor whose productivity economic logic says should be maximised. When we draw that containing boundary of the environment around the economy we move from 'empty-world' economics to 'full-world' economics. Economic logic stays the same, but the perceived pattern of scarcity changes radically, and policies must change radically if they are to remain economic. That is why there is such resistance to a simple picture. The fact that the picture is so simple and so obviously realistic is why it cannot be contemplated by the growth economists. That is why they react to it much the way vampires react to crucifixes – 'no, no, take it away, please! – that's not the right way to look at it!'

But let us persevere in looking at it that way, and turn now to consider some economic policies consistent with this 'full-world' vision.

3. FOUR POLICY SUGGESTIONS

1. Stop counting the consumption of natural capital as income.   Income is by definition the maximum amount that a society can consume this year and still be able to consume the same amount next year. That is, consumption this year, if it is to be called income, must leave intact the capacity to produce and consume the same amount next year. Thus sustainability is built into the very definition of income. But the productive capacity that must be maintained intact has traditionally been thought of as man-made capital only, excluding natural capital. We have habitually counted natural capital as a free good. This might have been justified in yesterday's empty world, but in today's full world it is anti-economic. The error of implicitly counting natural capital consumption as income is customary in three areas: (1) the System of National Accounts (SNA); (2) evaluation of projects that deplete natural capital; and (3) international balance of payments accounting.

The first (SNA) is well recognised and efforts are under way to correct it – indeed, the World Bank played a pioneering role in this important initiative, and I hope will regain its earlier interest in 'greening the GNP'.

The second (project evaluation) is well recognised by standard economics which has long taught the need to count 'user cost' (depletion charges) as part of the opportunity cost of projects that deplete natural capital. The World Bank's best practice counts user costs, but the Bank's average practice ignores it. Uncounted user costs show up in inflated net benefits and an overstated rate of return for depleting projects. This biases investment allocation toward projects that deplete natural capital, and away from more sustainable projects. Correcting this bias is the logical first step toward a policy of sustainable development. User cost must be counted not only for depletion of nonrenewables, but also for projects that divest renewable natural capital by exploiting it beyond sustainable yield. The sink, or absorptive services, of natural capital, as well as its source, or regenerative services, can also be depleted if used beyond sustainable capacity. Therefore a user cost must be charged to projects that deplete sink capacity, such as the capacity of a river to carry off wastes, or, most notably, the atmosphere's ability to absorb CO_2. Measuring user cost[1] is admittedly highly uncertain, but attempting to avoid the issue simply means that we assign to depleted natural capital the precise default value of zero, which is frequently not the best estimate. Even when zero is the best estimate it should be arrived at not by default, but by reasoned calculation based on explicit assumptions about backstop technologies, discount rates, and reserve lifetimes.[2]

Third, in balance of payments accounting the export of depleted natural capital, whether petroleum or timber cut beyond sustainable yield, is entered in the current account and thus treated entirely as income. This is an accounting error. Some portion of those nonsustainable exports should be treated as the sale of a capital asset, and entered on the capital account. If this were properly done, some countries would see their apparent balance of trade surplus converted into a true deficit, one that is being financed by drawdown and transfer abroad of their stock of natural capital. Reclassifying transactions in a way that might convert a country's balance of trade from a surplus to a deficit would trigger a whole different set of IMF recommendations and actions. This reform of balance of payments accounting should be the initial focus of the IMF's new interest in environmentally sustainable development. The World Bank should warmly encourage its sister institution to get busy on this – it does not come naturally to it.

2. Tax income less, and tax resource throughput more. In the past it has been customary for governments to subsidise resource throughput[3] to stimulate growth. Thus energy, water, fertiliser, and even deforestation, are even now frequently subsidised. To its credit the World Bank has generally opposed these subsidies. But it is necessary to go beyond removal of explicit financial subsidies to the removal of implicit environmental subsidies as well. By 'implicit environmental subsidies' I mean external costs to the community that are not charged to the commodities whose production generates them.

Economists have long advocated internalising external costs either by calculating and charging Pigouvian taxes (taxes which when added to marginal private costs make them equal to marginal social costs), or by Coasian redefinition of property rights (such that values that used to be public property and not valued in markets, become private property whose values are protected by their new owners). These solutions are elegant in theory, but often quite difficult in practice. A blunter, but much more operational, instrument would be simply to shift our tax base away from labour and income on to throughput. We have to raise public revenue somehow, and the present system is highly distortionary in that by taxing labour and income in the face of high unemployment in nearly all countries, we are discouraging exactly what we want more of. The present signal to firms is to shed labour and to substitute more capital and resource throughput, to the extent feasible. It would be better to economise on throughput because of the high external costs of its associated depletion and pollution, and at the same time to use more labour because of the high social benefits associated with reducing unemployment. There are limits to the substitutability of labour for resources, but we should take advantage of whatever substitution possibilities exist. Reducing the cost of labour to employers is bound to help increase employment. Nevertheless this policy will be more effective in increasing resource productivity than in increasing employment, because labour and resources are more complements than substitutes.

As a bumper sticker slogan the idea is, 'tax bads, not goods'. In more theoretical terms the idea is to stop taxing value added, and start taxing that to which value is added, namely the natural resource flow yielded by natural capital. Since the latter is the limiting factor in the long run (a point to be argued in the next section), and since its true opportunity cost is only poorly reflected in market prices, it is reasonable to raise its effective price through taxation. Shifting the tax base to throughput induces greater resource efficiency, and internalises, in a gross, blunt manner the externalities from depletion and pollution. It also avoids the distortions of taxing income. True, the exact external costs will not have been precisely calculated and attributed to exactly those activities that caused them, as with a Pigouvian tax that aims to equate marginal social costs and benefits for each activity. But those calculations and attributions are so difficult and uncertain that insisting on them in the interests of 'crackpot rigour' would be equivalent to a full-employment act for econometricians and prolonged unemployment and environmental degradation for everyone else.

Politically the shift toward ecological taxes could be sold under the banner of revenue neutrality: the same amount of money is taken from the public, but in a different way. Even so, there will be political resistance to such a change. However, the income tax structure should be maintained so as to keep progressivity in the overall tax structure by taxing very high incomes and subsidising very low incomes. But the bulk of public revenue would be raised from taxes on throughput either at the depletion or the pollution end, but especially the former. The goal of the vestigial income tax would be redistribution, not net public revenue. The shift could be carried out gradually by a pre-announced schedule to minimise disruption.[4] Ecological tax reform should be a key part of structural adjustment, but should be pioneered in the North. Indeed, sustainable development itself must be achieved in the North first. It is absurd to expect much sacrifice for sustainability in the South if similar measures have not first been taken in the North.[5] The major weakness in the World Bank's ability to foster environmentally sustainable development is that it only has leverage over the South, not the North. Some way must be found for the World Bank to serve as an honest broker, an agent for reflecting the legitimate demands of the South back to the North.

3. Maximise the productivity of natural capital in the short run and invest in increasing its supply in the long run. Economic logic requires that we behave in these two ways toward the limiting factor of production – that is, maximise its productivity today and invest in its increase tomorrow. Those principles are not in dispute. Disagreements do exist about whether natural capital is really the limiting factor. Some argue that man-made and natural capital are such good substitutes that the very idea of a limiting factor, which requires that the factors be complementary, is irrelevant.[6] It is true that without complementarity there is no limiting factor. So the question is, are man-made capital and natural capital basically complements or substitutes? Here again we can provide perpetual full employment for econometricians, and I would welcome more empirical work on this, even though I think it is sufficiently clear to common sense that natural and man-made capital are fundamentally complements and only marginally substitutable.[7]

In the past natural capital has been treated as superabundant and priced at zero, so it did not really matter whether it was a complement or a substitute for man-made capital. Now remaining natural capital appears to be both scarce and complementary, and therefore limiting. For example, the fish catch is limited not by the number of fishing boats, but by the remaining populations of fish in the sea. Cut timber is limited not by the number of sawmills, but by the remaining standing forests. Pumped crude oil is limited not by man-made pumping capacity, but by remaining stocks of petroleum in the ground. The natural capital of the atmosphere's capacity to serve as a sink for CO_2 is likely to be even more limiting to the rate at which petroleum can be burned than is the source limit of remaining oil in the ground.

In the short run raising the price of natural capital by taxing throughput, as advocated above, will give the incentive to maximise natural capital productivity. Investing in natural capital over the long run is also needed. But how do we invest in something which by definition we cannot make? If we could make it, it would be man-made capital! For renewable resources we have the possibility of 'fallowing investments' or, more generally, 'waiting' in the Marshallian sense – allowing this year's growth increment to be added to next year's stock rather than consuming it.[8] For nonrenewables we do not have this option. We can only liquidate them. So the question is how fast do we liquidate, and how much of the proceeds can we count as income if we invest the rest in the best available renewable substitute?[9] And of course how much of the correctly counted income do we then consume and how much do we invest?

One renewable substitute for natural capital is the mixture of natural and man-made capital represented by tree plantations, fish farms, and so on, which we may call 'cultivated natural capital'. But even within this important hybrid category we have a complementary combination of natural and man-made capital components – for example, a plantation forest may use man-made capital to plant trees, control pests and choose the proper rotation – but the complementary natural capital services of rainfall, sunlight, soil, and so on are still there, and eventually still become limiting. Also, cultivated natural capital usually requires a reduction in biodiversity relative to natural capital proper.[10]

For both renewable and nonrenewable resources, investments in enhancing throughput productivity are needed. Increasing resource productivity is indeed a good substitute for finding more of the resource.

But the main point is that investment should be in the limiting factor, and to the extent that natural capital has replaced man-made capital as the limiting factor, the World Bank's investment focus should shift correspondingly. I do not believe that it has. In fact, the failure to charge user cost on natural capital depletion, noted earlier, surely tends to turn investment away from replenishing projects.

The three policies suggested all require the recognition and counting of costs heretofore not counted. It is difficult to imagine a global authority imposing a more complete and uniform cost-accounting regime on all nations. It is also difficult to imagine nations agreeing on an international treaty to that effect. What is easy to imagine is just what we observe – different national cost-accounting standards leading to an international standards-lowering competition to reduce wages, environmental controls, social security standards, and so on. The best way to avoid the latter is to give up the ideology of global economic integration by free trade and free capital mobility, and accept the need for national tariffs to protect, not inefficient industries, but efficient national standards of cost accounting, as will be argued below.

4. Move away from the ideology of global-economic integration by free trade, free capital mobility, and export-led growth – and toward a more nationalist orientation that seeks to develop domestic production for internal markets as the first option, having recourse to international trade only when clearly much more efficient.[11]   At the present time global interdependence is celebrated as a self-evident good. The royal road to development, peace and harmony is thought to be the unrelenting conquest of each nation's market by all other nations. The word 'globalist' has politically correct connotations, while the word 'nationalist' has come to be pejorative. This is so much the case that it is necessary to remind ourselves that the World Bank exists to serve the interests of its members, which are nation states, national communities – not individuals, not corporations, not even NGOs. It has no charter to serve the 'one world without borders' cosmopolitan vision of global integration – of converting many relatively independent national economies, loosely dependent on international trade, into one tightly integrated world economic network upon which the weakened nations depend for even basic survival.

The model of international community upon which the Bretton Woods institutions rests is that of a 'community of communities', an international federation of *national* communities co-operating to solve global problems under the principle of *subsidiarity*. The model is not the cosmopolitan one of direct global citizenship in a single integrated world community without intermediation by nation states.

To globalise the economy by erasure of national economic boundaries *through* free trade, free capital *mobility*, and free, or at least uncontrolled migration, is to wound fatally the major unit of community capable of carrying out any policies for the common good. That includes not only national policies for purely domestic ends, but also international agreements required to deal with those environmental problems that are irreducibly global (CO_2 build-up, ozone depletion). International agreements presuppose the ability of national governments to carry out policies in their support. If nations have no control over their borders they are in a poor position to enforce national laws designed to serve the common good, including those laws necessary to secure national compliance with international treaties.[12]

Cosmopolitan globalism weakens national boundaries and the power of national and subnational communities, while strengthening the relative power of transnational corporations. Since there is no world government capable of regulating global capital in the global interest, and since the desirability and possibility of a world government are both highly doubtful, it will be necessary to make capital less global and more national.

I know that is an unthinkable thought right now, but take it as a prediction – ten years from now the buzz words will be 'renationalisation of capital' and the 'community rooting of capital for the development of national and local economies', not the current shibboleths of export-led growth stimulated by whatever adjustments are necessary to increase global competitiveness. 'Global competitiveness' (frequently a thought-substituting slogan) usually reflects not so much a real increase in resource productivity as a standards-lowering competition to reduce wages, externalise environmental and social costs, and export natural capital at low prices while calling it income.[13]

The World Bank should use the occasion of its fiftieth birthday to reflect deeply on the forgotten words of one of its founders, John Maynard Keynes:

> I sympathise therefore, with those who would minimise, rather than those who would maximise, economic entanglement between nations. Ideas, knowledge, art, hospitality, travel – these are the things which should of their nature be international. But let goods be homespun whenever it is reasonably and conveniently possible, and, above all, let finance be primarily national.[14]

NOTES

1. Depletion of a nonrenewable resource has two costs: the opportunity cost of labour, capital, and other resources used to extract the resource in question, and the opportunity cost of not having the resource tomorrow because we used it up today. The latter is referred to as 'user cost' and is calculated by estimating the extra cost per unit of the best substitute that will have to be used when the resource in question is depleted, and then discounting that amount from the estimated date of depletion back to the present. That discounted amount is then added to the current cost of extraction to get the proper price that measures full opportunity cost.

2. See J. Kellenberg and H. Daly, 'Counting user costs in evaluation of projects that deplete natural capital', Working paper, ENVPE, World Bank, 1994.

3. The term 'throughput' is an inelegant but highly useful derivative of the terms input and output. The matter-energy that goes in to a system and eventually comes out is what goes through – the 'throughput' as engineers have dubbed it. A biologist's synonym might be 'the metabolic flow' by which an organism maintains itself. This physical flow connects the economy to the environment at both ends, and is of course subject to the physical laws of conservation and entropy.

4. See Ernst von Weizsacker, *Ecological tax reform*, Zed Books, London, 1992.

5. Even in its 1992 World Development Report (*Development and the environment*) the World Bank has proved unable to face the most basic question: is it better or worse for the South if the North continues to grow in its resource use? The standard view is that it is better, because growth in the North increases markets for Southern resource exports, as well as funds for aid and investment by the North in the South. The alternative view is that it makes things worse by pre-empting the remaining resources and ecological space needed to support Southern growth. Northern growth also increases income inequality and world political tensions. The alternative view urges continued *development* in the North, but not *growth*. The two answers to the basic question cannot both be right. The absence of that fundamental question from World Bank policy research represents a failure of both nerve and intellect, as well as a continuing psychology of denial regarding limits to growth.

6. Both goods and factors of production can be either complements or substitutes. For consumer goods, shoes and socks are complements (used together); shoes and boots are substitutes (one used instead of the other). In building a house, bricks and wood are substitutes; bricks and masons are complements. If factors are good substitutes the absence of one does not limit the usefulness of the other. For complements, the absence of one greatly reduces the usefulness of the other. The complementary factor in short supply is then the *limiting factor*.

7. Keep in mind that no one questions that some resources can be substituted for others, for example, bricks for wood. But to substitute capital stock (saws and hammers) for wood is only very marginally possible if at all. Capital is the agent of transformation of the natural resource flow from raw material into finished product. Resources are the *material cause* of the finished product; capital is the *efficient cause*. One material cause may substitute for another (bricks for wood); one efficient cause may substitute for another (for example,

power saws for hand saws, or capital for labour); but efficient cause and material cause are related as complements rather than substitutes. If man-made capital is complementary with the natural resource flow, then it is also complementary with the natural capital stock that yields that flow.

8. Forgone consumption today in exchange for greater consumption tomorrow is the essence of investment. Consumption is reduced either by reducing per capita consumption or population. Therefore investment in natural capital regeneration includes investment in population control, and in technical and social structures that demand less resource use per capita.

9. Salah El Serafy has developed a practical way to answer this question.

10. From the familiar biological yield curve below it is clear that a sustainable harvest of H will be yielded either at a stock of P1 or P2.

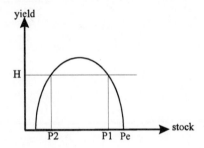

Figure 6.1 Sustainable Harvest

In general, P1 is the *natural capital* mode of exploitation of a wild population. P2 is the *cultivated natural capital* mode of exploitation of a bred population. At P1 we have a large population taking up a lot of ecological space, but providing, in addition to a yield of H, other natural services, as well as maintaining a larger amount of biodiversity and general resiliency. Costs are basically harvest cost of the wild population. At P2 we have a much smaller stock giving the same yield of H, requiring much less ecological space, but requiring greater maintenance, breeding, feeding, and confinement costs as cultivated natural capital. The appeal of cultivated natural capital is to get H from a low P, making ecological room for other exploited (or wild) populations. But management costs are high. The appeal of P1 and the mode of natural capital proper is that management service is free, and the biodiversity of larger stocks is greater. A large human scale forces more and more reliance on cultivated natural capital. In the limit, all other species become cultivated natural capital, bred and managed at the smaller population size to make more room for humans and their furniture. Instrumental values such as redundancy, resiliency, stability, sustainability, would be sacrificed, along with the intrinsic value of life enjoyment by sentient subhuman species, in the interests of 'efficiency' defined as anything that increases the human scale.

11. For an earlier analysis tending strongly in this direction see W. Arthur Lewis, *The evolution of the international economic order*, Princeton University Press, 1978.

12. As a thought experiment imagine first a world of free migration. What reason would there be in such a world for any country to try to reduce its birth rate? Now imagine that people do not migrate, but capital and goods, under free trade, migrate freely. With wages tending to equality world-wide, and cheap labour being a competitive advantage, what reason is there for any country to reduce its birth rate, especially that of its working-class majority? Does anyone think the United Nations will limit the global birth rate?

13. See H.E. Daly, 'The perils of free trade', *Scientific American*, November 1993.
14. J. M. Keynes, 'National self-sufficiency', in *The collected writings of John Maynard Keynes*, vol. 21, edited by Donald Moggeridge, London: Macmillan and Cambridge University Press, 1933.

7. Green Accounting and Macro-economic Policy

Salah El Serafy

1. THE SETTING

1. Different Objectives

By green accounting I mean estimating the deterioration of the natural environment through the degradation and decline of resource stocks, including pollution. Gradually green accounting has come to mean adjusting the national accounts to reflect such changes. Interest in green accounting has been rising, but its advocates vary greatly in perspective and objective. For a number of countries attempts have actually been made to adjust the conventional national accounts to reflect in them environmental change, or more accurately *part* of the environmental change. However, not all such attempts have been effected properly, and on the whole the revised numbers have failed to be taken seriously, and their implications for economic analysis have, generally speaking, neither been worked out nor brought to bear on policy. The central aim of this paper is to indicate the kind of economic policies that should be reassessed in the light of the green accounts and the likely impact the adjusted accounts will have on economic analysis. But it seems necessary beforehand to address a few issues relating to the recent efforts at 'integrating the environmental and economic accounts'.

It should be obvious that a comprehensive coverage of environmental deterioration in the national accounts is beyond realisation. A number of important environmental changes, such as the decline of biological diversity or the disintegration or loss of resilience of ecological systems, are difficult to gauge even in physical terms, let alone be assigned monetary values for their possible integration in the national accounts. Many aspects of the environment will continue to defy being monetised; thus even when the conventional accounts are said to have been greened we must not expect the new numbers to reflect a comprehensive adjustment, or to provide a panacea for environmental ills. The national accounts, after all, are an *economic* framework meant to produce macroeconomic magnitudes, and are not intended to turn out indicators of environmental change. Direct measurement of environmental deterioration in physical units, or in indices based on physical units, would serve the objective of monitoring the state of the environment much better than the national accounts will ever be able to do. True, physical measurements would not be easy to integrate into one aggregate indicator of the overall state of the environment, but taken piecemeal they can be, and actually have been, invaluable for serving the purposes of environmental policy.

And yet, adjusting the national accounts for environmental deterioration is necessary, and should be done urgently for numerous developing countries. The objective of greening the accounts should be perceived not merely as drawing attention to environmental decline, but primarily as a means to improving understanding of the economies the national accounts purport to describe. Once the national accounts have been properly adjusted for the major environmental changes, the revised estimates should be seriously assessed and used retrospectively to analyse past economic performance and formulate revised and more relevant future *economic* policies. Accurate or fairly accurate national accounts, it goes without saying, are essential for reliable economic analysis and for guiding those economic policies that are inevitably based on the macroeconomic aggregates revealed by the national accounts.

2. The Environment and the Economy

Environmental deterioration impinges on the national economy in varying degrees. The environment is being viewed increasingly as providing the very context within which all human activities take place, and is now recognised as sustaining fundamental life-support systems. Even from a narrowly defined economic perspective, the environment is the source of natural raw materials and energy and the ultimate recipient of the wastes generated by economic activities. When the world population and the scale of economic activity were small relative to nature's abundance, the bounty of nature seemed limitless, and it made sense for economists effectively to treat nature's services as free goods. But this outdated view can no longer be justified, particularly in respect of certain individual country situations where the stress on the environment is glaringly obvious, and the national accounts fail to reveal the unsustainability of their economies.

For many countries dependent on natural resources, environmental deterioration cannot be left out of the economic calculus without damage to the reality and relevance of economic analysis. Polluted air and water inflict harm on society – harm that translates into observable economic loss. Awareness of this fact has in many countries encouraged identification of pollution sources, and led increasingly to the internalisation of external costs of polluting activities. A combination of economic penalties, inducements and regulation is being put in place in a growing number of countries in an effort to curb pollution. For obvious reasons pollution abatement has been pursued much more vigorously in the richer than the poorer countries, a fact which has misled some writers into assuming that pollution will automatically be curtailed once income per capita has risen above a certain level. An example of such optimism is to be found in the World Bank's *World Development Report* (World Bank, 1992), but such optimism has been shown as groundless in a recent issue of *Science* (Arrow et al., 1995).

For the more affluent nations environmental concerns tend to be identified with pollution, and environmental protection is for them almost invariably tantamount to abating pollution. With some notable exceptions, much of their natural resource stocks have already been exhausted, and their domestic product now largely emanates from value added by secondary and tertiary activities. For the poorer nations pollution is not any less important or damaging, especially where large and rapidly rising populations are confined in a small space with a poor carrying capacity. Ignorance, poverty and ill health combine to enhance the damage caused by pollution, aggravating morbidity and lowering life expectancy, and altogether undermining economic productivity. For the developing countries, in addition to the enormous economic damage caused by pollution, the even more important function of the environment *as a source* is often also seriously threatened and overlooked in economic measurements and analysis. Agriculture, forestry, fishing, mineral extraction and similar primary activities tend to dominate or substantially contribute to the economies of the poorer countries. These activities are inextricably rooted in the physical environment and depend on its durability. When their environment deteriorates, the very basis of these economies is weakened, and it seems rather elementary that economists should awaken to such deterioration when analysing these economies and monitoring their progress.

3. Sustainability: Different Perspectives

The relationship between accounting and sustainability is profound. To the extent that accounting is built around the proper estimation of income, income has to be sustainable for it to be reckoned as income at all. Often without reference to accounting, sustainability has become a catch phrase in various fora and in different contexts, and is now a banner under which many agencies, corporations and multinational institutions claim to be operating or which they are at least attempting to pursue. Concern with sustainability gained much from the Brundtland Report *(Our Common Future,* 1987) and subsequently from the 1992 United Nations Conference on the Environment and Development (UNCED, the Earth Summit).

'Sustainable Development', a related concept, though difficult to define, has also become a slogan for many organisations working in the development field. Not long ago the World Bank created a Vice-Presidency for 'Environmentally Sustainable Development'. The early pursuit of unqualified economic growth is being tempered now by reference to environmental constraints – at least conceptually – with the view that growth should be confined within the limits imposed by environmental sustainability. The link between the national accounts and sustainability which had been developed earlier is also being recognised, albeit rather hesitantly (see Solow, 1992).

Sustainability means different things to different people, and it pertains to different levels and entities. One view concerns the *degree* of sustainability to be pursued, and this hinges on the target to be sustained. Is it *weak* or *strong* sustainability that should be the objective? *Weak sustainability*, has been described as a concept relevant to the measurement of *income* (El Serafy, 1996). It is in fact nothing more than a year-to-year *economic* sustainability to be achieved through the proper measurement of income. It has been dubbed 'weak' by environmentalists simply because it cannot deliver the stronger version revolving around environmental conservation. Advocates of weak sustainability insist that income must not be confused with asset sales. In order to estimate income from current receipts (some of which may be derived from natural asset liquidation including the excessive felling of trees, over-fishing or depleting stocks of mineral deposits), capital, including natural capital, must be *kept intact,* not as an end in itself, but as an instrument for income estimation. Capital in this sense is 'fundist capital' as defined by Hicks (1974). See also El Serafy (1991).

The accounting principle of keeping capital intact, which (without reference to natural capital) predates Adam Smith, has been acceptable to generations of economists, and finds expression in the notion that income must be sustainable from one accounting period to the next in order for it to qualify as income. This principle, however, is often flouted in respect of natural capital when the national accounts are being compiled.

Strong sustainability, on the other hand, concerns itself with the maintenance of the *stock* of natural resources as an objective on the argument that natural resources are indispensable for the continuation of economic activity, and that they provide the basic ingredients to which value added can be attached. If the stock of environmental resources is run down, economic activity will have to decline. True, some gains may be obtained from raising the productivity of the natural inputs, but this process is slow and limited and needs strong government encouragement which is not always forthcoming. Thus Daly, an advocate of strong sustainability, has argued that there is inevitably a relationship of complementarity between natural resources and human-made capital (Daly and Cobb, 1989) and that the latter capital cannot easily replace the former when natural resources continue to decline.

Some critics of 'weak sustainability' erroneously imagine that it rests on the assumption that both human-made and natural capital are '*perfect* substitutes'. But, if two goods are perfect substitutes for each other they cease to be two goods and become one. Using the injunction that capital should be kept intact for the proper estimation of income, as advocates of weak sustainability insist, does not at all mean that all forms of capital are substitutable for each other. It only means that from the limited perspective of the unit for which the accounts are being prepared, and from one accounting period to the next, a reduction of one form of capital must be offset by investing in another form of capital so that the income of this unit may be sustained. But strong sustainability comes into its own eventually, and in a broader perspective. This is because the situation would be untenable were every productive unit to run down its natural capital in the expectation that human-made capital would compensate for this decline and somehow income could still be sustained. An accounting device, namely 'keeping capital intact', which is needed for the limited purpose of estimating income, should not by any stretch of the imagination be taken as a normative injunction to liquidate natural capital on the dubious ground that it can be substituted for by produced capital. From the limited perspective of an individual productive unit, substitutability of one form of capital for another is certainly available for income generation, but this availability would not hold if all productive units were to embark simultaneously on liquidating their natural capital.

Another view of sustainability relates to the *level* or *entity* to which sustainability pertains. Already the national economy for which the *national* accounts are compiled has attracted accounting attention and this has led to the SEEA (see the next section). At a less aggregative level, some analysts have been promoting the concept of a sustainable *project*. Projects, however, are individual ventures which do not have to live for ever. Some of their sponsors may wish they will have an enduring impact on their surroundings, but this is a different point. Projects may operate for a time after which the resources invested in them can be shifted to other projects until these, in turn, will expire.

At yet another level, *regional sustainability* has been considered. Typically a region is a large sub-unit of the national economy, and may or may not coincide with a large enough *project* located in the same locality. Once those associated with the activity, including the staff, workers and their families, have built an integrated life around their work and in the process attracted ancillary activities to the region, regional sustainability assumes economic and social importance. The decline of a natural resource that sustains such an activity (for example, a forest or a mineral deposit) will obviously have a deleterious impact on the region as a whole and on the lives of its inhabitants. Some corporations, in Brazil as elsewhere, when faced with the problem of a declining natural resource base, have recognised their long-term responsibility towards the community that had formed around the project, and have sought to apply the principle of 'quasi-sustainability' to their operations: setting aside a proportion of their surpluses (akin to the user cost of the natural resource) to be invested in alternative ventures of a renewable nature in the same locality with the objective of sustaining the development of the region as a whole. Brazil is a large enough country where regional divisions are substantial and comparable in size to entire national economies. Regional sustainability can derive as much benefit from greening the regional accounts as national economies can from greening the national accounts.

2. THE SATELLITE ACCOUNTING FRAMEWORK

1. The SEEA

In the 1980s the World Bank and the United Nations Environment Programme (UNEP) organised a series of Joint Workshops with some international participation in order to explore the feasibility of adjusting the United Nations System of National Accounts (SNA) to reflect environmental change (Ahmad et al., 1989). In December 1993 this initiative appeared finally to mature, and the SNA, which had remained virtually unchanged since 1968, was amended and a novel set of 'Satellite Accounts' for the environment was born. The new *System of National Accounts 1993* came out under the aegis of five international agencies that included the World Bank and the International Monetary Fund (IMF). Guidance for implementing the new system was set out (also in December 1993) in a companion volume, Handbook of National Accounting, produced by the United Nations Statistics Division with the title, *Integrated Environmental and Economic Accounting*. This new 'integrated' system is often referred to by the initials 'SEEA' (System of Environmental and Economic Accounting).

The Handbook was meant to be a guide for implementing the proposed environmental satellite accounts, but its authors felt under an obligation to justify the new proposals by showing details of preparatory work that had indicated a variety of methodological suggestions. Unwilling or unable to resolve conflicting views they wisely called the Handbook an 'Interim Version'. Where they sought to resolve conflicts, they have not always been successful (see the following section). The Handbook thus came out long on concepts, but short on specific guidance as to how to put the new proposals into practice under a simple approach of general applicability. It has also become clear that the SEEA aimed primarily at exploring 'points of contact' between the environment and the economy and did not seek to adjust the national accounts as a central objective. In fact the new SNA gave the impression that the conventional national accounts are roughly adequate for economic purposes, and that the satellite accounts were enough to satisfy the environmentalists. Adjusting the macroeconomic estimates that make up the family of the national accounts turned out to be only one possible objective among many, whereas the goal of the UNEP-World Bank Joint Workshops had been all along concentrated on the production of an adjusted set of the central national accounting flows.

2. The Wrong Emphasis on Accounting for Stocks

It is clear from the Handbook that its authors were less concerned with accurately accounting for *income* as for accounting for a sustainable environmental stock. Stock accounting is certainly useful, but it should not be allowed to dominate and distort the estimation of the much more important flow accounts. This stock approach has oriented the SEEA in the direction of those environmentalists who wished to use the national accounts for drawing attention to environmental decline and is reflected in the emphasis the SEEA places on the estimation in value terms of the *stock* of natural assets as an initial step from which environmental accounting must ensue. By implication, the measurement of the *flow* accounts is downgraded and made derivative of the changed *values* of the stocks. Under the satellite account system each year's estimates have to start from the opening stock of natural resources. And the change in stock during the year is inferred by comparing the opening with the closing balances. Other 'troublesome' changes, due for instance to reassessments of the stock, are shunted to conciliation accounts, simply for informational purposes.

The weakness of beginning everything from the assessment of the stocks should be obvious. Since it is not possible to make a *comprehensive* list of environmental assets at either the beginning or the closure of the accounting period (and in fact even for produced capital no country has managed to compile a comprehensive list of such assets), it is not possible to infer the flows from changes in an incomplete asset list. The inappropriateness of this approach is especially enhanced when the stocks are valued (as recommended) at current prices that differ between the two dates, and only the values, but not the physical measurements, are shown. Very little *environmental* usefulness can be gained from changes in the value of the stock, and even less *economic* worth. Much more informative would be the quantification of the physical decline in the stock, especially in respect of those resources that are already covered in the national accounts (such as minerals or fish), while valuing the decline at the price at which it has actually been *transacted*. It is the flow, we must remember, that gets transacted, and not the stock. The price that the market sets relates to the flows and it is inappropriate to apply it to the stock since, if the stock were to be liquidated, the price would collapse. The stock approach, besides, would not take into account the 'imputed' cost of environmental resource use (that is, the *user cost*), which depends materially on the life expectancy of the resource at the current extraction rate. The impact of exploitation on the sustainability of the stock is thus overlooked under a stock approach, and this impact is the same whether annual exploitation represents 10 or 50 percent of the stock.

3. UNEP and the SEEA

It was mentioned earlier that the SEEA set its objective as indicating *points of contact* between the environment and the economy. While this may be taken as a useful objective capable of development in subsequent analysis, it can hardly be a worthwhile cause to inspire urgent action by hard-pressed and resource-short statistical offices the world over, especially in the developing countries. A new initiative, currently under way with the support of UNEP and the co-operation of the United Nations Statistics Division, aims at simplifying the SEEA while stressing the benefits to be gained from greening the accounts, specifically to serve *policy* objectives. It may be noted that hardly any study that produced significantly altered accounts has been used as a platform for reassessing policies that had been based on the unadjusted numbers. It is as if the end result of the process of green accounting was to produce altered numbers for their own sake. It is worth adding that before embarking on any new case studies, it would be advisable for previous case studies to be collected and subjected to systematic assessment. It does not make sense to embark on new and costly studies using different approaches before standing back to cull pertinent lessons from the experience of the past. Previous attempts at greening the national accounts do not seem to relate methodologically to one another, and neither their rigour nor their outcome has been properly evaluated.

4. What Should We Be Accounting For?

If accounting for the *state of the environment* is set as a goal, emphasis should understandably be placed on accounting for the *stock* of environmental assets at a point in time and as this changes periodically. But for best results the units of account should not be monetary but physical. Money values do fluctuate reflecting specific market conditions as well as the general price level, and little is gained by hiding meaningful physical changes under the obscuring veil of money. Many parts of the environment, as stated earlier, are not marketable at all, and others cannot readily be measured even in physical units. If accounting in physical units, or in indices based on physical units, is thought to be necessary to estimate environmental change, why can this not be done altogether outside the national accounting framework? A partial entering of physical estimates in satellite accounts, deliberately placed outside the 'economic' accounts, does not amount to 'integration'. In fact, if environmental deterioration is to be indicated through the national accounting framework, whether integrally in the core accounts, or peripherally in satellite accounts, the objective should unambiguously be to reflect environmental losses in the macroeconomic estimates. By relegating the environment to satellite accounts (though perhaps advisable at present, given the current state of methodological disagreement) the authors of the new SNA have in effect denied the need to adjust the economic accounts. As stated elsewhere in this paper, this conforms, perhaps inadvertently, with the outlook of the richer countries which would leave the conventional accounts unchanged while continuing to label them 'economic'.

5. Rich and Poor Countries: Different Interests

In respect of greening the accounts it is important to realise that there may be a genuine difference in objectives between the richer and more industrialised countries, on the one hand, and the poorer developing countries, on the other. The former appear to prefer leaving the conventional national accounts virtually unchanged, relying for their environmental (mainly pollution) concerns on physical accounting. By contrast, the developing countries, or at least several of them, even before the United Nations Statistics Division's Handbook came out, have demonstrated interest in adjusting their national accounts directly and integrally in money terms. For them, adjusting the economic accounts to reflect environmental losses is of urgent concern. The satellite accounting system, as issued, attempted to bridge the gap between the interests of developed and developing countries in this regard, so it came out as neither one thing nor the other. Although one might venture the judgement that the satellite accounting system was moulded to reflect the views of the industrialised countries, its authors have nevertheless left the door open for adjusting the flow accounts in money terms. In this sense, therefore, the new system cannot be said to have entirely neglected the interests of the developing countries.

6. Brazilian Measurements

Brazil is a vast and vibrant developing country endowed with rich natural resources that are being threatened with erosion and degradation. In parallel with others, Brazilian economists have turned their attention to adjusting the conventional national accounts to incorporate environmental change. One such attempt, confined to the mineral sector, has been published by Young and Serôa da Motta (1995). This study focused on the estimation of 'sustainable income' from eight minerals (iron, tin, gold, lead, chromium, manganese, tungsten and petroleum). It has the admirable quality over similar studies of spelling out the assumptions used for the calculations and, in being so open, it reveals some methodological weaknesses which, however, in no way detract from the empirical work. While it shows good judgement in making certain adjustments to older approaches (for instance removing the reassessments of reserves from directly influencing income estimation as done under the WRI study of Indonesia, 1989), and attempts besides to compare alternative approaches, it sometimes depicts these approaches incorrectly. The 'net price approach' (WRI, 1989), being built on the assumption of a discount rate of zero, is presented appropriately as a special case of the more general 'user cost method'. But the study is on dubious grounds in asserting that the 'El Serafy proposal is equivalent to assuming that unit rents and extraction levels are not expected to vary' (p. 117). The erroneous judgement is also offered (ibid.) to the effect that reassessments of reserves 'cannot be incorporated in the user cost'. Under the user cost approach any reassessment of reserves directly affects life expectancy and therefore the estimation of the user cost. Contrary to the assertion that this method relies on unrealistic 'rent expectations' in that it 'assumes that rents remain constant over time' (p. 125) no such expectations at all are involved either implicitly, or explicitly. In the context of national accounting the user cost approach is nothing but an *ex-post*, year by year, process that aims to convert any *past* year's net *receipts* into a perpetual *income* stream that is constant over time (a constancy needed to satisfy the condition that income must be sustainable). The receipts themselves are not constant, but are perfectly flexible depending on the owner's entrepreneurial (*ex-ante*) decisions regarding extraction, and the accountant takes them for granted after the event *as a fact*. Costs, likewise, are assessed *ex-post* and are therefore actual and not assumed. They are perfectly changeable whether the accountant likes it or not.

The paper's insistence on calling the surplus realised in mineral extraction 'value added' (whereas it is usually contaminated by the proceeds of asset sales) contradicts the intention of the authors to re-estimate income properly, the latter being identical inevitably with the correct estimation of value added.

Consideration of the discount rate in the study is also unfortunate. The discount rate that should be used for estimating the user cost is a real rate of interest conservatively expected to be earned from investing the equivalent of the user cost in order to generate future income. If invested domestically, the discount rate should be comparable with the real growth rate of the Brazilian economy which, in the period 1970–88, averaged about 5 percent a year, although it has tended to much lower levels afterwards. In a comparable study of Brazil's forestry sector for the period 1971–85 too high a discount rate (12 percent) was used (Serôa da Motta and May, 1995). The 5 percent discount rate which the Young and Serôa da Motta study considers as one of three choices of equal validity is roughly the magnitude that should be used to estimate the user cost (El Serafy, forthcoming). As stated before, however, the study sensibly shows all the relevant magnitudes needed for adjusting the calculations, and its transparency makes it a model that is rare in its field.

3. POLICY IMPLICATIONS OF GREENING THE NATIONAL ACCOUNTS

1. Impact on Policy

While pollution can be estimated in physical measurements, and may be mitigated by a combination of regulation and microeconomic measures such as selective taxation to dissuade perpetrators from polluting, running down environmental assets, by contrast, needs to be expressed directly in the macroeconomic measurements that make up the family of national accounts. The adjustment to the national accounts for natural resource declines should not be viewed as either environmental or novel, but simply as an overdue *correction* that needs to be effected in estimates that are, to say the least, economically misleading.

The purpose of adjusting the economic accounts must be seen as ultimately to reform economic policies, basing them on firm foundations that recognise relevant changes in the physical base of the economy. If, as a result of adjusting the accounts for environmental deterioration, the conventionally estimated macroeconomic magnitudes are found to change appreciably, a different view of the economy will be projected, implying a different set of macroeconomic policies. The policies indicated below are presented only summarily, with the purpose of highlighting the need to green the accounts for the benefit of economic analysis. Each one of them may be elaborated in detail in subsequent studies, but this cannot be done adequately in the space of this paper.

2. Market Failure to Indicate Ideal Prices

Once we realise that the unadjusted national accounts confuse natural asset sales with the creation of value added, we should be wary of the macroeconomic measurements produced conventionally by the national accounts. Leaving aside the issue of pollution, the faster a country cuts its forests, depletes its fossil aquifers, over-exploits its fish stocks and exhausts its mineral deposits, the higher its gross and national products will appear, and the faster the economy will be taken to be growing. To the extent that these activities are carried out in the public sector and the products sold on a world market insensitive to internalising domestic environmental costs, market forces will not indicate the problem of resource depletion and environmental unsustainability. Participation in world trade is no guarantee that international prices will be established which would fully reflect the environmental costs of natural resource extraction. Besides, international prices are often influenced by 'non-market' factors including, for instance, subsidisation by important exporters of agricultural exports, and political and military intervention by powerful importers that depresses the price of vital products such as petroleum. Furthermore, the poorer countries' supply curves for primary product exports can be backward rising on account of the poverty of the exporters and the lack of effective substitutes for natural resource exports. This means that lower prices would frequently induce greater rather than smaller exports, thus further depressing market prices. The international market for primary products certainly lacks anti-dumping mechanisms as effective as those available for internationally traded manufactures. Dumping, it should be realised, can be passive in the sense of products exchanging hands internationally at less than their full environmental costs.

If a country sells its natural assets and the economists set out to analyse the country's problems on the basis of the faulty national accounts, then their analysis may in fact be wrong as they misjudge economic performance, misread significant symptoms, and reach out for the wrong policy cures. The analysts would not even know if an economy is stagnating, declining, or growing. But this is not the whole story. For if the national output, as conventionally estimated, has to be substantially reduced because part of it is not value added, then the country in reality is poorer than the accounts make it out to be. Some studies have indicated that the degree of output exaggeration may amount to as much as 20 percent of the conventionally estimated GDP (El Serafy, 1993a), a percentage that is corroborated by estimates of 'genuine savings' made recently by the World Bank (1995).

When economists are unable to assess the level of economic activity, how can they reasonably estimate the productivity of the various natural resource inputs, whether for projects, sectors, or the national economy? Do conventional measurements of individual or total factor productivity have any validity when neither the products (inflated often by assets sales) nor the inputs (where natural resources are treated as costless) are measured properly? For projects exploiting natural deposits such as coal or petroleum, and where the cost of the resource itself is counted as nil, project appraisal would show meaninglessly high rates of return, sometimes upward of 100 percent. Likewise, what significance can be attached to an incremental capital–output ratio (ICOR) that indicates that liquidating natural assets as rapidly as possible represents desirable economic behaviour since ICORs would appear low, implying high input productivity? To what extent can building sophisticated macroeconomic models be justified as a tool for understanding an economy's industrial structure, its changes over time and much else if the numbers used in these models are seriously flawed? Such numbers may be good enough for the rough purposes of short-term demand management, such as guiding monetary policy, but they can be misleading for taking the pulse of an economy, and for managing its development over the longer term.

3. Depletion of Exhaustible Resources

How should the depletion of exhaustible resources be treated in the national accounts? If we include sale proceeds in the gross product and treat the decline of the stock due to exploitation as depreciation, we end up wiping out the contribution of this activity from the net product, besides keeping a flawed gross product inflated by asset sales. The proper way to estimate income from such resources as argued earlier is via the user cost method (El Serafy, 1981, 1989) which translates a natural asset as it depletes into a permanent income stream. Rival methods, including the Hotelling–Hartwick method (Hotelling, 1931; Hartwick, 1977; Hartwick and Hageman, 1993) that seek to estimate 'resource rent' as the difference between the market price and the marginal cost of extraction, while analytically impeccable and heuristically useful, are not operational (see, for example, Devarajan and Fisher, 1982). And marginal cost estimates are very rarely available. The user cost of a depletable resource therefore should be estimated and its equivalent re-invested at home or abroad in assets that would yield future income. The so-called 'El Serafy method' indicates the proportion of net current receipts that may legitimately be regarded as true (that is, sustainable) income, and which can be available for consumption. This level of income would be capable of being perpetuated, provided the user cost equivalent is re-invested. Once income has been adjusted, a whole set of macroeconomic measurements revolving around income has also to be re-estimated (El Serafy, 1995), and this leads to the next section.

4. Economic Policies to be Re-examined

At least four important policy issues need to be re-evaluated after the accounts have been greened. These relate first to savings and investment; second, to the Dutch Disease; third, to stabilisation of the general price level and the exchange rate; and fourth, to the balance of payments on current account. A fifth issue may be added, namely fiscal policy since the fiscal balance may be inaccurately estimated if exploitation is in the public sector and the receipts from natural resource sales flow directly into the public treasury, and get treated by the fiscal authorities as current revenue. All these issues are obviously interrelated.

5. Savings and Investment

It matters a great deal for income sustainability whether or not an economy is saving and investing enough. If the downward adjustment of GDP on account of resource depletion and degradation is large and if this is set against the apparent gross savings and investment, we could get a sobering picture of net capital accumulation (El Serafy, 1981, 1989, 1991). The attention belatedly given to genuine savings by the Environment Department of the World Bank (1995) is certainly welcome. But this is only one of several policy issues that had been repeatedly raised by the national account reformers since the mid-1980s, seeking to draw attention to adjusting the accounts to reflect environmental change. Furthermore, work on policy issues should not be confined to a consideration of net savings or net capital formation, but should extend to the whole family of the national accounts as explained below.

6. The Dutch Disease

If a country sells its environmental assets and does not institute measures to isolate the sale proceeds from the monetary flows associated with other activities, a phenomenon known as the Dutch Disease is likely to take hold, distorting the terms of trade between tradable and non-tradable goods to the detriment of traded goods activities. In other words the tradable goods sectors, other than resource extraction, will decline, and a process of 'de-development' sets in, shrinking previously productive sectors including manufacturing. Economists working on countries where significant revenues are derived from a rich, but impermanent source should be on the look out for the Dutch Disease syndrome. Some direct methods of assessing the incidence of this disease have been proposed (Gelb and Associates, 1988). To counteract it, active policies of monetary sterilisation are recommended. Public surpluses, when generated, should not be available for consumption, but instead invested locally in productive ventures to the extent that the domestic economy's absorptive capacity would allow. When this becomes limiting the surpluses should seek investment outlets abroad. Devaluing the domestic currency would be recommended in order to redress the unfavourable terms of trade that confront exportable goods and generally discourage tradable goods activities (see Corden, 1984). Turning a blind eye to the Dutch Disease symptoms in natural resource exporting countries has been quite common, and economic policies have therefore often been misdirected as discussed in the next section.

7. Price Stability and the Exchange Rate

A conventional procedure for assessing whether or not a domestic currency has appreciated *vis-à-vis* the currencies of its trading partners tends also to fail if the country is a natural resource exporter. This is due to the fact that proper attention is not given to the effect on the domestic price level of the availability of cheaper products imported from abroad and paid for not by current products but by exporting natural *assets* that have a limited life. This procedure, which is often used to determine whether or not devaluation of a domestic currency is called for, begins by selecting a year in the relatively recent past, judged to have been a 'normal' year from the point of view of the exchange rate. An index is then calculated of domestic inflation based on that year, extending it to the present and a comparison made between the index of local inflation and a composite index of inflation in the country's main trading partners based on the same year. Devaluation is indicated to the degree that domestic inflation, thus estimated, had exceeded foreign inflation. While this method (which is quite popular among IMF staff) may yield reasonably adequate results where the national accounts truly reflect reality, it will invariably fail for a resource-depleting economy. If the proceeds from the unsustainable exportation of natural assets are used to finance an import surplus, thereby suppressing a domestic inflation that would otherwise have become explicit in the absence of such imports, then the apparent stability or near-stability in the general price level, brought about by natural capital exports, cannot be genuine. In other words, the index of domestic inflation would underestimate genuine inflation. Devaluation, which may not have emerged as a policy option, could in fact have been indicated if a true assessment of the situation had been made, and, if effected, would have been instrumental in arresting the de-development process generated by the Dutch Disease phenomenon.

8. The Balance of Payments on Current Account

Looking at the same problem from a different angle, a free market for foreign exchange might be artificially sustaining an over-valued domestic currency owing to the simple fact that capital in the form of natural assets is being exported, and its value is recorded in the current account. The market for foreign exchange in any case tends to be too myopic to distinguish between current and capital flows, so that the inflow of foreign exchange, earned by natural resource exports, will push up the value of the domestic currency in terms of foreign exchange irrespective of the account in which it is recorded. Economic analysts should therefore be on the look out for the nature of these flows so that they may get a better grip on macroeconomic management, and should seriously consider devaluation as a policy option. Persistent over-valuation of a domestic currency is a sure recipe for stifling non-natural resource based exports, thus further impeding development.

The question as to whether exports of environmental assets should or should not be recorded in the current account of the balance of payments was broached by Haberler (1976: 184, note 12) but this issue has not since been taken up or developed. If, after adjusting the national income and product accounts, an attempt is made to cleanse the balance of payments on current account of flows of a capital nature, care should be exercised in this process. This is because conceptually the national or domestic product is made up (or should be made up) only of value added, whereas exports and imports contain within them, besides value added, the inputs used for their production. In other words the adjustment of balance of payments flows should not automatically parallel the adjustment of GDP.

The process of adjusting the balance of payments flows in the manner just described should instead focus on exports and not imports. This is because the importing country may be construed as requiring the imports in question: value added as well as the inputs they contain – a privilege that has to be paid for by exports. In the standard case of trade between two industrialised countries where exports are largely made up of value added on both sides of the exchange, one may ignore the distinction between value added and inputs for the purpose at hand. In such trade, the inputs are relatively small, and may be assumed to be roughly balanced in exports and imports. For a developing country, however, where part of exports (and GDP) represents a significant amount of natural resource declines, this part should be excluded from exports in parallel with its exclusion from GDP since exports are inevitably part of GDP. When adjustment to GDP is based on estimates of the user cost of natural resources, it is this quantity that has to be carried into the adjustment of exports. If this is done properly after careful examination of the various items exported, the current account of the balance of payments may look quite different, and a fresh set of policy options may in fact emerge. There will certainly be resistance by conventional economists against adjusting the balance of payments in the manner just described, but an analytical exercise to clarify the nature of the different balance of payments flows, even if effected outside the framework of the national accounts, would be analytically enlightening.

4. RELATED POLICY ISSUES

1. Structural Adjustment Programmes

For a number of countries, attention has been directed at finding out the deleterious impact of structural adjustment initiatives on the environment. Misguided blame, in my view, has been levelled at policies implemented under stabilisation and structural adjustment programmes, supported, *inter alia,* by the International Monetary Fund and the World Bank, on the ground that they have a harmful impact on the environment. Structural adjustment, it should be obvious, is unavoidable if an economy is living beyond its means, and in the process accumulating foreign liabilities which cannot be serviced. Short of the creditors actually writing off a significant part of the debt (and most creditors are reluctant to do so) the indebted country has no choice but to cut its expenditure in order to balance its accounts. These cuts may fall on the poor, health programmes, the environment or other vulnerable ends normally deserving protection. To protect all these worthy ends from the effect of cutting expenditure would defeat the structural adjustment process itself. The alternative is to work out a set of carefully selected expenditure cuts under which environmental concerns, being often of a longer-run nature, may indeed be sacrificed in order for more urgent needs to be met. This is not an uncommon phenomenon since even without adjustment programmes the poor are forced frequently to run down their natural assets in order to survive in a kind of Hobson's choice imposed on them by the severity of their conditions. If protection of the environment is thought to be of high priority to the critics, they could ask the creditors seriously to contemplate writing off part of the debt owed to them.

Much more productive than merely criticising the environmental after-effects of structural adjustment, would be to try and identify environmentally harmful policies already being pursued in countries that exhibit signs of environmental degradation. Policies, for example, leading to the wasteful use of water, settling landless peasants on forested land, subsidising ranching activities and cattle raising, and encouraging the export of underpriced natural resources and their products should be re-examined and their hidden environmental costs revealed and set against their apparent benefits. In Costa Rica, for instance, a minimal land tax that had remained constant in nominal terms for half a century was judged to be instrumental in the drive by landowners to extend their holdings, with land taken out of the virgin forest through a complex process of temporarily settling landless peasants – a process that ends up with the land being turned over to ranchers for wasteful cattle raising (El Serafy, 1988).

2. Should All Countries Green their National Accounts?

There are two important considerations to bear in mind in this regard. First, not all countries would benefit to the same degree from greening their national accounts. Second, not all environmental problems would be solved by adjusting the national accounts to reflect environmental change. On this latter point, enough has already been said, especially in respect of the importance of such adjustments for economic monitoring and analysis – quite apart from any environmental impact that may or may not be gained from a more realistic measurement of economic performance and a more accurate view of an economy's problems. One cannot be categorical *a priori* about which countries would benefit most from greening their accounts, and judgement has to be made, primarily by the countries themselves, as to the benefit, net of cost, of such an exercise. There may be a presumption, however, that countries whose economies rely to an appreciable degree on natural resources – countries whose industrial structure is dominated by primary activities, or whose exports are mainly or appreciably made up of primary commodities, would be a priority target for investigation (El Serafy, 1993, Table 2 lists fourteen developing countries where three primary commodities exported comprised upward of 40 percent of their exports by value in 1990). But such presumptions are not enough, and need to be corroborated by detailed expert knowledge at the level of the local economists who should apprise themselves of existing environmental studies, the country's environmental action plan if available, and any sectoral reports containing relevant information. Economists working on these countries should realise that it makes no sense to produce optimistic extrapolations of exports, say over a 10-year horizon, without examining the resource base from which these exports will have to emanate.

3. Physical Indicators

While many industrialised countries have given support to the notion of 'green accounting', their focus, with some notable exceptions, has largely been on pollution issues with little being done in those countries to assess the impact of resource depletion and degradation on their macroeconomic measurements and policies. The process of revising the SNA, which has so far been dominated by the industrialised countries, reflects, in my judgement, the view that the accounts, as conventionally reckoned, are roughly right, and that any adjustment to them may need to be carried out only in satellite accounts. It is also probably fair to say that opinion among the national income statisticians from the industrialised countries, especially those who have been involved in the process of revising the accounting system, has tended to lean in favour of leaving the conventional accounts unadjusted, preserving old time series while relying on physical indicators, especially of pollution, to direct attention to environmental deterioration. Physical indicators of pollution are indeed needed, and are often used as a tool for devising regulatory and economic policy measures to clean up the environment and also as a means of internalising pollution costs where these are external to individual or corporate economic units. In many instances such an approach has paid dividends and has led to cleaner environments. But resort to physical indicators, while quite effective for combating pollution, can hardly be adequate for the task of addressing the problems of resource deterioration in the less developed countries which are seeking economic and social development. Indeed physical indicators of deforestation, loss of fish stocks, mineral deposits, soil erosion and the like are necessary for drawing attention to environmental deterioration, and for being a basis for monetary valuation of economic losses, but clearly they are not sufficient to meet the accounting requirements as outlined above.

5. CONCLUDING REMARKS

1. Weak Sustainability: Economic, Not Environmental

At the risk of repetition it may be useful to recap some of the important issues already elaborated. Keeping capital intact, however approximately, is a *sine qua non* for estimating income, and does not imply that natural assets should be conserved. If natural capital is allowed to decline, then other forms of capital must be formed through saving and investment so that the total stock of capital can remain sufficient to sustain the current level of income into the future. Maintaining capital intact in this 'fundist' sense of capital is associated with 'weak sustainability'. It does not make conceptual sense to pretend that natural asset sales, conventionally included in GDP, are only counted in *gross* income, with the implication that GDP itself, as conventionally estimated, is correctly reckoned, and that 'depreciation' of the capital stock would be taken care of at the stage of estimating NDP. For this would lead us into even greater difficulties in that we will have neither a correct GDP nor a correct NDP since *using up* natural capital is not depreciation at all (El Serafy, 1993b).

This paper attempted to draw a distinction related to the target for sustainability made by two separate groups. Ecologists, together with those economists supporting a 'strong sustainability', would wish to preserve, to the extent possible, the stock of natural resources, including such things as clean air and water. Conscious of the fact that natural resources are needed *per se,* and are essential for maintaining life-support systems, the advocates of strong sustainability have achieved a certain degree of influence over public policy in a number of industrialised countries. In economic terms they have argued, quite rightly, that natural resources have few human-made substitutes, that the latter are slow to develop when they are needed, and that there is a certain degree of complementarity governing the relationship between natural resources and the other inputs required in many productive processes. The other group, made up of advocates of weak or economic sustainability, may or may not share the objectives of the former group, but they view their position as value free, needed for the proper accounting of income.

When the new SNA was being debated during the years preceding its formation, methodological disagreement among analysts reflected mainly these two points of view: that is, whether it is the weak or the strong variant of sustainability that should be the goal of greening the accounts. The conflict hinges on the following basic question: what are the 'green accounts' supposed to account for: the *environment,* or *income*? The view which is reflected in the new SNA, is that they should account for the *stock* of the environment. This view can be discerned from the very nature of the satellite accounts, deliberately placed outside the conventional accounts, with the latter dubbed 'economic' under the new initiative. The economic and the environmental worlds, if they must be united, can be married only *outside* the conventional national accounting measurements. When the Bureau of Economic Analysis of the US Department of Commerce attempted to green the US accounts for 1994 for depletable resources it went a step further than the SEEA and fully integrated the upward assessment of hydrocarbon stocks into the flow accounts – just as the study of Indonesia (WRI, 1989) had done five years earlier, and reached the dubious conclusion that since depletion, estimated also wrongly as straightforward depreciation, was compensated for by new finds, the adjustment to the accounts had been accomplished, and indicated little change from the conventional measurements. This well-intentioned initiative, if it had been done properly, might not have been abandoned as it now has (US Department of Commerce, 1994).

While the links between the environment and the economy are frequently delineated when economists focus on project and sectoral issues, the links between the environment and the macroeconomy are not sufficiently recognised or properly covered in most countries' macroeconomic work. For many developing countries the issue of the environment, including the supply of natural resources, is of primary importance and for some of them this issue is economically crucial. In order to ascertain whether an economy is growing at all, we need accounts that are capable of sifting asset sales from value added. Conventional national accounting confuses the two. But inability to ascertain *growth* is only one of several weaknesses of the conventional accounts. We need also an accurate measurement of the *level* of output. Moreover, GDP or GNP is routinely used as a denominator to gauge the significance of fiscal and balance of payments deficits, the incidence of domestic and external debt, and also for the illumination of structural relationships that accompany economic and social development. Analyses based on the wrong numbers inevitably lead to wrong insights about the very process of development.

REFERENCES

Ahmad, Yusuf J., El Serafy, Salah and Lutz, Ernst (eds) (1989), *Environmental accounting for sustainable development*, UNEP-World Bank, Washington, DC: World Bank.

Arrow, Kenneth et al. (1995), 'Economic growth, carrying capacity, and the environment', *Science*, **268**: 520–521.

Brundtland Report (1987), 'World commission on environment and development', *Our common future*, Oxford: Oxford University Press.

Commission of the European Communities, International Monetary Fund, Organisation for Economic Cooperation and Development, United Nations and World Bank (1993), *System of National Accounts 1993*, Brussels/Luxembourg, New York, Paris, Washington, DC.

Corden, W.M. (1984), 'Booming sector and Dutch disease economics: survey and consolidation', *Oxford Economic Papers* (36).

Daly, Herman E. and Cobb, John B. (1989), *For the common good*, Boston: Beacon Press.

Devarajan, Shantayanan and Fisher, Anthony (1982), 'Exploration and scarcity', *Journal of Political Economy*, **90** (6): 1279–1290.

El Serafy, Salah (1981), 'Absorptive capacity, the demand for revenue and the supply of petroleum', *Journal of Energy and Development*, **7** (1): 73–88.

El Serafy, Salah (1988), 'Environmental issues and the natural resource base', in *Costa Rica: Country Economic Memorandum*, World Bank, Report Number 7481-CR.

El Serafy, Salah (1989), 'The proper calculation of income from depletable natural resources', in Yusuf J. Ahmad, Salah El Serafy and Ernst Lutz (eds), *Environmental accounting for sustainable development*, UNEP-World Bank, Washington, DC: World Bank.

El Serafy, Salah (1991), 'Sustainability, income measurement and growth', Chapter 5 in Robert Goodland, Herman Daly, Salah El Serafy and Bern von Droste (eds), *Environmental sustainable economic development: building on Brundtland*, Paris: UNESCO.

El Serafy, Salah (1993a), *Country macroeconomic work and natural resources*, Environment Working Paper No. 58, Environment Department, The World Bank.

El Serafy, Salah (1993b), 'Depletable resources: fixed capital or inventories?', in Alfred Franz and Carsten Stahmer (eds), *Approaches to environmental accounting* (International Association of Research in Income and Wealth), Heidelberg: Physica-Verlag.

El Serafy, Salah (1995), 'Depletion of natural resources', Chapter 12 in Wouter van Dieren (ed.), *Taking nature into account: towards a sustainable national income – A Report to the Club of Rome*, New York: Copernicus-Verlag.

El Serafy, Salah (1996), 'In defence of weak sustainability – a response to Beckeman', *Environmental Values*, 5 (February): 75–81.

El Serafy, Salah (forthcoming), 'Natural resource accounting', Chapter in Jeroen C.J.M. van den Bergh (ed.), *Handbook of environmental and natural resource economics*, (in press).

Gelb, Alan and Associates (1988), *Oil windfalls: blessing or curse?*, Oxford: Oxford University Press for the World Bank.

Haberler, Gottfried (1976), 'Oil, inflation, recession and the international monetary system', *Journal of Energy and Development*, 1 (2) (Spring): 177–190.

Hartwick, John (1977), 'Intergenerational equity and the investing of rents from exhaustible resources', *American Economic Review*, 67 (5): 972–974.

Hartwick, John and Hagernan, Anja (1993), 'Economic depreciation of mineral stocks and the contribution of El Serafy', in Ernst Lutz (ed.), *Toward improved accounting for the environment*, Washington, DC: World Bank.

Hicks, John R. (1974), 'Capital controversies: ancient and modern', *American Economic Review*, 64 (May): 367–376.

Hotelling, Harold (1931), 'The economics of exhaustible resources', *Journal of Political Economy*, 39 (2): 137–175.

Serôa da Motta, Ronaldo and May, Peter (1995), 'Estimativas dos custos de exaustão dos recursos florestais no Brasil', Chapter 6 in Ronaldo Serôa da Motta (ed.), *Contabilidade ambiental: teoria, metodologia e estudos de casos no Brasil*, Rio de Janeiro: Instituto de Pesquisa Econômica Aplicada.

Solow, Robert (1992), 'An almost practical step toward sustainability', Resources for the Future, Washington, DC.

United Nations Statistical Division (1993), *Integrated environmental and economic accounting* (Interim Version), Studies in method, Handbook of National Accounting (Series F, No. 61), New York.

United States Department of Commerce (1994), 'Accounting for natural resources: issues and BEA's initial estimates', *Survey of Current Business*, Bureau of Economic Analysis, April.

World Bank (1992), *World Development Report: Development and the environment*, Oxford: Oxford University Press for the World Bank.

World Bank (1995), *Monitoring environmental progress – a report on work in progress*, Environmentally Sustainable Development Vice-Presidency, Washington, DC.

WRI (1989), Repetto, Robert et al. *Wasting assets: natural resources in the national income accounts*, Washington, DC: World Resources Institute.

Young, Carlos Eduardo Frickmann and Serôa da Motta, Ronaldo (1995), 'Measuring sustainable income from mineral extraction in Brazil', *Resource Policy,* **21** (2) June: 113–125.

8. A Politico-communicative Model to Overcome the Impasse of the Current Politico-technical Model for Environmental Negotiation in Brazil

Héctor Ricardo Leis

1. SCIENCE AND THE ENVIRONMENT

Current ecological problems have an importance for civilisation which is not found in other problems that may sometimes seem more urgent. This importance may be seen in the unusual fact that environmental problems simultaneously present a challenge at the ethical, religious, economic, political and scientific levels. However slowly, science has been responding to the ecological challenge by fighting the prevailing reductionism and overcoming the traditional clashes between disciplines. But the challenge is much larger than finding a viable interdisciplinarity. Recognising the complexity and dynamism of ecosystems implies building a science, the foundations of which may be uncertain, and which accepts a plurality of points of view as legitimate (Funtowicz and Ravetz, 1993). Scientists recognise this implicitly in their routine work when they seek hints for constructing their hypotheses in all possible forms of knowledge (including artistic and religious expression). Rigorously, this new type of science, capable of responding to the challenge thrown down by the ecological crisis, is not associated with a new paradigm, as many radical environmentalists still believe. More than a 'revolution' within science (borne by new axiomatic principles for formalised deduction), what is needed is a productive dialogue between scientists and civil society. In other words, the novelties of science are today both methodological and epistemological. When solving concrete problems, to uncertainties which are strictly cognitive must be added ethical uncertainties derived from conflicting values in society. The only way of solving the impasse brought about by traditional science (which, in the face of conflicting opinions, takes flight in the direction of a greater technical reductionism) is to conduct the evaluation of the scientific inputs for political decision-making in a 'democratic' communicative forum, made up not only of government, scientists and technicians, but also of representatives of civil society – including both non-governmental organisations (NGOs) and social and cultural movements, as well as the private business sector.

Ecological problems are different from those which challenged modern science when it began. Modern science allowed the successful prediction of the behaviours of those 'cuttings' from Nature which fit inside the laboratory, and therefore 'accept' to behave in a pure and stable form. Contrary to what was expected, the sum total of the enormous quantity of technologies derived from this science added up to a less-than-confident 'risk society' (Beck, 1992). In short, when we think of solutions for contemporary problems we cannot use the same scientific methodology which helped them come about (nor maintain the same 'alliance' between science and politics). The unexpected ecological problems which have arisen in recent decades have allowed Nature to be 'hauled out' of the laboratory and 'put back' once again in its proper place. The obvious consequence is that, if the scientist must now go and search for his object outside the laboratory, he loses the monopoly of 'exclusiveness' which he had hitherto. This does not lead to scientific discourse losing its specificity or value: it only loses its character of 'dominant knowledge'. The hypercomplexity of environmental problems obliges science to engage in a dialogue where the various existing pieces of knowledge may complement, instead of exclude, each other (Funtowicz and Ravetz, 1993). Scientific knowledge is useless and even dangerous if its ethical and epistemological uncertainties are not considered together. If we are to take ecological problems and the demands for 'sustainability' seriously, we must conclude that the priority goals of science have stopped being the 'conquest' of Nature. Today's priorities are much humbler and also much more complex: to establish a harmonious relationship between society and Nature. Whilst the old goals could perfectly well dispense with all actors other than scientists, today's ones simply cannot.

2. POLITICS AND THE ENVIRONMENT

Just as environmental problems seriously call the foundations of modern science into question, the same thing happens to politics (although in the latter case the ideological obstacles to perceiving it are greater). Normally, it is said that neither the international system, based on sovereign states, nor the management structure of the modern state, based on sectoral politics, is in a position to make a correct approach to environmental problems on their agendas, since these are mostly of a transnational or trans-sectoral type. But not always so, if one observes that the complexity of environmental problems goes much further. The fact that they exceed science and technology's capacity to provide answers brings political consequences that are perhaps of greater importance, given that one of the basic assumptions of the legitimacy of the modern state is its capacity to provide technical solutions to problems placed on its agenda. The problems which excited pre-modern Western societies (in the classical and medieval eras) always had numerous ramifications in areas external to politics, such as religion, philosophy and culture in general. Few remember precisely that our era has substituted *techne* for *praxis*; that is to say, hitherto, the objective of politics was understood as creating a good and just life, for which reason its doctrine was not rigorous as science, but prudent as morals. With modernity, politics would come to have a technical character, and its problems would (supposedly) be resolved in a definitive and rigorous form with the exclusive help of science (Habermas, 1966).

The much commented on and little understood crisis of the nation state refers above all to the fact just presented. It is not so much the vices (which are not few) of the idea of national sovereignty in an economically globalized world which are 'messing up' the state, but the latter's impossibility to continue to substitute ethics with technique, *vis-à-vis* the consequences of this 'political outlook'. From a certain point of view it may be stated that the social question has made this evident. But it does not possess by a long chalk the complexity of the ecological question, for which reason the technico-statist proposals (incidentally, hitched to economic performance, which is no less instrumental) still have legitimacy in the social field. Although there is no lack of authors who present environmental policies and the very concept of 'sustainable development' as a technical exercise, experience has consistently demonstrated that these proposals end up falling into the vicious circle of having to find reality 'guilty' due to the lack of actors able to implement it. Technical reductionism forgets that environmental policies suppose an essential component of learning and social participation which we still do not have. This is different from what happens to other government policies (including those in the social area), which can be sectoralised and subjected to a technical viewpoint because a certain consensus exists in relation to the means with which they are used and the objectives and benefits to be achieved. In the case of 'sustainability', rigorously defined, we know only that we must not continue doing things in the same way as hitherto.

3. ENVIRONMENTAL GOVERNABILITY

The statement that we do not know very well how to do things must not be understood as a romantic or anti-scientific posture but as a methodological requisite. The political treatment of environmental problems is an 'open' process, because it presupposes the undertaking of various trade-offs between the different options and values prevailing in society, which are very often exclusive and contradictory, and which demand taking decisions for the long term with consequences that are difficult to foresee (Carley and Christie, 1992). The realisation, for example, of the trade-off between the production of goods at low cost and the quality of environmental life can neither be derived from a process of self-regulation, nor from the market or the state. This trade-off (only one among many others which must also be made to achieve 'sustainability') can be thought through theoretically, just as institutional arenas for propitious participation can be created in the search for the parameters of policies aimed at its realisation; but no policy can be totally fixed beforehand nor can its results be totally pre-determined.

Despite their deficiencies and vacuousness in many aspects, the most important documents produced by the international community in recent years do not hesitate to point out, in a more or less explicit way, the necessity for environmental governability to be an open process which counts on the convergent participation of all sectors of society, both at the local and global levels (World Commission, 1987; Agenda 21, 1992). Also the recommendations of Brazil's government and NGOs in reports on the environment and development presented at the Rio-92 conference (Comissão Interministerial, 1991; Fórum Brasileiro, 1992) point towards the same objective. It is proper then to ask how the environmental question has been dealt with concretely in Brazil. Regrettably, Brazil is no exception among countries (especially in the Third World) that have been addressing this question in a predominantly technical and bureaucratic manner (Guimarães, 1991). What has arisen from the previous analyses of science and policy is that the context of environmental problems must be assumed to be one of conflict, and that the context of environmental solutions must be assumed to be co-operative. In view of this peculiarity of the environmental question (which prevails irrespectively of the ideological orientation of the actors involved), a technical proposition for environmental problems produces effects contrary to those which are intended, thus aggravating the conflicts and delaying solutions.

4. THE 'BACKWARDNESS' OF THE BRAZILIAN MODEL

Although in Brazil the progressive dissemination of concerns about the degradation of the environment has allowed environmentalism to make notable advances and to build itself up as a multi-sectoral movement since the mid-1980s, and although both the state and civil society have reached relative maturity in understanding environmental problems from the process of preparing for Rio-92, policies and public management in this area have remained stalled and significantly held back in relation to the real necessities and possibilities offered by the circumstances mentioned above. Albeit they are not solidified, the comparatively advanced characteristics of Brazilian legislation in this sphere (expressed clearly in the chapter dedicated to the environment in the 1988 Constitution), as well as the expressive consensus of Brazilian popular culture on the intrinsic value of Nature (demonstrated in opinion polls), are other indicators of the backwardness of policies and public management of environmental problems mentioned above (Constituição, 1988; Crespo and Leitão, 1993). There can be no doubt that the inactivity registered in this field must be included not only in sectoral difficulties but also in the general ones affecting the Brazilian state and society in responding to the challenges which they face. Nevertheless, we must insist on the idea of 'retardation', because it indicates the existence of opportunities which have not been grasped.

The axis for plotting initiatives which may permit lost time to be recovered in this field is to be found within an aspect astonishingly neglected by both the literature of the social sciences and by environmentalists themselves. From the foregoing it might be imagined that *environmental negotiation* was a central nucleus of debate and practice in the area in question, but this is not so. Although it is easy to understand that, without negotiation, it is not possible for environmental governability to exist, the practices institutionalised by the state minimise it by pushing it towards politico-technical instances which are generally at a loss, having very little influence on public policies. Brazilian legislation clearly consecrates the right of all citizens to an ecologically balanced environment by strongly emphasising their role in its protection and management. But, rigorously speaking, the existing legal articles reduce this role to a performance with scant results, due to both vices of origin which have arisen from the technical conception of the tools, and procedural vices brought about, on the one hand, by the 'extremism' of the traditional actors on the Brazilian stage (who have always been accustomed to imposing their will), and, on the other hand, by shortfalls in the practice of citizenship by the population in general.

5. CURRENT MECHANISMS OF PARTICIPATION

The participation of citizens and civil society organisations in the defence of the environment takes place mainly through three channels established almost at the same time in the last decade. These are: (1) the Evaluation of Environmental Impact (AIA, for short, in Portuguese), which includes procedures ranging from impact studies to public hearings; (2) Public Civil Action (ACP); (3) authorities such as the National Council for the Environment (CONAMA) and other state and municipal councils of the same type. None of these channels has in practice created a true space for negotiation. A round of negotiations needs to count on mechanisms which allow actions prior (*ex-ante*) to the final definition of a policy or project, and not just *ex-post*. It presupposes the existence of different actors having relatively equivalent abilities and resources to influence the decision-making process. There is no negotiation when civil society's participation is reduced to a corrective and/or defensive resource, without real conditions for producing any trade-offs and generating other alternatives. Although the intentions of the legislator in proposing the channels mentioned may have been different, they do not allow for anything else.

a. Evaluation of Environmental Impact

The study of environmental impact (EIA, for short, in Portuguese) is a public instrument which began to be legislated for in 1981, and was considered by law-makers as an example of *ex-ante* preventive policy (Machado, 1989). Later, in 1987, CONAMA made it obligatory to have a public hearing throughout the impact study process, when fifty or more citizens, the Public Ministry or some NGO so requested. But the habitual practice of this procedure is in contradiction with this epithet of preventive policy. Generally, the consummated-fact approach is adopted in studies and reports, to the extent that those using it do not supply technological or siting alternatives for the project and, much less, contemplate its non-execution (La Rovere, 1990). The large majority of EIAs are set up to justify the implementation of the project in its original form, and not in order to open a negotiation process. The EIAs are couched in a rhetoric aimed at convincing the public that all possible precautions have been taken to protect the environment. That is, the environmental impact is always presented as an inevitable counterpoint and condition in order that the benefits of undertaking the projects may be 'enjoyed'. Studies of this type do not permit the evaluation of the project to be (as it should be) a prior (*ex-ante*) probing of the final definition of the project, and not a bureaucratic routine in which the gathering together or not of the public audience scarcely makes a whit of difference. The greater technical resources of the consultants contracted by those charged with seeing that EIAs are undertaken, as well as the greater political resources of the latter, end up being imposed in the great majority of cases, in view of the ease of manipulating the populations affected and the under-equipment and lack of preparation both of the government's environmental bodies and the NGOs and others who represent civil society. Regrettably, public hearings thus remain closer to being shams of participation than authentic forums of environmental negotiation.

b. Public Civil Action

The majority of the Brazilian environmentalist community has traditionally not placed much confidence in the Brazilian juridical system as a means of solving problems (Viola and Nickel, 1994). Irrespective of the virtues and defects of the prevailing environmental legislation, it can be proved that this lack of confidence is not only a result of ecological radicalism which still exists in some sectors, but also of the normal lack of confidence which the layman feels towards the inefficiencies of the Brazilian juridical system. In general, citizens avoid appearing before courts of law to solve problems and there is nothing to indicate that environmental conflicts should be any different. There is no other sensible explanation for the fact that, despite the unmatched virtues of the law which regulates the ACP, passed in 1985, permitting the protection of the environment as a general interest (complemented by the instrument of Popular Action, consecrated by the 1988 Constitution, which allows any person or entity to bring legal action against those accused of damaging the environment without running the risk of having to meet the legal costs, should the case be lost), this article of law has been very little used. Surveys indicate that, in Brazil, legal actions to defend the environment are few, and the participation of civil society is practically restricted to directing isolated accusations at government bodies and/or some NGOs in the area (Carvalho and Scotto, 1995). When the inquests and cases of civil legal action of the state of Rio de Janeiro (a place certainly representative of Brazil's many environmental problems) are analysed, it can be shown that between 1985 and 1993 only 100 cases were taken up, 84 percent of which by the Public Ministry (Fuks, 1993). If we observe that surveys also indicate that the large majority of Brazilians think that the responsibility for protecting the environment rests in the first instance with the state, although they do not have much information about the agencies active in the sector, it is not difficult to show the important deficit in the citizenship of people passively delegating to others the solution of environmental problems (Crespo and Leitão, 1993; Fuks, 1993). Whereas legal action is essentially an (*ex-post*) corrective resource, it is obvious that greater participation on the part of citizens could bring important changes in the development of society and the economy, by pointing in the direction of a process of environmental negotiation. But, similarly to what happens in the case of AIA, the impasse of a relatively advanced technico-juridical mechanism such as the ACP indicates chiefly that it fails due to its inadequacy as a concrete means of participation and negotiation (or, put another way, its technical virtues do not in themselves make it a less abstract or more adequate mechanism).

c. The Collegiate Bodies

CONAMA, created by law in 1981 as the superior body of the National System for the Environment (SISNAMA, for short, in Portuguese), was conceived to be a forum for participation and environmental negotiation *par excellence*. It is a collegiate body integrated by representatives from several areas of government and civil society (comprising various sectors of the federal and state administrations, and representatives of the private business sector, workers, and environmental NGOs), aimed at centralising directives and norms of environmental policy. In view of the complexity of Brazilian problems and its existing legal and institutional labyrinths, it was to be hoped that CONAMA could assume an important role in the negotiation of the trade-offs necessary for governability in this area, but reality has shown that its members are not even meeting as frequently as laid down by the existing norms.[1] Curiously, CONAMA started running in 1984 as a relevant forum for environmental discussion, but its performance gradually lost its punch with the progressive institutionalisation of democracy (Acselrad, 1994). Of course, the vices of IBAMA (the Brazilian Institute for the Environment and Renewable Natural Resources), which makes up its Executive Secretariat, also contributed to leading CONAMA to its present paralysis. But, just as in the previous cases, CONAMA's principal problem is its inadequacy for current necessities. If we consider, on the one hand, that the agenda of environmental problems is becoming progressively more diversified and broader and, on the other hand, that since the tidying-up of Rio-92, it has been continually losing ground within the overall national agenda, we should not then find it strange that there has been a fall in the quality of government representation on CONAMA (both at the federal and state level), and that its traditional functions have begun to be dismembered and/or duplicated in new bodies with more specific functions. Instead of serving as a forum for environmental negotiation, CONAMA has begun to pursue facts and to adopt an increasingly bureaucratic formal role. The same thing, with few exceptions, can be said for all existing institutions which take on the 'Council' form at the state and municipal levels. An implicit recognition of the crisis of the current system which generates public environmental policies through bodies with excessive responsibilities, like CONAMA, comes from the very Ministry of the Environment trying to overcome the current impasse through Projects for Decentralised Execution or by creating a National Council for Natural Resources in order to deal with policies for the forestry, fishing and rubber sectors.

6. A COMMUNICATIVE PROPOSAL FOR ENVIRONMENTAL NEGOTIATION

Many environmentalists believe it is a priority to fight for the strengthening of the three channels of participation which we have just analysed (AIA, ACP, and the collegiate bodies like CONAMA and others). Paradoxically, this leads them to insist on a technico-formal vision of environmental problems which, regardless of its intrinsic merits and future potentialities, does not meet present needs and ends up feeding the impasse which they wish to overcome. In the current Brazilian context, these proposals have a strong utopian component, because they do not point to the challenges of environmental governability, which are not so much of a technico-formal type but rather of a communicative character. Environmental governability does not exist without negotiation, and there is no negotiation without a forum fit for participation based on efficient communicative action, where the best arguments have a real chance of prevailing before the instrumental visions of the traditional political and economic actors.[2] The realist-utopian proposal we are about to put forward is, therefore, justified by the necessity of getting out of the impasse of the current politico-technical model of environmental negotiation in Brazil, as well as by the potentialities of communicative action for the governability of environmental problems in contemporary society (Dryzeck, 1987, 1992).

In a previous paper, written in collaboration with Eduardo Viola, we presented numerous proposals for approaching the environmental question in an integrated way, situating it within the set of Brazilian public policies (especially in the agrarian, industrial, energy, financial, and science and technology areas) (Viola and Leis, 1995). In this paper we reached the conclusion that, despite the existing difficulties and disorientations within the environmentalist movement as well as in society and the state in Brazil, the country still has the ability to face up to its environmental challenges favourably.[3] We then suggested that to process better the existing opportunities and difficulties, the creation of a think-tank to deal with environmental matters has become imperative. The proposal which follows does not intend to eliminate the idea of a think-tank, nor to replace the prevailing environmental negotiation system, but to complement both in an integrated way with a view to greater environmental governability. The principal hypothesis of this paper is that under the prevailing articles of law, there is a problem of 'scale', which generates a loud 'noise' in the communication between participants. We believe, then, that our proposal will fill a vitally important vacuum in the processes of environmental negotiation.

a. The Process of Building Consensuses

It is worth remembering that in the processes of international discussion and negotiation it has been well demonstrated that, both in the construction of consensuses and in the search for technical solutions for environmental problems, governments cannot do without the contribution of many non-traditional actors, such as citizens' and scientists' groups, economic corporations, the media, religious institutions, intergovernmental agencies and NGOs. But we must not conclude from this that good communication between these actors has been possible in all cases. Communication really functioned when the strict rules of diplomatic discussion were applied in well-defined and not excessively wide spaces and agendas. We can then verify that the communicative competence of the participants was augmented, and greater consensus was progressively obtained, irrespective of the diversity of interests and values at stake.[4] The appropriate definition of the negotiation space, according to the requisites of communicative competence, is an essential aspect, although very often neglected, of the process of negotiation. This does not mean by any measure that all the actors must possess x or y pieces of technical knowledge about the theme in question, but the simple fact that the rules, the problems to be considered and the level of representation of the actors present in the space must contribute to the constitution of an authentic communicative community with real negotiation conditions. Although this is obvious, few stop to think, for example, that for the success of a negotiation the legitimacy of the representation of the participants is just as, or more, essential than the technical means available for solving the problems on the agenda.

The creation of consensus presupposes prolonged 'face-to-face' meetings, in which the participants may construct relations of trust and knowledge which, added to their common interest in finding solutions for the problems, generate a high rejection of any attempt at discursive instrumentality. The correct dimensioning of the communication forum guarantees the validity of the participants' communicative action, since it impedes the transformation of the action into one exclusively aimed at carrying out one's own intentions. By way of illustration, let us say that the participants of the existing channels of negotiation in Brazil normally have at their disposal a high quota of 'impunity', in the sense that they seldom meet, the levels of representation are not equivalent and many of them possess scant legitimacy, in addition to their being obliged to speak about an agenda that is either far too wide or far too restricted. That the participants do or do not use this impunity depends more on their good judgement than on the sanctions which can one day be imposed on them and their interests. What Habermas calls the 'discourse ideal situation' is precisely characterised as being an interaction where the claim of validity of the participants' discourse (basically: truth, correction and sincerity) can be criticised in such a way that each interlocutor may recognise the responsibility, sincerity and coherence of each one (Habermas, 1984). To a large degree, the secret of any negotiation therefore resides in the correct dimensioning of the communication space so that no one can be misled with impunity.

b. Characteristics of the Appropriate Spaces for Environmental Negotiation

Our proposal is aimed at questions to be negotiated and decided in intermediate (*meso*) instances, neither very *macro* nor very *micro* (as has been happening until now), organised on the basis of the problems of the environmental agenda and of its 'natural' actors (leaving to one side the politico-legal 'scales' which characterise the existing devices). The negotiation processes within the *meso* and *ad hoc* structures constitute a practice recognised and accepted in many places, but unfortunately not in Brazil.[5] The bureaucratic-centraliser patrimonialism of the Brazilian State traditionally leads it to resist the (democratic or not) division of its grasp of power in the definition of public policies. The brief environmental history of Brazil does not register significant instances which might justify the type of negotiation which is being argued for here, but it is opportune to comment that recent political history has revealed a notable example of negotiation in a relatively 'informal' space as that suggested. We refer to the so-called 'sectoral chambers' (in particular that of the automobile sector), which have been examples not only of a democratic relationship among diverse actors with contradictory interests but also efficient and beneficial for everyone (Arbix, 1995). Let us remember that these chambers (which had their best performance from 1992 to 1994, during the Collor and Itamar Franco governments) were explicitly constructed as consensual negotiation spaces (basically, between government agencies, trade unions and business), thus favouring communicative competence. Let it be said that the current Fernando Henrique Cardoso government has been emptying these sectoral chambers, thus ruining their innovative political potentiality for these and many other problems and actors of Brazilian society.

We do not intend to make here any forced comparison between policies in the environmental area and in the automobile sector, but we have introduced the 'sectoral chambers' because they are a very successful example of co-operation in a non-formal space between actors with specific pieces of knowledge and contradictory values stakes, so giving adequate conditions for communicative competence. Despite the fact that the complexity of the environmental problems is qualitatively superior to those which arise from labour relations (we said before that in the social area technical solutions will continue to have legitimacy), we believe that the way out of the impasse of Brazilian environmental policy is not qualitatively different from the way out found to overcome the impasse in which the automobile sector was to be found at the time of the emergence of the 'chambers' at the beginning of the 1990s. The secret of this similarity, besides the enormous differences which separate one case from the other, resides in the fact that in both *the way out of the impasse is situated in the creation of an appropriate negotiation space which may serve both to solve problems and to create the means for their solution (in other words, that it be political and pedagogical, because it is communicative).*

c. Integrating Communicative Communities into Environmental Negotiation

Let us now render concrete our proposal. It is a question of integrating the politico-technical model of existing environmental negotiation with a politico-communicative model (therefore, of a consensual nature), which must be applied to perfectly defined problems on a *meso* scale and in an *ad hoc* fashion. The environmental negotiation spaces (ENAs, for short, in Portuguese) created from this model will allow the diverse political, technical, social and ethical aspects of problems and/or very concrete projects to be approached with communicative competence, thus generating the opportunity of reaching a consensus capable of carrying out the necessary trade-offs which environmental governability demands. An essential difference in the composition of ENAs in relation to the 'sectoral chamber' (derived basically from the public and private character of the assets in dispute in one and the other structure, respectively) is that in the first case a single technical team will have to exist, in contrast to the other case, where various teams exist (since each of the parties takes along its own advisers). As a dispute over common assets, the ENA proposal does not correspond to a 'privatisation' of the scientific-technical discourse (it would be equally as absurd as the wish that each traditional actor took along his own environmental NGO to the debate). This possibility must be totally avoided in the treatment of complex problems which, therefore, admit a multiplicity of approaches and demand the discursive autonomy of each one of the various participating communicative communities. Depending on the case to be negotiated, the ENA will admit the participation of various communicative communities (CCs), which may go from a maximum of six to a minimum of three. In more complex cases, it will have to count on representations from the actors more directly involved, from:

(a) governmental bodies (political CCs, in a strict sense);
(b) environmental NGOs (environmental CCs, in a strict sense);
(c) scientific-technical entities (epistemological CCs);
(d) economic corporations (business CCs);
(e) trade unions (workers' CCs);

(f) other NGOs and entities of civil society which are representative of the
     stakes of the population affected (ethico-social CCs).

In less complex cases ENAs will be able to count on at least representations
stemming from the first three CCs (political, environmental, and
epistemological). In anticipated response to possible criticisms, we add in
relation to this point that the ENA proposal is not aimed at diluting the role of
the Ministry of the Environment. Nothing could be further from reality than
this, to the extent that the latter will have to carry out the difficult task of
taking the initiative and defining exactly the themes and dimensions of the
ENAs, as well as inviting and legitimising the various representations and
conducting the negotiation process itself.

     With respect to the launch of the ENAs, let us say that it is not suitable for
there to be many at the start. The ENAs presuppose a relatively lengthy
process of apprenticeship on the part of the actors involved, which suggests it
is a better use of human and material resources available to go 'slowly', in
order to take better advantage of the know-how of the first experiences. By
way of example, we list below some themes from the current environmental
agenda, simply to give an idea of the type and diversity of the problem areas
which can be tackled within the ENAs:

(a) project for the Brazil-Argentina hydro-way (the *hidrovia*);
(b) project for the diversion of the waters of the river São Francisco;
(c) programme for energy conservation and production of solar energy;
(d) national reforestation programme;
(e) programme of sustainable agriculture;
(f) setting and control of environmental norms for the production of food;
(g) setting and control of environmental norms for the quality of life in the
     large cities.

     Obviously, we cannot in the brief space of this paper give an account of
the 'engineering' necessary to make the ENAs viable within the existing
political-juridical system. Certainly, this aspect will have to be studied at a
later date, if the political will to carry out this proposal emerges. Here we are
only trying to justify it theoretically. At any rate, by way of conclusion, we
would like to add that perhaps the best form of analysing the suitability
and/or viability of this (or other similar) proposals, as well as the
characteristics and the objectives of its possible implementation, would be to
give priority to the above-mentioned creation of a think-tank for
sustainability, in such a way that amongst its first tasks we might include the
discussion of the intricate problem of environmental negotiation.

NOTES

1. According to Assis (1992), at the legal level, apart from the chapter of the 1988 Constitution and various specific laws, we have in Brazil: the Waters Code, the Forest Code, the Hunting Code, the Fishing Code, the Mineral Exploitation Code, the National Policy for Sanitation, the Land Statute, and so on; and at the institutional level, in addition to the Ministry for the Environment and IBAMA, we have: SUDEPE, IBGE, DNOS, DNOCS (now defunct), the Superintendencies for Development of the Ministry of the Interior, and others, all of them with some capacity to get in each other's way on environmental subjects.
2. According to Habermas (1984), the concept of 'communicative action' explains an action where the participants are seeking to reach an understanding on a question and also to co-ordinate their plans through consensus. Communicative action represents the ideal form of social action to the extent that all those involved have equality of opportunity to decide the guidelines that will determine collective life. This action supposes, therefore, the absence of any coercion since the diverse positions of any one of the participants will have to take into account the possibility of being contested by the others, thus having to be proved through the presentation of the best arguments and not by the use of force. For a more recent analysis of communicative action from the perspective of the social movements and civil society see Cohen and Arato, 1992.
3. In addition to the work cited, for a vision from a sustainability point of view of Brazil in the future see Viola, 1995.
4. For some examples of the importance of communicative action (although not always presented conceptually under this name) for the range of environmental problems at the international level see Benedick, 1992; Caldwell, 1993; Haas, 1993; Haas et al., 1994; and Leis, 1995.
5. The United States is perhaps the country with the highest degree of historical acknowledgement of this type of practice (see the case studies contained in Lake, 1980, and Talbot, 1983). As a rule, we may say that in the less developed countries, even when no formal and/or legal restrictions exist, those practices have been less frequent than in the countries with more advanced economies. A possible explanation for this fact could be found in the various factors which result from the state's more centralising role, and from the weaknesses of civil society, in the more economically backward countries (see D'Amato, 1996).

REFERENCES

Acselrad, H. (1994), 'Dados para um diagnóstico sobre o CONAMA', *Políticas Ambientais*, 2 (5).

Agenda 21: The United Nations programme of action from Rio (1992), New York: UN Publications.

Arbix, G. (1995), 'Social-democracia sem concertação?', *Novos Estudos*, **43**.

Assis, L.F.S. de (1992), 'Meio ambiente e políticas públicas', Brasília, Comissão de Defesa do Consumidor, Meio Ambiente e Minorias, Chamber of Deputies (mimeo).

Beck, U. (1992), *Risk society: towards a new modernity*, London: Sage.

Benedick, R.E. (1992), 'Inner workings of the new global negotiations', *The Columbia Journal of World Business*.

Caldwell, L.K. (1993), *Ecología, ciencia y política medioambiental*, Madrid: McGraw-Hill.

Carley, M. and Christie, I. (1992), *Managing sustainable development*, London: Earthscan.

Carvalho, I. and Scotto, G. (1995), *Conflitos sócio-ambientais no Brasil*, Vol. 1, Rio de Janeiro: IBASE.

Cohen, J. and Arato, A. (1992), *Civil society and political theory*, Cambridge, MA: MIT Press.

Comissão Interministerial para reparação da Conferência das Nações Unidas sobre Meio Ambiente e Desenvolvimento (1991), *O Desafio do desenvolvimento sustentável: relatório do Brasil para a Conferência das Nações Unidas sobre o meio ambiente e desenvolvimento*, Brasília: Secretaria de Imprensa, Presidência da República.

Constituição da República Federativa do Brasil (1988), Brasília: Secretaria de Imprensa, Presidência da República.

Crespo, S. and Leitão, P. (1993), *O que o Brasileiro pensa da ecologia*, Rio de Janeiro: ISER.

D'Amato, J.L. (1996), *Reflexiones desde el campo y la ciudad*, Córdoba: GADU (mimeo).

Dryzeck, J.S. (1987), *Rational ecology: environment and political economy*, Oxford: Basil Blackwell.

Dryzeck, J.S. (1992), 'Ecology and discursive democracy: beyond liberal capitalism and the administrative state', *Capitalism, Nature, Socialism*, **3** (10).

Fórum Brasileiro de ONGs e Movimentos Sociais para a Conferência da Sociedade Civil sobre Meio Ambiente e Desenvolvimento (1992), *Meio ambiente e desenvolvimento: uma visão das ONGs e dos Movimentos Sociais Brasileiros*, Rio de Janeiro.

Fuks, M. (1993), 'Ação civil pública – uma conquista a ser assegurada', *Políticas Ambientais*, **1** (2/3).

Funtowicz, S. and Ravetz, R. (1993), *Epistomología política*, Buenos Aires: Centro Editor de América Latina.

Guimarães, R. (1991), *The ecopolitics of development in the Third World: politics and environment in Brazil*, Boulder, CO: Lynne Rienner.

Haas, P.M. (1993), 'Epistemic communities and the dynamics of international environmental co-operation', in V. Rittenberger (ed.), *Regime theory and international relations*, Oxford: Clarendon Press.

Hass, P.M. et al. (eds) (1994), *Institutions for the earth: sources of effective international environmental protection*, Cambridge, MA: MIT Press.

Habermas, J. (1966), *Teoría y praxis*, Buenos Aires: Sur.

Habermas, J. (1984), *The theory of communicative action*, Vols. I and II, Boston, MA: Beacon Press.

Lake, L.M. (ed.) (1980), *Environmental mediation: the search for consensus*, Boulder, CO: Westview Press.

La Rovere, E.L. (1990), 'A universidade e a avaliação de impactos ambientais', in Antônio C.R. Moraes et al. (eds), *Universidade e sociedade face à política ambiental Brasileira*, Florianópolis: UFSC.

Leis, H.R. (1995), 'Globalização e democracia: necessidade e oportunidade de um espaço público transnacional', *Revista Brasileria de Ciências Sociais* (ANPOCS), year 10, no. 28.

Machado, P.A.L. (1989), *Direito ambiental Brasileiro*, São Paulo: Editora Revista dos Tribunais.

Talbot, A.R. (1983), *Settling things: six case studies in environmental mediation*, Washington, DC: Conservation Foundation.

Viola, E.J. (1995), 'Essay on Brazil', in T. Nagpal and C. Folts (eds), *Choosing our future: visions of a sustainable world*, Baltimore, MD: WRI.

Viola, E.J. and Leis, H.R. (1995), 'O ambientalismo multissetorial no Brasil para além da Rio-92: o desafio de uma estratégia globalista viável', in Héctor Leis et al. (eds), *Meio ambiente, desenvolvimento e cidadania: desafios para as ciências sociais*, São Paulo/Florianópolis: Cortez/UFSC.

Viola, E.J. and Nickel, J. (1994), 'Integrando a defesa dos direitos humanos e do meio ambiente: lições do Brasil', *Novos Estudos*, **40**.

World Commission on Environment and Development (1987), *Our common future*, Oxford: Oxford University Press.

9. Agenda 21: A Sustainable Development Strategy Supported by Participatory Decision-making Processes

Sérgio C. Trindade

1. INTRODUCTION

Agenda 21 is a useful tool to organise the efforts of society to achieve sustainable development. However, Agenda 21's structure is fragmented and requires careful analysis to extract practical instruments for the implementation of sustainable development. The need to convert the good intentions of Agenda 21 into practical achievements led to the introduction in it (as its Chapter 37) of the notion of the national Agenda 21, which deals with capacity building. What makes the national Agenda 21 singular is the transparent and participatory nature of the process that generates it.

Chapter 28 of Agenda 21, on the local authorities, borrowed these concepts and applied them to local situations, such as communities, municipalities, states, provinces, and so on. The Agenda 21 concept can be stretched to address thematic issues. Although not explicitly considered in the draft of the global Agenda 21, one could think of thematic Agendas 21, for instance, a Water Agenda 21 applied to a specific body of water, an Air Agenda 21 for a specific urban agglomeration suffering from severe air pollution, and so on. In July 1994, the UNEP International Environmental Technology Centre, in Japan, proposed the Water Agenda 21 of Katowice, in Poland and the Agenda 21 of the City of Shenyang, the capital of the Liaoning province in China.

The discussion that follows focuses initially on the key feature of the national (or local) Agenda 21, namely the participatory decision-making process it employs. Extensive practical examples are provided. The discussion continues with the presentation of the global Agenda 21. The national Agenda 21 is later introduced, as well as the local and thematic agendas. Reviews of the China and Bolivia national Agendas 21 are presented, as they are among the few national Agendas 21 completed so far. China was the first country in the world to complete a national Agenda 21. And, in Latin America, Bolivia is the only country that has concluded a national Agenda 21.

In Brazil, efforts at a national Agenda 21 started in 1995. In 1997 a Commission on Sustainable Development and Agenda 21 was established within the Office of the President, with stakeholders from government and society. The large size and diversity of Brazil suggested an approach by broad ecosystems, if possible coinciding with geographical regions, and perhaps an urban thematic approach. So far the only regional Agenda 21 within Brazil that has advanced is the Brazilian Amazonia Agenda 21. Efforts are under way to complete the Brazilian national Agenda 21 by December 1998 and use the findings to shape the next pluriannual development plan.

An exciting proposal to develop the Agenda 21 of the Greater Amazonia, an area the size of Australia in Northern South America, with the largest biodiversity on earth, is presented as well. The Annex is especially important as it discusses the prerequisites for successful Agenda 21 processes, based on the practical experience achieved throughout the world since the Rio Conference in 1992.

2. PARTICIPATORY DECISION-MAKING PROCESSES

Participatory decision-making processes are natural processes among social groups, are especially common in democratic societies, and can be stimulated in societies in transition. Dialogues among relevant stakeholders are an important form of the participatory decision-making process and define the minimum space where there is consensus. Dialogues are more effective when the themes and issues under discussion are concrete and meaningful and when no relevant stakeholder is left out of the process.

'Stakeholders' are interested social parties in situations where there are inherent conflicts. For instance, in public transportation the relevant stakeholders are the users, the public transport companies, the vehicle manufacturers, the fuel suppliers, and the regulatory agent.

3. TAXONOMY OF PARTICIPATORY DECISION-MAKING PROCESSES

Participatory decision-making processes take place at various levels. The hierarchy presented below is illustrated with the case of hydro resources.

1. Social, Organisational

Determines the priorities. For example, in the case of hydro resources of a given basin, a hydro resource council integrated by the relevant stakeholders:

2. Managerial, Operational

Dedicated to execution and implementation. In the above example, the basin management committees.

3. Technical, Scientific

Provides the knowledge base. Perhaps, in the above example, the basin agencies.

In the hierarchy of decision-making processes, the 'sovereignty' of the stakeholders should prevail over the 'dictatorship' of the experts. Nevertheless, the stakeholders' consensus is not an absolute perennial understanding. Once consensus over priority initiatives is achieved among stakeholders, it must be reviewed and revised, via renegotiation, from time to time.

4. EXAMPLES OF PARTICIPATORY DECISION-MAKING PROCESSES

1. Science and Technology for Development

The United Nations Centre for Science and Technology for Development – CSTD – originated the stakeholders' dialogues concept during 1986–91 and applied it to the decision-making process on science and technology policies of countries and regions. The starting point of the process is the definition, by consensus among stakeholders, of the sustainable development demands and later the answers which technology and science can bring, through investment, international trade, technology transfer, education and training, to meet the above demands.

Under this conceptual framework, ten countries (Cape Verde, Jamaica, Jordan, Nepal, Pakistan, Thailand, Tanzania, Togo, Uganda and Vietnam) and one region (Daqing, China) began dialogues among 'stakeholders'. Unfortunately, there was not sufficient continuity in the processes for the cycle of decision on priority initiatives and implementation to run its full course. Nevertheless, in many of these countries and in Daqing, concrete benefits were achieved. For example, in Nepal, the Royal Nepali Academy of Science and Technology – RONAST – previously insulated from the productive sectors, as a result of the dialogues began to interact with the

Agricultural Development Bank, the main vehicle of technology transfer in the country. In Daqing, the future of this region, the largest oil-producing area of China, albeit at escalating costs, was extensively considered and discussed among the key 'stakeholders'. In Jamaica, the process led to a heightened awareness of the role of technology and science in the sustainable development process of the country, and to the establishment of the National Commission of Science and Technology, headed by the Prime Minister.

2. Agenda 21

Chapters 37 (national) and 28 (local) invite countries and regions to conduct 'stakeholders' dialogues' to define priorities for sustainable development. In the end, the implementation of the global Agenda 21 requires the implementation of the ensemble of the national Agendas 21. Thus, if the global Agenda 21 had been edited, instead of remaining a collection of sectoral chapters, Chapter 37 should have become a sort of umbrella chapter, through which interested countries would organise their efforts to implement, at national level, the many recommendations of the global Agenda 21.

3. Public Hearings and Regulatory Negotiations – RegNegs

Originating from legislative and/or administrative initiatives, public hearings are happening in Brazil, and have been in place for a considerable time in the USA and other countries.

The decision about the composition of reformulated gasoline in the United States resulted from negotiations among the relevant stakeholders; that is, the vehicle manufacturers, the oil refineries, and the producers of oxygenated fuels (alcohols and ethers), presided over by the regulatory entity, in this case the Environmental Protection Agency – EPA.

In conclusion, participatory decision-making processes do not mean the complete absence of the state. On the contrary, such processes value the intelligent state, effective and efficient, and the residual decision-making power is always in the hands of the state, to intervene, but only when necessary.

4. Technology Missions in Minas Gerais

The Administration of the state of Minas Gerais (1995–98) defined science and technology as one of their structuring programmes. The science and technology structuring programmes, known more simply as 'Technology Missions', establish sustainable development priorities, focused on problems/ opportunities, sub-regions and markets, wherever they may be located, and promotes initiatives in response to the demands identified in the process, which can be seen as true technology missions, employing a variety of mechanisms and institutional synergies aiming at articulating, co-ordinating and amplifying human, material and financial resources; public and private, national and international; and thus contributes to improving the quality of life of all the people in the state, and to the growth of the economy.

Initial rounds of dialogues among stakeholders, relevant to Minas Gerais society, were organised on the basis of the Minas Gerais Integrated Development Plan (PMDI), the Pluri-Annual Government Action Plan for 1996–99, the sectoral priorities and the other structuring programmes, for a preliminary indication of sustainable development priorities focused on problems/opportunities, sub-regions and markets, and their demands for scientific, technological, financial, managerial support, and so on. These rounds of dialogue identified, on a preliminary basis, the portfolios of priority initiatives, that is, the Technology Missions which will respond to the demands perceived by the stakeholders. These are: gem and jewels, aquaculture, renewable forests, biotechnology and urban waste management. After experience was gained, an integrative Mission was added, which can serve as a basis for the PMDI for the next Administration. This Mission is the Agenda 21 of the state of Minas Gerais.

In some cases, it was possible to initiate promptly the concrete actions required by some of the Technology Missions. However, in other situations, it was prudent to re-examine problems/opportunities, sub-regions and markets, and resubmit them, with adequate preparation, to further rounds of dialogues among stakeholders closer to the issues, to confirm known demands and/or to identify demands not perceived by the first set of stakeholders.

At the end of this 24-month process, the limited set of Technology Missions which make up the science and technology structuring programme was established and important initial results began to show up. Taxation on gems and jewels has been reduced, while overall fiscal revenue is expected to rise as the sector formalises, trains manpower and expands markets. A programme has been agreed for higher value-added labour-intensive management of planted forest resources in a pocket of poverty in the state. Ornamental fish exports are expanding, food fish for export is being planned and development of trout food ration is taking place. Some 400 municipalities in the state, with less than 10,000 inhabitants, will have for the first time, urban waste management systems, including separate processing for hospital wastes. Biotechnology start-up firms are being incubated to address human and animal health needs, as well as agricultural needs. And the state Agenda 21 is being made ready for launch.

The Technology Missions must be implemented in a flexible way, by a varied ensemble of institutional and financial instruments, either existing, to be leveraged or to be created. Such instruments, however, only acquire definitive contours through the stakeholders' dialogue process, which defines the Missions. Thus, there is ample room for the participation of a variety of entities, municipal, state, federal; public and private; national, foreign and multilateral, in the implementation of the Missions. The Missions provide opportunities for institutional innovation and for the development of creative financial mechanisms to leverage existing and available resources.

5. Stakeholders' Platforms

Probably inspired by the Minas Gerais Technology Missions, the technology development component of the Brazilian Programme to Support Science and Technology Development (PADCT), funded by the World Bank, is another example of participatory decision-making processes based on the consensus of the relevant stakeholders. The platforms, to be launched in 1998, aim at promoting diffusion and technological innovation to improve the competitiveness of the Brazilian productive sector. To achieve this goal it seeks to set up partnerships between research institutions and Brazilian enterprises, through stakeholders' platforms.

Platforms are consensual decision-making processes among the stakeholders, open to all relevant organised groups in society. The platforms will involve seminars, studies, working groups, and other activities to identify and induce demand and promote business development. They provide for communication mechanisms between the stakeholders in specific sectors, to identify technological innovation needs of enterprises and the setting up of partnerships to respond to them. From the priority agendas defined by these platforms, specific technological innovation activities (for example, research, development, demonstration, diffusion, incubation and so on) will ensue from a series of requests for proposals, where partnerships between all kinds of research entities and Brazilian enterprises are eligible to implement co-operative projects.

5. AGENDA 21, THE PROGRAMME OF ACTION OF THE RIO CONFERENCE

The global Agenda 21 is an all-encompassing programme of action for sustainable development in the 21st century, which considers the complex relationship between development and environment in a variety of fields. The global Agenda 21 is one of the documents developed for the United Nations Conference on Environment and Development of 1992, through a preparatory process which took two years of extensive negotiations among member states. Agenda 21 includes a statement of objectives and goals, as well as a set of strategies and actions to be followed to fulfil them. The Conference was only the first step of a long process of building up understanding among nations about concrete measures to 'reconcile economic activities with the need to protect the planet and ensure a sustainable future for all peoples'.

6. THE NATIONAL AGENDA 21

Paragraph 37.5 of the global Agenda 21 points out that

> as an important aspect of overall planning, each country should seek internal consensus at all levels of society on policies and programs needed for short- and long-term capacity building to implement its Agenda 21 program. This consensus should result from a participatory dialogue of relevant interest groups and lead to an identification of skills gaps, institutional capacities and capabilities, technological and scientific requirements and resource needs to enhance environmental knowledge and administration to integrate environment and development.

The participatory process of prioritising development initiatives, based on stakeholders' dialogues, is described in detail in OECD's publication of October 1991, entitled 'Managing Technological Change in Less-Advanced Developing Countries' (actually applicable to all countries), which resulted from a discussion in Paris in May 1990, in which I took part. If the word 'technology' in this publication is replaced by the word 'environment', we come to the origins of the concept of national Agenda 21. The global Agenda 21 only acquires practical meaning when interpreted at national level (Chapter 37). The national Agenda 21 is essentially a sustainable development agenda (and *not* an environmental agenda), and it should naturally converge into the national development plan, as long as the latter emphasises transparency and the participation of the relevant 'stakeholders'.

7. THE LOCAL AGENDA 21 (OR THEMATIC AGENDA 21)

Paragraph 28.2 of the global Agenda 21 proposes that 'by 1996, most local authorities in each country should have undertaken a consultative process with their populations and achieved a consensus on a "local Agenda 21" for the community'. Paragraph 28.3 invites more explicitly 'each local authority' to

> enter into a dialogue with its citizens, local organisations and private enterprises and adopt a 'local Agenda 21'. Through consultation and consensus-building, local authorities would learn from citizens and from local, civic, community, business and industrial organisations and acquire the information needed for formulating the best strategies.

8. IMPLEMENTATION OF THE AGENDAS 21

Thus, the national (local, thematic) Agenda 21 is a potentially integrative concept of the activities of the authorities responsible for the environment and for broad government planning. Again, Agenda 21 is more a *sustainable development agenda* than an environmental agenda. The *process* of preparing Agenda 21 is more important than the Agenda *per se*. Thus the preparation of national (local, thematic) Agenda 21 must result from the consensus stemming out of *broad dialogue among the relevant stakeholders* in the society considered. Evidently, the quality of this decision-making process will depend, in part, on the inclusion of the minimum set of relevant stakeholders and on information and analyses on the issues selected by the stakeholders.

The national (local, thematic) Agenda 21 is thus an instrument of planning and analysis, at national, local and thematic levels. The Agendas 21 support integrative efforts and the concentration of resources to address problem areas. The Agenda 21 process mobilises financial resources, local, national and international.

The full development of Agenda 21 processes will nevertheless face many problems such as:

(i) government and civilian society do not possess sufficient knowledge about negotiations and agreements related to sustainable development;
(ii) the tradition of a participatory culture is often non-existing or incipient.

Consequently, the minimum requirements for the successful development and implementation of national (local, thematic) Agendas 21 include:

(i) institutional partnerships within the government, which legitimate the initiative in the national (local, thematic) frame and facilitate the implementation of the priority programmes out of Agenda 21; for instance, the environmental authorities should not steer the Agenda 21 process alone, since, again, Agenda 21 is a sustainable development agenda, and not an environmental agenda;
(ii) establishment of a small, but representative, *Co-ordinating Committee*, engaging the national (local, thematic) institutional partners, to monitor the process, and a small *Executive Secretariat* for Agenda 21, with an extensive network of contacts, to keep the memory of the process and to provide continuity of efforts, follow things up, and delegate executive initiatives required for the completion of the Agenda 21 process;
(iii) for each topic selected, the minimum set of relevant stakeholders should be involved, given the key feature of Agenda 21; that is, the

participatory, broad and transparent nature of the decision-making processes;

(iv) mobilisation of resources for the implementation of Agenda 21, by engaging at the earliest possible stage, those stakeholders, local, national and international, who could be potential implementation agents of the initiatives prioritised in Agenda 21.

Furthermore, the implementation of national (local, thematic) Agendas 21 could benefit from the following initiatives:

(i) promotion of the preparation and implementation of national (local, thematic) Agendas 21, by identifying specific ecosystems and biomass, relevant stakeholders and resources;

(ii) incorporation of the sustainable development priorities of national (local, thematic) Agendas 21 to national (local, thematic) development plans;

(iii) dissemination of methodologies for the management of national (local, thematic) sustainable development;

(iv) encouragement of the exchange of knowledge and experiences among the participating stakeholders;

(v) strengthening an adequate national (local, thematic) participating capacity.

9. NATIONAL AGENDAS 21 OF BOLIVIA AND CHINA

The prerequisites of successful Agendas 21 are discussed in the Appendix. The following presentation of the development and implementation of the Agendas 21 of Bolivia and China follows the main headings of the discussion in the Appendix.

1. Joint efforts of co-ordination, budgeting and planning

In Bolivia, the participatory nature of the planning process, in accordance with the precepts of Agenda 21, was a valuable and concrete innovation worth mentioning, as it involved the experience of organised society and its decision to participate and contribute to the process of construction and sustainable development of the country.

The success of this approach in Bolivia helped remove persistent doubts about the feasibility of the joint and productive participation between government and the society. Thus this approach assisted in building up a consensus from divergent positions, real or presumed, based on productive complementarities.

The rapid response of China to the challenge of UNCED seems to be motivated by the conviction of the most senior political leaders and of the Communist Party, that the fast rates of economic growth obtained in China in recent years, while desirable, were not sustainable in the long run.

The co-operation between the two State Commissions (Planning – SPC – and Science and Technology – SSTC) is rare in China, but proved to be invaluable with respect to implementing the Agenda. It is worth mentioning that the National Environmental Protection Agency (NEPA) was not a partner at the highest level of the institutional coalition, confirming the view that Agenda 21 deals with sustainable development, and not in a narrow sense with the environment.

One important difference between the global Agenda 21 and the Agenda 21 of China is the absence, in the Chinese Agenda, of any attempt to estimate the cost of the portfolio of priority initiatives which, despite the inevitable imprecision, would have a didactic effect on the reflection process of the Agenda 21. On the other hand, it is worthwhile remembering that the Agenda 21 process is as important, if not more important, than the final product itself. Thus, the final document must be 'owned' by all the relevant stakeholders, and should not be seen as the document of consultants, national and international, of a given ministry or the central government alone. In China, the preparation of the national Agenda 21 contributed to harmonise policies and to resolve conflicts between rival agencies and ministries.

2. Executive Secretariat

In March 1993, the Administrative Centre of China's Agenda 21 (ACCA21) was established as the Secretariat of the Agenda 21 of China. Initially, its staff numbered 8 full time professionals, fluent in English and competent in several areas of sustainable development, originating from SPC, SSTC and from research and academic institutions. The work of ACCA21 was crucial to the success of the Agenda, through the harmonisation between the Leading Group (described below) and the Working Group, as well as by drafting the final text of the Agenda and promoting its implementation.

3. Role of Stakeholders in the Choice of Themes and Approaches

In Bolivia, the Bolivian Council of Sustainable development was established, to respond to the need to provide an environment for harmonisation and dialogue between the government and the organised society. With these objectives in mind, the Council has been working regularly since its inception. Its multisectoral structure and its 9 intersectoral departmental councils, have produced a dynamic setting which allows progress in the building up of a culture of dialogue among all sectors of Bolivian society around the complex topic of sustainable development.

In China, a Leading Group was established, with more than 300 individuals from commissions, ministries, agencies, mass organisations, and non-governmental organisations to promote a broad and participatory dialogue, leading towards a consensus among different interest groups and individuals, exactly as proposed in the global Agenda 21. However, relevant stakeholders, such as the farmers, enterprise managers, non-governmental environmental organisations, and so on, have not participated in the process. Their engagement in the building up of China's Agenda 21 would have helped accomplish the change in the development strategy, as proposed in Agenda 21, and would have facilitated its implementation.

In China, the Leading Group developed a list of 20 programmatic areas and assigned the task of drafting each chapter to specific ministries, which missed the opportunity of proposing an integrated strategy for the sustainable development of China in a way incurring the same shortcoming as the global Agenda which is fragmented in its presentation. More intense work with the relevant stakeholders, at the onset of the process, would have spared time and effort at later stages. After all, Agenda 21 applies to the totality of society, and not just to the government and its departments. Parallel to the Leading Group, SPC and SSTC established a Working Group for China's Agenda 21, supported by an inter-ministerial Administrative Centre (a Secretariat), whose task consisted in co-ordinating and integrating the work of the Agenda 21 of China.

4. Implementation Strategies

In China, the first draft of the national Agenda 21 was completed in May 1993 by the joint work of the two Groups, with the assistance of national consultants. The text was revised by consultants hired by the United Nations Development Programme (UNDP) and the second draft was finished in August 1993. After a third revision by the same consultants, working together with the drafters of the various chapters, the text was assessed in October 1993 by a high-level team of national and international consultants in a workshop promoted by UNDP. The final product entitled 'Agenda 21 of China – White Paper on Population, Environment and Development in China in the 21st Century' received the approval of the State Council on 25 March 1994.

Immediately after the workshop. in November 1993, UNDP supported a 3-day training programme on sustainable development for 62 participants from a number of planning commissions and science and technology commissions at the provincial and municipal levels.

After the conclusion of the China Agenda 21, SSTC and SPC, with ACCA21 support, reviewed more than 500 projects to define 62 priority initiatives, whose implementation will be supported by the State Commission on Economy and Trade and NEPA. The projects will be implemented jointly by national and local agencies, as well as international partners, and should involve broad stakeholders' participation.

All project proposals were summarised in English and Chinese for dissemination in China and abroad, in preparation for the first round of mobilisation of a coalition of resources for their implementation. In practice, however, given the hurry with which SSTC and SPC produced an ensemble of projects, even before completing China's Agenda 21, many of the proposals which were requested and submitted did not meet the requirements of the strategy or the priorities of the China Agenda. The process of requesting proposals could have been much more open, to a broader range of stakeholders and more transparent to the general public, and selected on a more arms-length basis. Nevertheless, despite its imperfections, the Priority Programme fulfils the important role of signalling, domestically and internationally, the priorities of China for its sustainable development.

5. National and International Mobilisation of Resources

China plans to cover some 60 percent of the cost of implementing its Agenda 21 with its own resources, and seeks international co-operation for the balance of the financial requirements, in the form of loans, bilateral and multilateral donations, foreign direct investment and joint ventures, as well as build-operate-transfer (BOT) arrangements.

China's Priority Programme derived from its national Agenda 21 is useful communication mechanism with the international community on the level of 'new and additional resources' required by the sustainable development of China. The first set of 62 projects prepared for the first round of resource mobilisation in July 1994 involved US$4.5 billion, 40 percent of which was expected to come, in one form or another, from the international community.

To ensure the success of the first round in July 1994, three missions were sent to Europe, North America and Asia, in May–June 1994, perhaps too close to the date of the event. The missions revealed something which could have been detected earlier; that is, the need to promote foreign direct investment by the international business community, besides the traditional forms of co-operation of subsidised credits and donations, exclusively for the Priority Programme. With the flow of foreign direct investment to China in recent years, to the tune of US$30 billion annually, and the economy growing at rates of 10 percent per year, the introduction of cleaner technologies would play a much more significant role than the standard co-operation flows. Thus, the need arose to broaden the participation of foreign private enterprise already in the first mobilisation round. In the end, the July 1994 event resulted in the pledge of financial and technical assistance by the Asian Development Bank, the World Bank, 10 organisations of the United Nations system, 15 foreign governments, 8 foreign private companies and 4 international non-governmental organisations, to 50 of the 62 project proposals of the Priority Programme. However, the 'new and additional' feature of the resources mobilised remained unclear, the impression remaining that a large part of the resources pledged had already been reserved for China previously, or perhaps would have been re-allocated from other priorities already agreed between the donor community and the Chinese bodies which are engaged in dealing with foreign assistance.

6. Merger Between Agenda 21 and Plans and Budgets

In view of the progressive decentralisation of power in China, the engagement of provincial and municipal governments is especially crucial. In the beginning it was planned to request each province and each municipality to develop their respective Agenda 21, but the idea was later discontinued given its practical complexity, especially the difficulty in keeping methodological consistency. Nevertheless, it is expected that all the most important provinces and municipalities will incorporate the concepts of Agenda 21 in the planning for the 9th Five-Year Plan and, in addition, support the process of implementing China's Agenda 21.

In the second phase of assistance to China by the Capacity 21 Programme of UNDP, employing national and international consultants, the emphasis switched to the integration of China's Agenda 21 into the planning process and the plans derived thereof, at all levels of government. The scope included: (a) preparing a broad strategy to integrate Agenda 21 in all stages of the planning process, local, provincial and national; (b) preparing reports recommending operational policies and a series of indicators of sustainable development; (c) intensive training of civil servants in government departments at national and provincial level, economic development agencies and other key organisations; (d) establishment of a system of management of the portfolio of priority initiatives – the Priority Programme – of Agenda 21. The participants in the training programme will, in the future, train other people in their respective organisations. A limited effort of training abroad will be carried out, in developed and developing countries, for a limited number of planners previously trained in phase 2. This phase will also reinforce the capacity and the capability of ACCA21, which will play a bridging role between governmental agencies and potential investors and donors, within and outside China. It is important to note that the economic reform China is undergoing is leading to gradually decreasing importance of government planning. Thus, the principles of Agenda 21 need to be disseminated in the broadest possible way in the midst of the economy and society of China.

10. AGENDA 21 OF GREATER AMAZONIA

The project aims at developing the Greater Amazonia Agenda 21 as a blueprint for sustainable development action by the Amazonian Co-operation Treaty (TCA) member countries. All TCA countries – Bolivia, Brazil, Colombia, Ecuador, Guyana, Peru, Surinam and Venezuela – are expected to participate in building up sustainable development plans for their Amazonian regions and mobilising resources; budgetary and non-budgetary, public and private, national and international; to implement them. A new vision for Amazonia as a modern biomass-based civilisation for the 21st century is expected to arise from this project. Given the size and diversity of the region, equivalent in surface area to Australia, the Greater Amazonia Agenda 21 will be built on the basis of bilateral and trilateral Amazonia Agendas 21 among TCA countries.

International co-operation, both intra- and extra-regional, will be crucial for the success of the project. The project will be guided by the Amazonian stakeholders, an Advisory Committee and the TCA political mechanisms. It will be co-ordinated and executed by an International Executive Task Force, on behalf of the TCA. The project will also serve the purpose of facilitating the establishment of the Permanent Secretariat of the TCA in Brazil, a move previously agreed by the TCA. There are also several special considerations imbedded in the design of the project, such as improved governance; integration of native peoples and women in sustainable development; environmental issues; technical co-operation among developing countries; engagement of non-governmental organisations; involvement of the private sector; pre-investment and/or investment potential, and so on.

APPENDIX I: PREREQUISITES FOR THE SUCCESS OF REGIONAL, NATIONAL OR LOCAL AGENDAS 21

1. Political Alliance among Government Bodies Responsible for Planning and Co-ordination, Budgeting and the Environment

The experience of the countries which attempted to re-orientate their development on the basis of the sustainable development concepts contained in the global Agenda 21, shows clearly the need for a political alliance among the government bodies responsible for the budget; for planning; for inter-governmental co-ordination; and for the environment. Such alliance operates through an inter-ministerial structure which leads the process, engaging, directly and indirectly, the ensemble of relevant stakeholders to society and the issues concerned. This alliance kicks off the process of designing the features of Agenda 21, whose definitive traits and colours are painted by the emerging consensus of the stakeholders achieved through systematic dialogues.

In spite of all the discussion and the efforts to disseminate pertinent information, the understanding of Agenda 21 as a sustainable development agenda has eluded many and has not been absorbed by national and international communities. Thus, to achieve full success in the Agenda 21 process, it is crucial to translate the strategic formulation of the regional, national and local Agendas 21, in terms of public budgets, and to stimulate the non-governmental sector, especially the private productive sector, to allocate resources for the implementation of the Agenda. Agenda 21 should not be perceived simply as an environmental agenda, which could, potentially, even threaten the economic development perspectives of a nation or region. Much to the contrary, Agenda 21 is the tool for initiatives supporting sustainable development, for a new approach, for a new perception of the relationship between humanity and its original home, the planet Earth.

Here it is fitting to bring up a subtle, but important point. Not all countries which attempted to re-orientate their development along the lines of sustainable development, prepared their formal national Agendas 21, but all, without exception, reviewed and revised their ongoing policies to check them against the criteria of sustainable development which emanated from the global Agenda 21. Thus, the country profiles submitted to the annual meetings of the United Nations Inter-Governmental Commission on Sustainable Development are narratives of successes and failures of each country in the implementation of the global Agenda 21 at national level. On the other hand, the national Agenda 21 as such is an explicit plan for sustainable development at national level, which, if successfully implemented, will result in country profiles gradually moving closer to the applicable recommendations of the global Agenda 21. Finally, for the countries which prepare pluriannual development plans, the national Agenda 21 and the Pluriannual Plan must coincide in full. Even if prepared separately from the Plan in its original version, the national Agenda 21 should, gradually, over the years, merge with the Pluriannual Plan, since the latter in the future must necessarily be a Sustainable Development Plan.

2. Project Co-ordination and International Secretariat

Unanimously, in all countries which seriously considered tuning up their development plans with the requirements of the global Agenda 21, the experience confirms that the conceptualisation, discussion, dissemination, resource mobilisation and implementation of Agendas 21 constitutes a complex and demanding proposition which needs a minimal Secretariat structure entirely dedicated to the many tasks involved. This Secretariat, preferably inter-ministerial in composition, and open to other inputs, including non-governmental contributions, must prepare and move initiatives, mobilise institutions, resources and stakeholders, and keep the memory of the process which originates and implements the national Agenda 21. The Secretariat must also energise the building up of coalitions of resources, mobilised, nationally and internationally, to implement the portfolio of prioritised initiatives, which makes up the Priority Programme derived from the national Agenda 21; the Secretariat must also stimulate, and/or organise, and/or carry out training activities to permeate throughout society the concept and the practice of sustainable development. Most importantly, a lively Secretariat constitutes the essential prerequisite to engaging in international co-operation, in support of the Agenda 21 process. For international co-operation to work effectively, it is necessary that the sides involved be well structured to allow for the absorption of the exchange of experiences and knowledge.

3. Selection and Performance of the Stakeholders

Without adequate participation of relevant stakeholders, Agenda 21 would not add anything to traditional governmental action. The novelty that Agenda 21 brings to the concept of development is not only the concept of sustainable development, but especially the direct engagement of the relevant stakeholders in the decision-making process in the selection of priorities and the implementation of the initiatives resulting from them. In many cultures there is the habit of restricting the decision-making process to limited groups of power and to experts, under the allegation, in relation to the latter, of the esoteric nature of matters to be decided upon. It must be emphasised that experts have a lot to contribute to decision-making processes, especially by providing expert information and analysis in their respective areas of expertise. However, global Agenda 21 reminds us that decisions which affect a range of diverse stakeholders, have a higher probability of sustainable implementation if they result from the consensus of the stakeholders on what course and priorities to pursue. The inter-ministerial alliance which launches the Agenda 21 process should, together with a select group of relevant stakeholders, with the support of the Executive Secretariat, define the macro concept of the Agenda. Alternative choices include, for instance, if the Agenda should consider the country as a whole or treat regions and/or relevant eco-systems separately, or by a thematic approach (for example, urban Agenda 21; water Agenda 21; energy Agenda 21, and so on.). Always with the support of the Executive Secretariat, and from the macro concept of the Agenda, the regions, eco-systems, themes and chosen issues should be studied and analysed, in preparation for the dialogues among relevant stakeholders, whose consensus defines the priority initiatives which constitute the Priority Programme to be implemented.

4. Implementation Strategies

From the very beginning of the Agenda 21 process, the issue of its implementation must be present, although its practical relevance will only materialise as the Agenda evolves towards completion. The implementation strategies will naturally depend on the macro concept of the Agenda; on the Agenda proper; and on the relevant stakeholders engaged in its conceptualisation and implementation. Actually, the experience of many countries reveals that, in many cases, implementation is a weak element of existing Agenda 21 processes, perhaps because the Agenda 21 process is new in many societies, and because the incorporation of the priorities agreed upon by the stakeholders' consensus into public and private budgets and plans takes time along a learning curve, even in the countries which have a favourable disposition towards sustainable development. There is ample room, to be explored strategically, for international co-operation, public and private, bilateral and multilateral. Again the Executive Secretariat will be crucial to the execution of the resource mobilisation strategy decided upon.

5. Mobilisation of Resources, National and International

Among the country experiences reviewed, regarding the implementation of the global Agenda 21, both in the cases of national Agendas 21 and in their absence, the adjustment of policies, plans and budgets to the principles of the Global Agenda 21 originates a portfolio of priority initiatives – the Priority Programme – which evidently requires an ensemble of resources for its implementation. The engagement in the consensus building process on priorities of stakeholders who are potentially interested in the implementation of priority initiatives, may facilitate the mobilisation of resources for the materialisation of the Priority Programme. Likewise, the engagement of stakeholders with influence on the formulation of public budgets, from the outset of the preparation of the Agenda and its Priority Programme, facilitates the mobilisation of national public resources. International co-operation has an important role to play to augment domestic resources; to promote technology transfer and management skills; and to stimulate trade, always in support of sustainable development. It may be convenient to organise explicitly rounds of international resource mobilisation based on the contents of the Priority Programme.

6. Merger between Agenda 21, Plans and Budgets

Since the United Nations Conference on Environment and Development, which took place in Rio de Janeiro in 1992, it is not acceptable, at least officially, to have development that is not sustainable, because about 180 sovereign countries approved many agreements, all in support of sustainable development, including the Global Agenda 21. Thus, the national Agendas 21, which are sustainable development plans, cannot be distinguished from policies and plans for social and economic development. Therefore, countries which decided to develop their national Agendas 21 are engaged in the integration of their Agendas into the existing national policies, plans and public budgets. Those countries which revised their policies and plans to incorporate in them the principles of the global Agenda 21, even when not preparing their national Agendas 21, have effectively introduced the criteria of sustainability into the steering of their development process.

10. International Private Finance and Sustainable Development: Policy Instruments for Brazil[1]

Peter H. May

1. INTERNATIONAL CAPITAL FLOWS AND SUSTAINABLE DEVELOPMENT IN BRAZIL

Over the past few years there has been a transformation in the origin of capital for development investment, from public multilateral and commercial credit to private financial capital. Despite the commitments assumed by the parties to the Rio Declaration at UNCED in 1992 to dedicate a growing proportion of the GNP of Northern economies toward official assistance for sustainable development, this commitment has actually declined. Flows of private capital, in contrast, have quintupled since 1990, reaching $243 billion in 1996 (World Bank, 1997). Growth in external direct investment has been a function of the continuous integration of the world economy, and reflects factors such as liberalization and economic reform, export-oriented growth models, increased capital mobility, and globalization of technical parameters and product quality restrictions (Gentry, 1998).

Brazil's tendency toward integration in global markets has followed a trajectory similar to that of other developing nations. During the decade after the collapse of the economic 'miracle' pursued by the military regime in the 1960s and 70s, the nation succumbed to a series of fiscal crises and adjustments. These were associated with the debt crisis, redemocratisation and macroeconomic adjustments of the 1980s, and the swing toward trade liberalisation and monetary stability in the mid-1990s (Coes, 1995). Financial uncertainty and political instability accelerated inflationary pressures and stimulated capital flight during the earlier part of this period, while signs of stronger economic performance, regional trade co-operation and stability over the past few years have brought capital investors flocking into financial markets at an unprecedented rate. According to the UN Economic Council for Latin America (ECLAC), the inflow of external capital into Brazil in 1995 already accounted for over 70 percent of all such financial flows into

Latin America and the Caribbean in that year, somewhat short of 20 percent of the global figure (*Folha de São Paulo*, 22 Jan. 1996).

The question then arises: to what extent can private capital flows be conceived as an appropriate substitute for public commitments toward development? What is the environmental 'content' of such flows, and to what degree does Brazil possess instruments capable of directing these new resources toward investments that will have a positive repercussion on the nation's search for sustainable development?

In assessing the environmental content of private financial investment in Brazil, it is necessary to make a distinction between 'productive' versus 'speculative' investment in Brazilian capital markets. The recent tendency of international finance to seek opportunities for rapid turnover of footloose capital ('hot money') is troublesome from the perspective of sustainability. Such opportunistic trade in financial paper leads mobile capital toward highest profits rather than investments that reflect societal concerns for employment and environmental quality (Daly and Goodland, 1994); its mobility was disastrous to Mexico and continues to threaten Argentina's monetary stability. As described in a recent report on transnational investment in the Americas: 'The world of nations is woven into a single world economy ... through the financial markets. Countries that commit themselves to a policy of free capital flows must realize that they've put themselves at the mercy of these often whimsical, unaccountable forces' (Henwood, 1996).

The volatility of Latin American equity and bond markets is not only due to footlooseness of foreign investments, however. Domestic investment is weak in instruments other than the 'overnight', which promises immediate liquidity. Furthermore, most Latin American bond offerings are public rather than private (*The Economist*, 9 Dec. 1995).

The search for fiscal balance through disposal of fixed capital assets from the state sector, accepting 'rotten paper' at cash parity in the haste to relieve the state's burden, represents a further source of concern for the sustainability of liberalisation. The nebulous treatment in the privatisation process to date of outstanding environmental liabilities, or of natural resource assets whose extraction rates have heretofore been managed by the state sector, is another preoccupation. On the other hand, such state administration of common resources has not always been so benign. Some state enterprises are known to have skirted investment in environmental management to avoid costs that would have to be publicly financed or risk the inflationary effects of being passed directly through to consumer prices, a problem notorious in Brazil's petroleum industry.

It is to be hoped that exposure to international markets, where environmental contents of processes and products have become essential components of quality standards, will drive newly privatised firms to internalise outstanding liabilities and husband dwindling natural capital assets. The record to date on this desirable response to external market forces is not clear, however, and may be limited to those sectors which perceive distinct and immediate advantages from an upgrade in their environmental profile. A recent survey by the World Business Council for Sustainable Development found that:

> Given low resource prices and the ability of businesses to keep costs for much environmental damage 'external' to their own balance sheets, the profitability of becoming eco-efficient is reduced. Eco-efficient companies are often not preferred by financial markets ... Sustainable development is concerned with the importance of the future. Financial markets discount the future routinely and heavily. (Schmidheiny et. al., 1996: 8)

Liberalisation policies and monetary stability may offer greater security to investors, lengthening their investment horizons. However, such policies in combination tend to overvalue domestic currencies, leading to pressures to open the doors to cheap imports. While beneficial for controlling inflationary pressures and offering consumers a wider choice of goods thus stimulating healthy competition, the process may excessively expose producers and lead them to 'overgraze' the commons. The response to stability in Brazil, at least in this early phase, has been for economic actors, accustomed to high inflation, to perceive the moment as ephemeral, stimulating them to put their momentarily revalued savings into immediate consumption. The result has been more cars on the highways, greater energy consumption, and an explosive expansion at the agropastoral frontier.[2]

In the next section, we explore the pattern of overseas investment flows into Brazil over the past decade, examining its sectoral distribution as a basis for considering the implications of such flows for sustainable development.

2. RECENT TRENDS IN FOREIGN CAPITAL FLOWS TO BRAZIL

The growing importance of private capital in overall international financial flows in recent years is dramatically evident. In 1992, the Rio 'Earth Summit' called on industrialised countries to make an additional US$125 billion available each year to developing countries to help place them on the path to sustainable development. Since then, total flows of capital to the developing world have exceeded this target every year, but through private investment, not foreign aid ('ODA' or Official Development Assistance). See Figure 10.1 (World Bank, 1997).

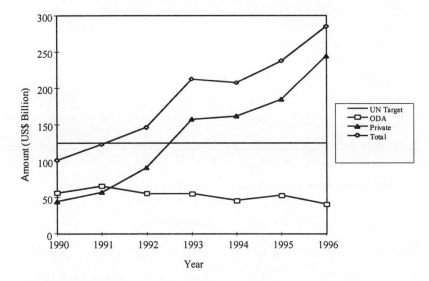

Source: World Bank (1997).

Figure 10.1: International financial flows to developing nations: 1990–96

Globalisation of private financial capital manifests itself through flows of foreign direct investment (FDI) as well as other modalities, including international credit, development assistance payments and foreign portfolio (equity and fixed return) investments. A great deal of private capital flowing into emerging markets is attracted to volatile investments such as portfolios rather than longer-term commitments toward building industrial capacity and competitiveness. Volatile investment lends instability to the national economy, which can have serious repercussions in crises such as those faced by the Southeast Asian economies since late 1997.

In the case of Brazil, there has not only been a significant upturn in the volume, but also a shift in the composition of foreign investment. In 1991 about 40 percent of the total inflow was accounted for by portfolio investments, whose predominance over FDI was maintained over the ensuing years; by 1993, 90 percent of gross inflows were constituted by such investments. Individual investors (households, persons or their legal representatives) and not institutions, constitute the principal source of these resources (Figure 10.2). It is not possible to identify exactly who these 'individual' investors are, and where their interests lie. One must assume that these capitals are in search of the greatest short-term yield on their portfolio investments, and will have no qualms concerning their rapid dislocation to more profitable markets.

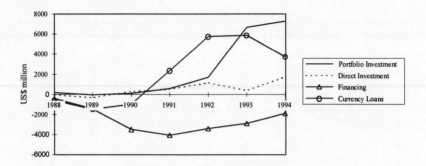

Source: *Boletim do Banco Central do Brasil*, Vol. 32, March 1996.

Figure 10.2: Composition of net foreign financial flows to Brazil: 1988-94

Before reflecting on the significance of these numbers, we will observe more closely the performance of Brazil's capital balance. This balance demonstrates the following pattern over time: net inflows of capital were negative in most years between 1985 and 1991 (with the exception of 1988), and from this year onward, the entry of capital registers positive increments ($25 million in 1992 and about $14 million in 1994). These values are due to growth of investments and the restoration of financing and loans in foreign currencies (financing and currency loans), that have made possible an intensification in flows of international trade (imports and exports) and both short- and long-term loans.

Between 1989 and 1991, the outflow of capital due to amortizations and other purposes (payments of financial as well as currency loans, from multilateral, bilateral and National Banks – Eximbanks) exceeded the entry of capital. From 1992 onward, this movement reversed itself, with an entry of $41 billion in 1994, and a return flow of around $31 billion, leaving the nation with a net balance of nearly $10 billion. As far as investment *per se* is concerned, portfolio investment was considerably more important than direct investment, especially from 1992 onward. Investments in goods were very inexpressive, and the conversion of debt to investments was also significantly reduced.

Flows of direct foreign investment to Brazil were quite modest until the very recent past, when compared with previous periods. The economic difficulties facing the nation during the period from 1980 through 1993 (a decline in the level of economic activity combined with spiralling inflation, and with the foreign debt crisis), led to a substantial reduction of net capital inflows. If we consider Brazil's share in absorption of global direct investments between 1970 and 1995, inflows to Brazil continually declined from 7.6 percent of total flows in 1977, to 0.7 percent in 1993. This share recovered to 1.4 percent in 1995 owing to increased political and monetary stability, but is still relatively modest when compared with other nations. When one considers the participation of Brazil in direct investment flows toward developing nations over the same period, when capital flows toward the so-called emerging markets expanded quickly, Brazil's participation dropped from 32.3 percent of the total in 1977, to 1.9 percent in 1993, recovering to a timid position of 3.4 percent in 1995.

In absolute terms, from 1988 to 1993, foreign direct investment in Brazil remained nearly stagnant at an average of $1.4 billion. In 1994, with the Real Plan there began a recovery which has been sustained up to the present. According to recent Central Bank estimates, this amount exceeded $5 billion in 1996 and had reached $10 billion in 1997. Coupled with this growth in FDI, the foreign debt load grew continuously between 1985 and 1995, but net external debt has remained static at around $106 billion between 1990 and 1995, while GDP grew steadily over the same period. The net foreign debt/GNP ratio has hence declined, an indicator of improving economic health.

Capital flows were attracted to different strategic sectors in different periods in Brazil's recent history, through governmental subsidies and other incentives. The roles of infrastructure financing (transport, storage, electrical generating capacity, and so on) and privatisation were critical to capital attraction.

Despite the low level of flows perceived in the past, the stock of direct foreign investment is significant in certain sectors. The increased net flows over the past few years have been accompanied by a change in the sectoral composition of these investments (Figure 10.3). If we compare its distribution by industrial subsectors, we see the following trends. In the case of the automotive industry, whose net investment was negative (minus 5.2 percent) in the period 1986–90, this performance is dramatically reversed between 1991 and 1994, when the sector received 54.6 percent of all direct investments and reinvestments. Chemical products, in turn, maintained the same level of participation in the sectoral distribution of FDI of about 14.5 percent during the overall period. Medical, pharmaceutical and veterinary products, on the other hand, saw a reduction in their participation during the most recent period (declining from 7.9 percent in 1986–90 to 3 percent between 1991 and 1994). The participation of food products has remained even between the two periods (about 7 percent), while investments in metallurgy declined from 14.5 percent in the first period to only 4.3 percent in the second, as did electronics, electrical and communication equipment, whose amount is reduced from 17.9 percent to 7.3 percent in the second period. This last result, however, masks the cheapening of products that occurred in this sector, that was accompanied by a substantial improvement in quality, capacity, power and productivity in this industry and its products.

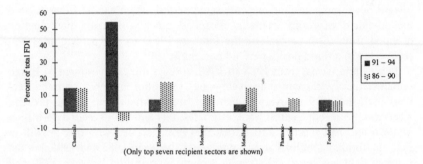

(Only top seven recipient sectors are shown)

Source: Banco Central, FIRCE.

Figure 10.3: Sectoral distribution of FDI in Brazil: 1986–90 and 1991–94

It is apparent that the sectoral strategy for capital investment anticipated by the federal government over the coming decade will rely strongly on private international capital flows. Besides efforts to attract capital toward strategic investments in private industry, plans place emphasis on joint public/private ventures in transportation, power and communications.

The intentions for investment of foreign private enterprises between 1995 and 1999, if they are maintained and confirmed, reveal the following profile (Figure 10.4): 38 percent of investment will tend to occur in the automotive industry; 16 percent in the chemical-pharmaceutical complex; 10 percent in the electronic, electrical and communications area; 6 percent in food products and 4 percent in pulp and paper. These investment intentions suggest the need for a specific regulatory framework to guarantee sustainable investments in these sectors.

Finally, the percentage distribution of investment and reinvestment flows into Brazil by country of origin between 1991 and 1994 shows a greater stability of German direct investments in first place, and of French sources, second, in comparison with North American, British and other nationalities. Despite a relatively similar behaviour in rates of annual growth in average annual sales by German and North American firms in Brazil (with the Americans showing greater growth rates), the North American pattern has been less stable. A high rate of transmission of profits and dividends demonstrates, especially from 1989 onward, the absence of barriers to the outflow of productive capital. Those barriers remaining had been effectively

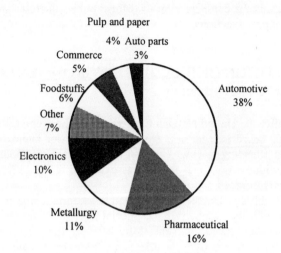

Pulp and paper

4% Auto parts
Commerce   3%
5%

Foodstuffs
6%

Other
7%

Automotive
38%

Electronics
10%

Metallurgy
11%

Pharmaceutical
16%

Note: 'Other' refers to the following sectors: Drinks and Tobacco; Capital Goods; Plastic and Rubber; Mineral Extraction; Hygiene, Cleaning and Cosmetics.

Source: Ministério de Indústria, Comércio e do Turismo, Brazil.

Figure 10.4: Investment intentions of private foreign firms as a percentage of total FDI (1995–99)

dismantled through constitutional amendments in 1995.

Although the statistics reported above do not yet reflect the current wave of private licensing of public infrastructure and communications facilities, private investment in public works could have mixed results for the environment. Licensing of public utilities and services to private firms, an emerging line to attract private investment, could have positive environmental consequences if it were possible thereby to reduce congestion and accident rates, improve service efficiency and limit wastage.

The issue remains whether the assumption of such investment by the private sector will imply reduced access for civil organisations which act as sentinels, demanding recourse against environmental damages. According to a leading Brazilian watchdog group, 'to channel the effects of this new capitalist wave, new models of confrontation and collaboration will be necessary between civil society and the government' (Schwartzman, 1995). The course of evolution of Brazilian policy and the implementation of environmental safeguards affecting investment in industry and infrastructure, and provisions for compensation of diffuse public interests are reviewed in the following two sections.

3. EVOLUTION OF BRAZIL'S ENVIRONMENTAL POLICY FRAMEWORK

In 1972, after the United Nations Conference on the Human Environment in Stockholm, concern regarding environmental issues intensified in Brazil. Legislation attending to environmental themes, up to this point limited only to preservation of flora and fauna, was extended to the utilisation of water and mineral resources.

In 1973, through Decree 73.030, another important step in this direction was taken with the creation of the Special Secretariat for the Environment (SEMA), subordinated to the Ministry of the Interior. This was complemented by creation in the same period of state agencies with responsibilities in this area, such as the State Foundation for Engineering and Environment (FEEMA) in Rio de Janeiro, and the Company for Environmental Technology and Sanitation (CETESB) in São Paulo. The two agencies were structured principally to respond to industrial pollution problems, through licensing procedures based on a System for Licensing of Polluting Activities (SLAP).

In 1975, the environmental theme was incorporated within the Brazilian national development plan (II PND), whose identification of critical pollution problem areas (later ratified by Decree No. 76.389) conditioned the approval of industrial projects on observance of pollution control norms.

In the 1980s, environmental consciousness in Brazil was intensified when industrial health disasters erupted at Cubatão in São Paulo, and extensive burning in the Amazon provoked international concern over CO_2 emissions and possible global warming. The National Environmental Policy of 1981 (Federal Law No. 6.938) reflected Brazil's legislative response to these concerns. The former policy proclaimed that:

> All citizens have the right to an ecologically balanced environment, that is a collective good for use by the people, essential to their health and quality of life, making imperative that public agencies and society as a whole defend and preserve it for the present and for future generations. [Translation by the author.]

This policy provided for decentralisation of technical-administrative functions regarding the environment among the different spheres of government, for ample dissemination of information to the public regarding environmental issues, as well as their participation in review of projects and related activities.

The 1981 law established a range of instruments for achieving its broad objectives:

- environmental quality standards;
- environmental zoning;
- assessment of environmental impacts (EIA);
- licensing and monitoring of currently or potentially polluting activities; and
- disciplinary or compensatory penalties against infractions.

To assure a more complete integration and co-ordination of national environmental policy among federal, state and local governments, the 1981 law created the National Environmental System (SISNAMA) and the National Environmental Council (CONAMA). The former is made up of government agencies responsible for oversight of policies affecting natural resource use or improvement of environmental quality. CONAMA establishes technical and administrative guidelines for implementing environmental policy. Besides government agency officials, members of CONAMA include presidents of the principal trade unions, industrial and agricultural federations, two non-governmental environmental organisations, and five civil organisations representing environmental concerns pertinent to distinct macro-regions.

Among environmental policy instruments, the most polemical has been EIA, applicable to a wide range of activities which might result in alterations in physical, chemical or biological properties of the environment. CONAMA Resolution 001 of January 1986 required preparation of an EIA and summary public review report (RIMA) to obtain government licensing for such activities, whether in the public or private domain. Among projects subject to EIA were included agropastoral establishments of over 1,000 hectares, as well as activities causing significant deforestation and all significant industrial facilities.

In regulating the federal legislation for impact assessment, CONAMA defined the requirements for carrying out public hearings as a channel for participation by individuals or groups concerned with the decisions to be taken, regarding licensing of projects that might significantly modify the human environment. As a result of such hearings, project characteristics might be altered or an entire project even be halted entirely.

The 1988 Constitution reinforced the perception that environmental protection is an essential corollary of socio-economic development, making it obligatory at all levels of public administration to assure that such development does not degrade the natural environment (Art. 170, VI; Art. 225). In an important change superseding the 1981 legislation, the Constitution delegated to the states significant authority to legislate regarding environmental questions. In an oblique fashion, the new Constitution also delegated to municipalities the legislative competence to solve local problems.

The constitution also provides for class action for the defence of diffuse interests (Art. 5, LXXIII; Art. 129, III), and makes corporations and governmental authorities subject to sanctions if their actions degrade the environment, providing for criminal penalties (Art. 22, I). Among other sections referring to environmental protection, the Constitution conditions the social function of property on environmental preservation, suggesting that activities that satisfy environmental criteria (among other criteria related to labour relations and productive land use) be exempted from expropriation for land reform purposes.

In 1989, the federal government adopted new measures related to the environment, among which was included the creation of a government agency with broad responsibilities in the conduct of environmental policy, the Brazilian Institute for Environment and Renewable Natural Resources (IBAMA). This super-agency was made up of several existing departments scattered among several ministries responsible for ecological reserves, pollution control, environmental education, forestry, natural rubber policy, and fisheries.

Finally, influenced by the public concern aroused by the realisation of UNCED in Rio de Janeiro in June 1992, the Brazilian government created a Ministry of the Environment later that year, to which IBAMA was subordinated. In 1994, specific responsibility for coordinating policy relative to the Amazon region was added to the MMA mandate, and in 1995, with the Cardoso government, responsibility over water resource development was also included within this framework.

Based on Article 23 of the constitution, and precedent in legislation of 1975, 1977 and 1980, industries are required to prevent and correct damages caused by pollution emissions. Environmental licensing by state authorities is provided if the required EIA-RIMA and environmental standards and norms are observed. The latter refer to emissions of gases, vapours, noise, vibrations, radiation, risk of explosion, fire, leakage and other emergencies, raw material volume and quality, employment generation, operating hours and traffic, patterns of land use, and availability of basic infrastructure.

In Brazilian constitutional law, agricultural projects and plantation forestry are conditioned by the adequate establishment of erosion control measures as preparatory activities, as well as agroecological zoning, use of native varieties, and environmental education. Law No. 7.802 of 1989, regulated by Decree 98.062 of 1990 provides for production, marketing and use of pesticides, requiring prior registry with the federal government, to determine the degree to which their production and use may endanger the environment.[3]

4. EFFECTIVENESS OF ENVIRONMENTAL POLICY

Widely considered one of the most advanced environmental frameworks in the world, Brazilian legislation has however been found difficult to implement, principally due to problems caused by weak intergovernmental co-ordination, the lack of definition of responsibility among federal, state and municipal authorities, as well as the chronic shortage of resources.

In fact, to the extent that environmental restrictions interfere in sectoral interests of each governmental authority, such interference is often rejected. It has thus been extremely difficult to integrate environmental restrictions in the formulation of macroeconomic or sectoral policies. Due to the regulatory nature of such restrictions, their effectiveness has been subject to political pressures from stakeholders, further impeding initiatives for integration among government agencies, whether at the state or federal level. Although intergovernmental responsibilities are spelled out in legislation, they are difficult to fulfil, particularly when this implies transfer of resources or reallocation of responsibilities (Serôa da Motta, 1993b).

To date, the Environment Ministry lacks resources and political support to advance the environmental agenda. In the context of current efforts to redirect and stabilise the national economy, involving reduced government expenditure, fortification of environmental management has been relegated to a back burner.

The Constitutional delegation of authority to municipalities only confused matters more thoroughly. This duplication has generated dispute and conflict regarding industrial and facility licensing and monitoring responsibilities, resulting simultaneously in lack of definition and in regulatory omission.

The chronic shortage of resources has in part been overcome through external financing, although the national counterpart funds required to match these have been severely restricted by fiscal control policies. Funds derived from environmental penalties and fines, often minuscule and ineffective as incentives toward technological adaptation, are not always used to cover expenses in environmental administration, being aggregated as part of general revenues. In the same way, revenues derived from national timber extraction taxes, from sewerage service fees and other such charges, are so minimal that they offer little incentive to restrain resource extraction or discharge.[4] Royalties derived from natural resource extraction in Brazil are only nominally applied toward abatement of environmental spillovers.

IBAMA has not succeeded in playing its role as a federal environmental super-agency, despite its broad scope for action. With the increasing outcry over deforestation, IBAMA devoted much of its attention towards forest resource management. In consequence, federal support and monitoring of pollution control have suffered.

The experience of controlling industrial pollutants through command and control measures such as standards and penalties has been diverse among

Brazilian states. The most wealthy states have been most effective, although the correlation between state product and environmental control shows some exceptions. The industrial structure, age of capital stock, and both the institutional arrangements and public mobilisation in the environmental arena determine the level of control achieved by each state.

For example, in São Paulo, public complaints guide the government agency responsible for environmental enforcement – CETESB – to violating industries. After reviewing compliance with legally established emissions standards, the agency advises the firm to bring its process technology into line in one month. If standards are still in violation after three repeat monthly inspections, subject to progressively increasing fines, the firm may be shut down by the state environmental secretariat. Although the fines themselves are minuscule in comparison to the probable cost of adopting control technology, firms find it is in their interest to avoid consumer dissatisfaction or legal battles in the public eye (Neder, 1992).

5. HOW INTERNATIONAL FLOWS OF PRIVATE CAPITAL INTO BRAZIL AFFECT THE ENVIRONMENT

The geographical impact of capital flows is directed by resource opportunities given Brazil's substantial land and subsurface resources, and the still haphazard application of environmental legislation in the more backward regions. The nation's sheer immensity and diversity make a general assessment of the environmental effects of private international investment rather premature. In general terms, however, these effects may have been significant in certain areas, such as pulp and paper derived from plantation forests; chemicals and pesticides; iron, bauxite and tin mining; ranching and other agribusinesses. Concern persists regarding the growth in tropical timber extraction which may come to replace that derived from Southeast Asia.

Table 10.1 provides estimates of current levels of control based on the technology used to manage principal pollutants emitted by Brazilian industries. Certain export industries, particularly those related to metallurgy and plastics, are significantly energy and pollutant-intensive. Some food industries are high in particulate emissions and in BOD, as has been demonstrated for soluble coffee manufacturing (May, 1994a).

Water polluting characteristics of broad sectoral groupings, when compared against sectoral investment data, demonstrate to what extent investors may be choosing sectors that are particularly pollutant-intensive, or that have drawn down natural resource stocks to an undesirable extent. Sectors which, after treatment levels existent in 1988, had most residual

Table 10.1: Control levels for principal pollutants: 1988

Pollutant	% Controlled
Biological oxygen demand (BOD)	75.2
Heavy metals	59.9
Particulates	57.2
Sulphur dioxide (SO$_2$)	1.0
Nitrogen oxide (NO$_x$)	0.1
Hydrocarbons (HC)	43.7
Carbon monoxide (CO)	6.5

Source: Serôa da Motta (1993a).

oxygen-demanding water pollutants were primarily traditional industries such as food processing, sugar and alcohol, but steel manufacture, other metallurgical industries, tanning and chemicals constitute significant residual sources of heavy metals deposition to water courses (Mendes, 1994; see Table 10.2).

The majority of foreign direct investment is in modern subsectors such as the automotive industry and chemicals, although there is a significant attraction for such capital in resource based agribusiness, pulp and paper and mineral industries where resource costs are significantly lower than those found in other regions, due to their relative abundance in Brazil. Table 10.2 suggests that the overall pollutant intensity for those sectors for which data are available was already fairly low in 1988. Some foreign investors concentrated on sectors whose pollution control levels in Brazil were relatively higher (automotive and mechanical), but others (chemicals, food products, pulp and paper) demonstrated a high intensity of BOD per dollar of foreign investment, and the metallurgical sector exhibited alarming rates of residual heavy metals deposition.

Investment in environmental control technology manufacture in Brazil as yet is extremely weak. For the most part, such technology is purchased abroad, or licensed for fabrication (Tigre et al., 1994). The domestic market, despite fairly advanced environmental legislation, remains small. Transnationals have led investment in control technology adoption. Such investments have not merely focused on 'end-of-pipe' solutions, but increasingly seek process renovation as a means of improving production efficiency, reducing waste of raw materials and energy. For example,

Table 10.2: Residual water pollutant intensity and foreign investment in Brazilian industry: 1988

Sector	Stock of FDI (US$ million) [a]	Intensity of Residual Biological Oxygen Demand (BOD)		Intensity of Residual Heavy Metals	
		tons/ year	g/US$ invested	tons/ year	G/US$ invested
Metallurgy	2,497.3	448	0.2	9,872	4.00
Mechanical	2,789.0	8,891	3.2	996	0.40
Transport. equipment	4,002.1	1,385	0.3	371	0.10
Wood	393.4	11,132	28.3	–	–
Pulp and paper	656.4	52,107	79.4	1	0.00
Chemicals[b]	4,451.4	256,784	57.7	427	0.10
Pharmaceu- ticals	1,416.3	2,820	2.0	–	–
Textiles	530.4	22,706	42.8	5	0.00
Food products	1,488.6	154,775	104.0	–	–
Beverages	156.8	57,898	369.2	–	–
TOTAL	18,381.7	568,946	31.0	718	0.04

Notes:
(a)   Investment data used in constructing the index of pollutant intensity refer to net investment stocks rather than flows, averaged over the period 1986–90 for each sector.
(b)   Includes sugar and alcohol.

Sources: Mendes (1994); Boletim do Banco Central (various numbers).

Aracruz Celulose, the world's largest producer of hardwood short-fibre investors, recently put $250 million into a dramatic upgrading of its process, enabling production of Total Chlorine Free (TCF) cellulose in part of its plant. As a result, emissions loads would be nearly completely eliminated in favour of a 'closed cycle' production process (Gertner et al., 1997).

In other industries, trends in ambient atmospheric pollution levels demonstrate reduced pollutant levels. This trend is particularly notable in the complex at Cubatão, formerly considered a 'valley of death' due to health effects of ambient toxic substances and the dying off of hillside vegetation, putting settlements at risk (Serôa da Motta and Mendes, 1996). In some cases, firms are committing themselves to environmental management investment in a preventative fashion, prior to any imposition of regulatory controls, in efforts to establish a 'clean' image as well as to avert future costs. However, such investment is quite limited, and depends on availability of capital at concessionary rates, since returns from these long-term tactics are vulnerable to risk in international and domestic markets.

Another area in which environmental concern has been complementary with productivity enhancement and process innovation is that of agribusiness. Advances in soybean breeding conducted by the government agricultural research corporation EMBRAPA have led to improved productivities on infertile savanna (*cerrado*) soils, and the transgenic modification of seed to breed in resistance to the damaging effects of pesticides. Soybeans in Brazil's cerrado are produced using low-till methods, integrated soil management and rotations which restrain soil erosion as well as having lower energy requirements than traditional 'green revolution' technologies. These enhancements, linked vertically to greater industrial yields, modification in oil and feedmeal characteristics in response to consumer health concerns, and diversification in final uses of soybeans toward 'ozone-friendly' markets such as inks and bio-diesel fuel, are expected to improve the industry's competitiveness and environmental sustainability in the long term.

6. INSTRUMENTS TO INFLUENCE THE ENVIRONMENTAL CONTENT OF PRIVATE CAPITAL FLOWS

In the context of the Plano Real, privatisation, trade liberalisation and regional market agreements, Brazil has placed considerable policy attention toward attracting new sources of capital. In general, the demand for investment has been more intense than any particular efforts to manage its geographical destination or sectoral concentration. Recent policy reforms are designed to strengthen the relative contribution of international private investment, including upward revision in the proportion of shares open for international participation in privatised enterprises, the opening of mineral exploration rights to external investors, and the deregulation and privatisation of telecommunications.

Measures being proposed to limit capital mobility and avert the 'tequila effect' include encouragement for firms to reinvest in-country rather than repatriate profits, through such instruments as differential taxation. In general it has been clear to investors that rates of return tend to be higher (albeit riskier) here – the average return on positions held by US corporations in Brazil in 1994 was 25.4 percent, the highest such rate in the world

(Henwood, 1996 based on data from the US Commerce Dept. *Review of Current Business*) – and a good share of profits have been ploughed into new investment.

Multilateral aid and trade agencies have been instrumental over the years in conditioning adjustment assistance on trade liberalisation and opening the doors to overseas investors. In this sense, the World Bank group has leveraged substantial private and bilateral investment. Such leverage can also condition investment on adequate incorporation of environmental concerns in project planning. A case in point is that of the Carajás iron mine, railroad and port project executed in the early 1980s, in which the World Bank offered a proportionately small loan to Companhia Vale do Rio Doce (CVRD), leveraging more substantial investments by Japan and Germany. Due to the Bank's environmental procedures, the project incorporated regularisation of indigenous land claims and prevention of environmental impacts in the areas under direct control of CVRD.[5]

Another channel to conduct private international capital toward environmental improvement in industry is the International Finance Corporation (IFC). The current IFC portfolio in Brazil totals $602 million in loans and $175 million in equity, with the largest number of commitments in the areas of agribusiness and forestry, pulp and paper, and chemicals; all sectors with expressive environmental content (IFC, 1995). Although not formerly an issue of particular concern in lending, the IFC has developed a stronger interest in environmental effects of its investments over the past two years. Environmental diligence has become an intrinsic element in the assessment of lending risks.

The World Bank has also provided capital toward a substantial programme to finance private corporations' installation of environmental control technology, administered by the National Bank for Economic and Social Development (BNDES). Since initiation of its credit line in this area five years ago, BNDES has made loans for environmental control totalling in the order of $1.2 billion (BNDES, 1995).

The recent establishment of a 'Green Protocol' to redirect federal public lending toward environmentally friendly investments could also be adopted as a parameter throughout Brazilian capital markets (*Diário Oficial*, 12 Nov. 1995). This could thus affect the content of international private capital flows insofar as these operate through joint ventures and/or seek local financial contributions in Brazil. For commercial banks to assume such a role would require the improvement of capacity to assess the environmental risks and opportunities associated with such investments. In its capital markets portfolio, the IFC has provided capitalisation for loan funds for small and medium enterprises, operating through indirect loans to commercial banks (Itaú, Bradesco and Unibanco are the principal takers), and is currently providing specific training to credit managers in these banks to enhance their capacity to assess environmental variables associated with private investments (Leticia Oliveira, IFC, personal communication; IFC, 1994).

Although relatively stringent, Brazil's environmental legislation is not perceived as a hindrance toward attracting new investment, as most investors are aware of the limitations of local enforcement. International investors are required to adhere to domestic rules which are in general enforced on a rather selective basis. The licensing phase is usually more effective than monitoring and enforcement in scrutinising investments to ensure environmental risks are considered. Licensing can, however, become a very tedious process limited by the incapacity of state and municipal environmental agencies to process licensing documents expediently (Laura Tlaiye, World Bank, personal communication). Although licensing procedures are there to ensure a clear identification of impacts and of safeguards necessary to avoid risks to the neighbouring community and to a firm's environmental profile, review is seldom rigorous and does not necessarily result in improved enforcement.

Penalties for noncompliance are generally inconsequential relative to the profits derived from dirty practices. In the past, dispute resolution procedures have responded to the nation's corporativist political structure, thus encouraging firms to search for individual favours in government circles. Although there has been a growing reaction against such influence and rent-seeking, it must be conceded that such practices are still rife in Brazil.

Efforts are urgently needed to improve governmental capacity to streamline and limit favouritism in licensing procedures. The ranking system used by BNDES to pinpoint those investments that may in fact have detrimental environmental effects signalling the need for more rigorous analysis, could serve as one means to facilitate this process, a procedure that would answer part of the objectives of the Green Protocol (Isaura Frondisi, BNDES, personal communication). Environmental auditing and self-regulation such as that practised in the chemical complex at Camaçari in Bahia, could also avert some of the delays and place the ball firmly in the camp of the polluting industry to identify lowest cost solutions. Recent proposals by the pulp and paper and industrial silviculture industries to 'de-bureaucratise' requirements affecting the establishment of tree plantations represents another approach in this regard (see Box 10.1).

Public scrutiny of project proposals and residuals monitoring are also essential to environmental enforcement. NGOs have become more active as watchdogs over new investment, particularly that by transnationals in natural resource sectors such as mining and forestry. Access through international networks to consumer groups in principal Northern markets has resulted in significant pressures to alter production techniques. Negotiations that build constructive partnerships between NGOs and private firms have been found a useful approach to neutralise the negative public relations effects of environmental campaigns (Ros, 1994). In the case of Aracruz Celulose, for example, forest ecologists have been invited to conduct research on the environmental effects of eucalyptus plantations and assist in the reintroduction of native vegetation and fauna (Gertner et al., 1997).

An important area for development of collaborative strategies in environmental protection is that of the intensification of tropical timber exploitation. Over the past year, Southeast Asian timber operators displaced by increased control over logging and unprocessed wood exports, have begun to rapidly occupy areas in the western Amazon where they purport to conduct 'sustainable forestry'. There, the capacity of NGOs to monitor such developments will be extremely fortuitous to prospects for environmental protection. The lack of any serious governmental forest policy for native timber resources leaves a serious vacuum that in the medium term is being filled in part by nongovernmental and grass roots organisations.

With the removal of import restrictions and tariffs between nations that form the Mercosul trading block (Brazil, Argentina, Uruguay, Paraguay and soon, Chile), the volume of intra-regional trade has increased rapidly, quadrupling its volume between Brazil and Argentina, for example. The need for harmonisation of environmental and product quality controls among trading partners has hence emerged as a concern. Investors may choose to establish operations attracted by laxity in the regulatory framework by one of the trading partners so as to dominate the regional market, a form of 'ecological dumping'. One case in point is that of the production and utilisation of pesticides. Brazilian legislation, and the norms to register a new product, are much more severe than those in Argentina and Uruguay. Under Mercosul, pesticides banned in Brazil could move freely from neighbouring nations, that could be prejudicial to product standards, worker health and safety, and efforts to decontaminate streamflows. Products imported from these nations into Brazil would also be suspect due to pesticide residues. Efforts have finally begun to establish protocols for harmonisation of environmental codes within Mercosul, but this process clearly takes a low priority when compared with the 'fast track' removal of border restrictions to accelerate growth in trade.

Transnational enterprises, accounting for the majority of foreign direct investment worldwide, have tended to be more sensitive than are many domestic firms to environmental scrutiny as well as to the demands of international markets. Adoption of auditing procedures and adherence to ISO 9000 and, more recently, ISO 14000 criteria have become fairly widespread as incentives toward adoption of environmentally friendly processes. Some firms have adopted environmental auditing and other self-regulatory mechanisms to gradually adapt technology and product parameters to increasingly demanding international criteria.

Intellectual property issues remain a significant source of contention in the attraction of international investment. The Brazilian Congress recently approved industrial patent legislation that defines rights over foreign sourced products and technologies. In the past the lack of clarity created friction with pharmaceuticals and informatics investors leading to threats to drop Brazil's favoured nation status by the US Trade Representative.

Opposition to patenting has arisen from environmental and farmer support organisations concerned over the homogenisation of genetic resources, rights over biological organisms, and other concerns associated with capturing benefits from investments in biodiversity prospecting. Although it might be thought that Brazil's megadiversity would have attracted pharmaceuticals and others interested in cashing in on such biodiversity prospecting options, this is not yet the case, due to the lack of intellectual property rights criteria. The federal government recently established a forum to facilitate and finance partnerships of business, NGOs and universities through a GEF fund (FUNBIO) for biodiversity research and development based at the prestigious Getúlio Vargas Foundation. Current plans by the IFC to finance private ventures in the management of biological diversity, such as ecotourism and private nature reserves (IFC, 1996), make the adequate definition of such rights imperative to ensure that Brazilians do not once again lose potential revenues from their unparalleled natural resource base, which accounts for over 25 percent of the world's tropical forests, a significant part of the remaining global biodiversity.

7. POLICY TOOLS AND MECHANISMS TO INCREASE THE ENVIRONMENTAL CONTENT OF INTERNATIONAL PRIVATE CAPITAL FLOWS INTO BRAZIL

There are a number of mechanisms that could be considered in efforts to expand the environmental character of frameworks for private international investment in Brazil. One area whose exploitation is still incipient is that of attracting venture capital to environmental investments. This can be accomplished through such instruments as (a) differential treatment of capital gains taxation for investments in environmentally certified industries, and (b) establishment of Brazilian environmental venture capitalisation fund(s) such as those already existent in the USA and Europe. Such environmental funds could have initial capital subscribed by a multilateral agency such as the World Bank group, but would gradually be capitalised through public bond offerings. Resources from such funds would be available for investment in environmental control technologies, biodiversity prospecting and capacity development, and so on.

Box 10.1: Expansion of Brazil's Plantation-based Pulp and Paper Industry

The Brazilian pulp and paper sector is privileged in that the cost of raw material is extremely low, due to climatic factors and hybridisation that have increased the productivity of eucalyptus well beyond that feasible in other regions of the world, as well as low labour costs. For many years, this competitive edge made Brazilian short fibre hardwood cellulose cheaper to produce than any competing raw materials for the industry. (Finland has been able to reduce its raw materials costs using advanced harvesting and digital processing systems.) Furthermore, a governmental fiscal incentive program during the 1970s–80s stimulated planting of significant areas in plantation forest monocrops, thus providing an extensive raw material base for expansion of the industry, which is based exclusively on planted pine and eucalyptus forests that today total over 4 million hectares, of which 1.4 million are controlled directly by the industry.

Brazil's pulp and paper industry is currently composed of 235 firms, most involved solely in paper manufacture, with a small group of integrated pulp and paper facilities and several cellulose-only operations. Output in 1995 was 5.5 million tonnes of cellulose and 5.9 million tonnes of paper (about 3 percent of global production). The industry serves a strong domestic market, and also exports 38 percent of its cellulose and 26 percent of paper production. Total annual output value was $5.6 billion in 1994, corresponding to about 1 percent of Brazil's GDP (*Agroanálise*, 1995).

The availability and potential for expansion in the industry derived from available raw material supply base attracted international capital investment through different modalities over the years. Foreign direct investment was responsible for the initiation of a number of significant industrial facilities in early years, such as those under majority control of Champion and Jarí (today CAEMI). The latter appropriated an immense central Amazon property and devastated considerable areas of native forest to plant tropical monocultures. The domestic backlash against this project forced the government to hand it over to national investors, and has led to a reticence to approve further projects under sole multinational control. Instead, the majority of investors are engaged in joint ventures (for example, Aracruz: Brazil/Norway) or sole-owned family enterprise (Klabin: Klabin Paper and Riocel). The only state-owned enterprise was Cenibra, in fact jointly owned by CVRD and Celulose Nipo Brasileira (CVRD was privatised in mid-1997). Capital for expansion in these enterprises came principally from federal credit sources, chiefly BNDES, complemented with IFC credits (current portfolio value: $238.3 million in 9 projects).

The principal cost factor in pulp and paper is not the raw material, but the conversion to pulp and paper, responsible for 90 percent of overall enterprise cost. Pulp and paper is an extremely capital-intensive enterprise with significant economies of scale, requiring an initial investment in a minimum 350,000 tonnes per year plant capacity to achieve financial viability on the order of $700 million. Such substantial capital and scale requirements lead to cyclicity in the market, due to oversupply when new plants come on stream, and many Brazilian firms have experienced idle capacity problems during the recent volatility in global pulp and paper markets. Investment decisions made during a growth phase (1989) were substantially committed when the market plummeted in the 1990–93 period, resulting in idle capacity of 17 percent (BNDES, 1993).

Market volatility, and large up-front capital requirements in the sector have led to new thinking regarding the options for forest-based development. In some areas, such as southern Bahia and Amapá, planted forests are being used for production of wood chips for direct export in unprocessed form to complement insufficient regional raw material supplies in the southeastern US and Japan. Early in 1996, responding to yet another downturn in the cellulose market, Aracruz Celulose S.A. determined to proceed with planned investments in wood products manufacture using excess eucalyptus derived from its plantations.

Over the past decade, to remain competitive with international market demands, the pulp and paper industry in Brazil has been obliged to invest substantially in environmental management, and has generally adopted total quality procedures to satisfy ISO 9000 standards. One company, Bahia Sul, with investment by CVRD and Suzano, anticipated environmental management standards still under discussion and attained certification by the British Industrial Standards Association in 1995.

Although the sector is competitive in international markets, and has successfully adapted to the rigorous environmental norms demanded by consuming nations, there are a number of factors linked to raw material production that have restrained growth in the industry. First, the fact that land in Brazil cannot be purchased outright for industrial purposes by foreign firms, a damper on foreign investment in a sector which requires vertical integration to maintain productive efficiency. Second, the cost of expanded plantation area, approximately $1,400/hectare in eucalyptus, is superior to the present value of raw materials once harvested, due to the extremely high domestic cost of capital; although this problem could conceivably be partly overcome by joint ventures with overseas investors with access to low interest credits, this option has not been seriously explored to date. Third, efforts to introduce outgrower systems involving farm forestry under contract to the industry have been frustrated by bureaucratic obstacles that require the same treatment of small areas as those required for extensive plantations, as well as opposition from environmental and farm labour groups, concerned that farm forestry could be an insidious method for the industry to expand its land holdings.

In an effort to advance the prospects for the industry to maintain its competitive footing, sectoral associations have formed a working programme in partnership with government, in efforts to identify means to reduce bureaucratic obstacles toward growth in forest plantations on small and medium-sized areas. The overall proposal is aimed to define conditions under which silvicultural production could again become eligible for federal subsidies or 'green' credit facilities that would counter the high costs of domestic capital. Coupled with this proposal, the industry has sought to establish a framework for certification of sustainable wood production from forest plantations, in association with the national standards agency and the Forest Stewardship Council. A National Certification System made up of sectoral interest groups, government and NGOs would establish norms and certify producers and products. On the basis of this structure and an analysis of industrial growth potential, proposals would be formulated for support by government to stimulate expansion in reforested areas for industrial purposes.

Another area for policy development is that of incorporation of environmental considerations into support programmes for specific sectors. 'Sectoral chambers' have recently been established as a mechanism to establish norms and stimulate environmentally appropriate investment and performance. One recent example of such a mechanism is the organisation of an institutional framework to allow certification of origin of forest raw materials which would ensure production processes meet environmental norms satisfactory to importers, and proposals to remove bureaucratic obstacles toward expansion in forest-based industries (see Box 10.1).

Finally, it is important to broaden the base of information relevant to the making of sustainable private investments in Brazil. Information is needed to guide strategic investment to forestall environmental risks and sustain production in the long term. This should be based on environmental accounting at a national/regional level to monitor the economic implications of natural resource exploitation and absorption of residuals, requiring maintenance of physical environment and natural resource stock information. Ideally, these would be an agglomeration of firms' environmental audits, production data and ambient environmental monitoring by government. At present, such information gathering and dissemination, a role of the Brazilian Institute for Geography and Statistics, is very weak. Failure to maintain the economic census since 1985 makes sectoral analysis difficult particularly in the agriculture and natural resources sectors. A recent initiative by the Ministry of the Environment to establish a National Programme of Indicators of Sustainability would assemble information from pertinent sources and expert information, to monitor progress within a 'pressure, state, response' framework such as that proposed by the OECD (Tolmasquim et al., 1996).

To make plausible a movement by industry in developing nations toward sustainable enterprise, consumer nations have a role in rewarding use of environmentally friendly technologies for goods they import. This is particularly true in the case of organically produced foodstuffs and natural products, which can serve as substitutes for raw materials obtained using chemical pesticides and fertilisers, or petroleum-based synthetics. However, there is a tension between demands for product quality and environmental content of production processes which make necessary the establishment of certification procedures (May, 1995). Government policy should establish the framework for monitoring and certification of compliance with environmental norms, placing emphasis on self-regulation based on market advantage, as well as fortifying opportunities for collaborative partnerships with civil society and industrial representatives.

NOTES

1. This paper presents a review of issues under study in the project 'International Financial Capital Flows and the Environment', coordinated by Bradford Gentry of the Center for Environmental Law and Policy at Yale University with funding from the Avina Foundation, with case studies in Brazil, Mexico, Argentina and Costa Rica, whose full results are to be published in Gentry (forthcoming). The Tinker Foundation supported a series of seminars to discuss the implications of this study in each of the participating nations, and in Washington, DC. Ana Célia Castro and Antônio Barros de Castro formed part of the Brazil case study team for this project, and their contributions are acknowledged.
2. In 1995, the global press reported a five-fold increase in Amazon burning over the previous several years with 72,719 fire points sighted just during the first part of August with NOAA satellite imagery, possibly heralding the greatest expansion in deforestation to date (*Veja*, 8 Nov. 1995). This expansion was later confirmed by official deforestation statistics, which reported a doubling of new Amazon clearing in 1995 over the average for 1991–94 (INPE, 26 Jan. 1998). Although this rate of deforestation slowed somewhat in 1996 and is projected to slow still further in 1997, there is no doubt that the severity of this process has continued unabated, despite the commitments at UNCED.
3. According to this legislation, 'Registry is not permitted in the case that antidotes are not readily available in Brazil for those substances that may cause disease such as cancer, genetic mutations or hormonal disturbance, or which may cause environmental damages. Products should be sold with correct labelling that provides access to full information regarding their dangers, possible side effects, precautions and instructions for cases of accidents. The government may impugn and request cancellation of pesticide registration, arguing damage to the environment, natural resources or public health. Quantity and quality standards are maintained."
4. A case in point is that of pollutant-intensity sewerage charges on industrial users established in the 1980–82 period by the state water and sewerage authority of São Paulo, SABESP, that devised this system as a means of raising revenues to subsidize households. When industries found they were being charged on the basis of the intensity of BOD or suspended solids discharges, they moved rapidly to adopt pollution reducing technology to cut their charges. However, this resulted in SABESP no longer generating the additional funds needed for its incremental operating expenses. The progressive charge system was hence abandoned (Miglino and Harrington, 1984).
5. This is not to say that such leverage necessarily resolved environmental problems. In the Carajás case itself, indirect effects of land occupation have been internationally decried as a source of devastation of remaining tropical forests. Ancillary pig iron, cement and silicate industries promoted by government, based on charcoal derived from native forest, prompted many years of international criticism that has been particularly virulent in Europe, where CVRD sells a good part of its high grade iron ore from Carajás (May, 1994b). Subsidies were subsequently removed for Grande Carajás regional investment, affecting growth in private investment in enterprises in this region. CVRD has been prompted to work with existing downstream industries to improve their environmental profile, and has recently received a $100 million loan from the World Bank to finance general environmental improvements in its operations (May, 1997).

REFERENCES

Agroanálise (1995), 'Celulose e papel'.
BNDES (1993), *Segmento de celulose do mercado*, Rio de Janeiro: Banco Nacional de Desenvolvimento Econômico e Social, Área de Planejamento, Depto. de Estudos Setoriais-DEEST.

BNDES (1995), 'Ação ambiental do BNDES – informe estatístico', Rio de Janeiro: Banco Nacional de Desenvolvimento Econômico e Social.

Coes, Donald V. (1995), *Macroeconomic crises, policies, and growth in Brazil, 1964–90*, Washington, DC: The World Bank.

Daly, Herman and Goodland, Robert (1994), 'An ecological-economic assessment of deregulation of international commerce under GATT', *Ecological Economics*, **9** (1): 73–92.

Gentry, Bradford (ed.) (1998), *Private capital flows and the environment: lessons from Latin America*, Northampton, MA: Edward Elgar Publishing.

Gertner, David, May, Peter, Castro, Ana Célia, Leme, Celso Funcia and Vinha, Valéria (1997), 'Aracruz Celulose, S.A. (A business case in corporate communication)', in Susan Ward and Lawrence Pratt (eds), *Sustainable enterprise in Latin America*, Washington, DC: Management Institute for Environment and Business/World Resources Institute.

Henwood, Doug (1996), 'The free flow of money', *NACLA Report on the Americas*, **29** (4), Jan/Feb: 11–17.

IFC (1994), 'Environmental risk management for financial institutions', *IFC Brief*, Washington, DC.

IFC (1995), *Annual Report*, Washington, DC: International Finance Corporation.

IFC (1996), 'Biodiversity enterprise fund for Latin America and the Caribbean', Mimeo.

May, Peter (1994a), *Environmental issues in coffee and cocoa production and processing in Brazil*, Geneva: UNCTAD Commodities Division.

May, Peter (1994b*), Relatório ambiental: opções energéticas para o pólo siderúrgico de Carajás*, Washington, DC: World Bank Environment Department.

May, Peter (1995), *A survey of environmentally friendly products of Brazil*, Geneva: UNCTAD.

May, Peter (1997), 'Devastação ou empreendimentos sustentáveis no Carajás', in *Coherent public policies for the Amazon region*, São Paulo: FOE/GTA.

Mendes, Francisco Eduardo (1994), 'Uma avaliação dos custos de controle da poluição hídrica de orígem industrial no Brasil', Tese de Mestrado, COPPE-UFRJ.

Miglino, L.C.P. and Harrington, J.J. (1984), 'The impact of tariffs in generation of industrial effluents', *Revista DAE*, **44** (138), São Paulo.

Neder, Ricardo T. (1992), 'Há política ambiental para a indústria brasileira?', *Revista de Administração de Empresas*, **32** (2), Apr/Jun: 6–13.

Ros, Luiz Carlos Fo. (1994), *Financiamentos para o meio ambiente*, Brasília: Instituto de Estudos Amazônicos e Ambientais.

Schmidheiny, Stephan et al. (1996), *Financing change: the financial community, eco-efficiency, and sustainable development*, Cambridge, MA: MIT Press.

Schwartzman, Steven (1995), 'Investimento privado em obras públicas terá impacto ambiental', *Parabólicas*, Instituto Sócio-Ambiental, São Paulo, December: 3.

Serôa da Motta, R. (1993a), 'Indicadores de poluição na indústria brasileira', *Perspectivas da Economia Brasileira – 1994*, Rio de Janeiro: IPEA.

Serôa da Motta, R. (1993b), *Estudo da competitividade da indústria Brasileira*, Consórcio IEI-UFRJ/IE – UNICAMP, Campinas: São Paulo.

Serôa da Motta, Ronaldo and Mendes, Ana Paula (1996), 'Health impacts of air pollution', in Peter H. May and Ronaldo Serôa da Motta (eds), *Pricing the planet: economic analysis for sustainable development*, New York: Columbia University Press, pp. 101–122.

Tigre, Paulo B., Wanderley, Anibal, Ferraz, João Carlos and Rush, Howard (1994), *Tecnologia e meio ambiente; oportunidades para a indústria*, Rio de Janeiro: Ed. UFRJ.

Tolmasquim, Maurício (ed.) (1996), *Estrutura conceitual da elaboração de indicadores de sustentabilidade ambiental para o Brasil*, Brasília: Ministério do Meio Ambiente, Recursos Hídricos e Amazônia Legal.

World Bank (1997), *Global development finance 1997*, Washington, DC.

11. Environmental Services as a Strategy for Sustainable Development in Rural Amazonia

Philip M. Fearnside

1. INTRODUCTION

Sustainable Development

What is 'sustainable development'? 'Development' refers to a change, implying an improvement, in the way that people support themselves. Although the term is frequently misused as synonymous with 'growth', it does not necessarily imply an increase in the throughput of matter and energy in an economy (Goodland and Ledec, 1987). Indeed, if a continual increase in either flows or stocks were a requirement, then 'sustainable development' would be a contradiction in terms. Since 'limits to growth' constrain the use of both renewable and non-renewable resources, strategies for sustainable development must, in the long run, concentrate on reorganisation of how resources are used and how benefits are shared.

Much discourse on sustainable development has implied that this can be achieved with unending growth, adding only the caveat that environmental quality standards will somehow be respected (see review by Willers, 1994). Sustainable development is seen as a means of not admitting to the existence of limits. Recognising limits is resisted by the rich as a potential cap on their profit making, while the poor and those who work on their behalf often have an ideological aversion to recognising limits for fear that doing so condemns the poor to poverty. Unfortunately, limits to what can be removed and sold from Amazonia or any other region exist, independent of what people may think about the matter. 'Continual' growth is not an option; the option that is often confused with this is merely a postponement of restraining the offtake of products to within the bounds that limit their sustainable production. What must be answered is the question of how and when 'growth' will cease, and what kind of society one wants to have when this transition has passed.

Rather than condemning the poor to poverty, recognising the existence of limits condemns the rich to facing up to dividing the pie (see Fearnside, 1993a).

'Development' implies creation of an economic basis for support of a population. It is essential to define clearly what population is to be benefited. I have long argued that, in the case of Brazilian Amazonia, this should be limited to the present population of the region and their descendants. From the perspective of the local population, a cattle ranch for an absentee landlord is not development. Neither, for example, are the aluminium smelters in Barcarena, Pará, and São Luís, Maranhão, that export (mostly to Japan) two-thirds of the power from Tucuruí Dam, in the form of aluminium ingots. Most of the output of the US$ 8 billion dam goes to support an industry that employs less than 2,000 people (Fearnside, 1989a).

In order to be 'sustainable', the basis of support must be maintained for a long time. Ideally this would be forever, but in practice it must be defined in terms of a finite time horizon; for example, a period in the order of hundreds of years. It must also be recognised that nothing is certain – the probability is always less than one that the activity will last for the specified time period. One must define the maximum acceptable probability of failing to last this period. The choice of a value for the probability criterion depends on the magnitude of impacts in the event of a failure and a social decision regarding the relationship between magnitude of impacts and acceptable risk (see Fearnside, 1997a).

Elements of a Strategy

One must decide on a *strategy* for attaining sustainable development; that is, a broad indication of the direction of activities, rather than a specific recipe for sustainability. The approach to be taken must be based on what is most likely to yield the long-term result that defines sustainable development. Cattle pasture, the dominant system at present, is unlikely to prove sustainable over the long run (Fearnside, 1997a). Soybeans, the crop currently favoured by government agencies for a future support base, also has a high probability of proving unsustainable, no matter how correctly specified the technical formulae of fertilisers, pesticides, and so on, may be. Some future change, such as a disease, pest, or change in price, is likely to intervene. Once the forest has been thrown away to plant such a crop, there is no return to the security offered by the original diversity. As a general rule it is better to make something sustainable into development than to try to make an unsustainable form of development sustainable. Rather than try to extend the life of cattle pastures by means of fertilisers and changes in pasture grass species, it is better to start with tropical forest, which has proved itself sustainable by thousands of years of existence, and find ways to market the services that rainforest provides.

Sustainable use is most likely if the country maintains control over what is sold. Brazil must sell what it wants to sell rather than what the world wants to buy. The world may want to buy jaguar skins, pig iron and mahogany, but, as with jaguar skins, Brazil can decide that these are not what the country wants to sell. The fact that a country has a given resource in no way implies that the country in question is under some sort of moral obligation to supply it to the world. The situation is analogous to prostitution: everyone, no matter how physically endowed, has at least some potential to supply the market's demand for prostitutes – but most people decide not to sell this particular service. In the same way, a country may have tropical hardwoods and decide, without any qualms, not to sell them. What Brazil would be wiser to sell are the environmental services of its forests.

Long-term versus Short-term Objectives

While it is all well and good to pursue a long-term strategy of tapping the value of environmental services as the foundation of sustainable development in rural Amazonia, under the best of assumptions this can only be expected to bring results years in the future. What are rural Amazonians to do in the meantime? One is reminded of the famous remark by Harry Hopkins to US President Franklin D. Roosevelt: 'People do not eat, in the long run, nor, on the average; they eat every day'.

Attention must be paid to *both* short-term and long-term concerns. If concern is only with the long term, people will starve in the meantime. The temptation is therefore strong for all effort to be devoted to dealing with the day-to-day crises of survival. However, if thought is given only to these immediate demands, then long-term sustainability will never be achieved.

A variety of mechanisms for short- and medium-term support have been suggested, such as use of non-timber forest products (NTFPs), ecotourism, and so on. Whatever short-term solutions are adopted, it is essential that the options chosen do not destroy the resource base of the long-term strategy (the forest), nor the credibility of local groups. Amerindians have the best record of maintaining forest, and in certain regions the only forest left is that on indigenous lands. However, sale of timber by tribes is increasing as leaders succumb to the temptations that money offers (Fearnside, 1997b). The loss from selling resources such as logs is much more than the value the tribes can receive from the sales, even if they were not subject to unfavourable terms and outright cheating on the part of timber merchants. In addition to losing trees and damaging forest, they also lose part of their most valuable future resource: credibility for maintaining environmental services.

2. CRITERIA FOR SUSTAINABILITY

Biological Sustainability

In order to be sustainable, any form of forest use or other land use must meet certain criteria. One class of such criteria relates to biological sustainability, or the long-term maintenance of biological processes that keep the ecosystem in a stable state that is unlikely to collapse in the face of foreseeable stresses. Population biology is one area in which a balance must be achieved: if trees or other ecosystem components are harvested at rates greater than the regenerative processes of the population can replenish, then the forest will inevitably become depleted. Nutrient balance must also be maintained, as a drain of nutrients greater than that which is input and captured by the system will lead to impoverishment and inability of living components of the ecosystem to survive. The system must have a stable biomass, as any tendency to decline will eventually degrade the forest and its environmental function as a carbon store. Genetic quality of the populations of trees or other taxa must be maintained, as degradation, for example, by repeated harvesting of individuals with the best form, will eventually worsen the quality of the remaining population even if the numbers of individuals and species represented remain the same. Keeping forest intact requires a low probability of fire, this being one way that forests can quickly be decimated, even if they are not deliberately felled. Finally, provision of an adequate number, diversity and area of fully protected reserves must be included as part of any strategy for making economic use of the forest.

Social Sustainability

If a system implies a social injustice that represents the seeds of its own destruction, then it will be unsustainable on social grounds. For example, the charcoal industry for manufacture of pig iron in the Grande Carajás area of eastern Amazonia is based on a form of debt slavery that must sooner or later come to an end, even if the system were technically sound. Brazil's charcoal industry has provoked national and international scandal following charges brought before the International Labour Organisation in 1994 (Pachauski, 1994; Ribeiro, 1994; Sutton, 1994; Pamplona and Rodrigues, 1995).

3. ENVIRONMENTAL SERVICES AS SUSTAINABLE DEVELOPMENT

Types of Environmental Service

Biodiversity

Maintenance of biological diversity constitutes an environmental service for which beneficiaries around the world might be willing to pay. Biodiversity maintenance has some direct local benefits, such as providing non-timber forest products (Fearnside, 1989b; Grimes et al., 1994; Hecht, 1992; Peters et al., 1989; Pimentel et al., 1997a; Richards, 1993; Vásquez and Gentry, 1989; Whitehead and Godoy, 1991). Local benefits also accrue from the stock of genetic material of plants and animals needed to give a degree of adaptability to forest management and to agricultural systems that sacrifice biodiversity in nearby unprotected areas (Myers, 1989). However, many benefits of biodiversity are global rather than local. The stock of useful chemical compounds, and of genetic materials for other than local use, represents an investment in protecting future generations in distant places from the consequences of lacking that material when it is needed one day. This value is different from the commercial value of products that may be marketed in the future (which would represent a lost local opportunity should biodiversity be destroyed). A medicinal use, such as a cure for some dreaded disease, is worth more to humanity than money that can be earned from selling the drug. An estimate of the opportunity cost for medicinal uses for rainforests in Mexico arrived at a figure of US$6.4/hectares/year, with a range from US$1 to US$90 (Adger et al., 1995). Substantial potential exists for identifying chemical models for pharmacological products based on Amazonian plants (Cordell, 1995; Elisabetsky and Shanley, 1994; Kaplan and Gottlieb, 1990). It is important to realise, however, that the financial value of pharmaceutical products, although clearly important, is not sufficiently large to support conservation on the scale sometimes envisioned. Existence value is also something that accrues mostly to populations who are either very close to the forest, such as indigenous peoples, or who are far removed from it, such as urban dwellers elsewhere. Whether or not one believes that biodiversity is worth spending money to protect, it is sufficient to know that many people in the world do believe it is important, and that it therefore can be converted into a source of income to support the population and protect the forest in Amazonia.

Negotiating for protection of biodiversity is especially complicated because it represents a balance between two opposing lines of argument, both of which are inadmissible. On the side of countries with biodiversity, there is the implied threat of blackmail: either 'developed' countries pay whatever is demanded or forests will be cut and the species they contain sacrificed. On the other side, there is the implication that countries with biodiversity should be protecting their natural heritage anyway, so any payments from outside are strictly optional.

One difficult point is the question of national sovereignty. It is often said that by agreeing to set aside reserves and abstain from 'development' in these areas, countries like Brazil are giving away their national sovereignty. However, there is no difference between the sovereignty effects of entering into an agreement on reserves and biodiversity and the effects of entering into any other sort of commercial contract. If a country contracts to sell *anything*, including both traditional commodities and environmental services, it is in effect exchanging the assurance of a monetary flow for the option to do whatever it wants with part of its land. For example, when Brazil agrees to sell a certain quantity of soybeans in a future year at a given price, it is giving up the option to plant some other crop in a given part of its territory. Nor is the permanence of protected areas a significant difference from most commercial contracts, which are usually temporary: the changes from a commercial contract may be just as permanent as those brought about by a contract for permanent maintenance of an area of natural habitat. For example, if forest is cut or inundated as part of a development project it cannot be brought back should the country later change its mind.

The value of biodiversity is poorly quantified, and severe methodological constraints limit our ability to assign meaningful monetary values to it (Norton, 1988; Stirling, 1993). While one knows that its monetary value is very high (Costanza et al., 1997; Pimentel et al., 1997b), the willingness of the world at large to pay is the limiting factor on how much of this value can be translated into a monetary flow. That willingness to pay has, in general, been increasing, and it may be hoped that it will increase substantially in the future.

One problem is that what individuals and governments are willing to spend on biodiversity is constrained by other priorities these money sources have. The total allotted to biodiversity, even though it may increase both proportionally and in absolute terms, is, in effect, a pie over which potential beneficiaries compete. It is a zero-sum game: what is spent on saving the rhinoceros is not spent on slowing Amazonian deforestation, and vice versa. It is rare when true 'new and additional funds' are provided, as demanded by Agenda 21 – the 800-page internationally negotiated document that provides for implementation of conventions signed at the United Nations Conference on Environment and Development (UNCED) held in Rio de Janeiro in 1992.

Biodiversity assessment and monitoring, although plagued by difficulties, can be approached quantitatively in a hierarchical manner (Noss, 1990). Monitoring protocols must capture the three primary attributes of ecosystems: composition, structure and function. The monitoring must be done over a range of levels of organisation and at different temporal and spatial scales.

Among the difficulties in assessing biodiversity protection value is the question of how time preference should be treated. Discounting may be applied, similar to the discounting of monetary values routinely done by bankers in financial calculations. However, biodiversity has a unique characteristic that makes it different from money and other environmental services, such as maintaining carbon stocks. Biodiversity is not substitutable or interchangeable. Once a species or an ecosystem becomes extinct, there is no going back. This fact provides an argument against discounting in the case of biodiversity.

The criterion for achievement in biodiversity protection, however, must include some kind of reward for long-term maintenance. Should weight be given for the number of species-years of survival achieved as compared to a 'business-as-usual' reference scenario, or should one make a count of the biodiversity present at some future time, say 100 years from now, and compare this to the biodiversity that would be present in the reference scenario? If any kind of discounting were applied, this would give advantage to places like Rondônia, where the threat of extinction is more imminent, as compared to relatively untouched areas in the interior of the state of Amazonas. Countries like Costa Rica, where the last remnants of rainforest are under threat of destruction, also have an advantage. It is true that, from the point of view of biodiversity, a hectare of forest loss in Costa Rica implies a much greater loss of species than does a hectare in many parts of Brazilian Amazonia, where extensive rainforest is still standing.

How much might the world be willing to pay for maintenance of biodiversity in Amazonia? Considerable research effort would be needed to answer such a question with reliable numbers, and this has yet to be done. As a starting point for discussion, however, one may take the value of US$20/hectares/year suggested by Cartwright (1985: 185) as what would be needed to convince tropical countries to enter into agreements for biodiversity maintenance. Cartwright believes such a value is feasible. Table 11.1 presents data on deforestation and on the population of the Legal Amazon used in subsequent calculations for the values of biodiversity, carbon and water cycling. This makes it possible to explore the implications of these values for supporting the human population, considering the value of the standing stock of forest, the annual environmental damage at the 1990 deforestation rate, and the part of this damaged caused by the small farmer population. Small farmers are defined in Brazilian Amazonia by the Brazilian Institute for Geography and Statistics (IBGE) as those having less than 100 hectares of land. The distribution of deforestation among states with varying degrees of land tenure concentration indicates that 30.5 percent of clearing is done by small farmers, with the remainder done by either medium or large ranchers (Fearnside, 1993b).

Table 11.1: Constants used in calculations of forest value

Area deforested in 1990 (Millions of ha)	1.38[a]
Forest remaining in 1990 (Millions of ha)	337.72
Deforestation in 1990 caused by small farmers (%)	30.5[a]
Rural population (Millions of individuals)	7.65[b]
Properties (= families) of small farmers (%)	83.2[c]
Population of small farmers (Millions of individuals)	6.4[d]
Average family size (Individuals)	5
Discount rate (%/year)	5

Notes:
(a) Fearnside, 1993b.
(b) Brazil, IBGE, 1992.
(c) Brazil, IBGE, 1989.
(d) Calculated from rural population and percentage of small farmers.

Contrary to recent statements by the head of the Brazilian Institute for Environment and Renewable Natural Resources (IBAMA) (Traumann, 1998), deforestation data for 1995 and 1996 released by INPE (Brazil, INPE, 1998) do not indicate that small farmers are now the primary agents of deforestation. The fact that about half (59 percent in 1995 and 53 percent in 1996) of the area of new *clearings* (as distinct from the area of the *properties* in which the clearings were located) have areas under 100 hectares reinforces the conclusion that most of the deforestation is being done by large ranchers, as no small farmer can clear anywhere near 100 hectares in a single year. Only 21 percent of the area of new clearings in 1995 and 18 percent in 1996 were under 15 hectares. The average small farmer family is only capable of clearing about 3 hectares/year with family labour (Fearnside, 1980). During the period of rapid deforestation by small farmers opening the colonisation areas on the Transamazon Highway (in Pará) and the BR-364 Highway (in Rondônia) in the 1970s, the mean clearing rate per family ranged from 2.3 to 5.4 hectares/year in the settlement areas (Fearnside, 1984). In fact, clearings this size are below the detection limits of the satellite (6.25 hectares).

Because most deforestation is done by the rich, distribution of benefits derived from a government decision to halt further clearing would lend itself well to a 'Robin Hood solution': a means of taking from the rich to give to the poor. No qualms need be felt about removing the profitability of land speculation for ranchland without compensating the large landholders

Table 11.2: Value of biodiversity maintenance

Type	Environmental value basis	Description	Units	Value		
				Low	Medium	High
Assumption						
	Damage in 1990 caused by total population	Value of biodiversity maintenance[a]	US$/ha/yr	10	20	30
Calculated values						
	Damage in 1990 caused by total population	NPV[b]	US$ million	276	552	828
		NPV per small farmer family[b]	US$/family	217	434	650
		Total annuity[c]	US$ million/yr	14	28	41
		Annuity per small farmer family[c]	US$/family/yr	11	22	33
	1990 damage caused by small farmer population	NPV[b]	US$ million	84	168	253
		NPV per small farmer family[b]	US$/family	66	132	198
	1990 and all future damage caused by the total population	NPV[b]	US$ billion	5.5	11.1	16.6
		NPV per small farmer family[b]	US$ thousand/family	4.4	8.7	13.1
		Total annuity[c]	US$ million/yr	277	554	831

Table 11.2 continued

1990 and all future damage caused by small farmer population				
Annuity per small farmer family[c]	US$/family/yr	218	435	653
NPV[b]	US$ billion	1.7	3.4	5.1
Value of forest stock in 1990				
NPV per small farmer family[b]	US$ thousand/family	1.3	2.7	4.0
NPV[b]	US$ billion	68	135	203
NPV per small farmer family[b]	US$ thousand/family	53	106	159
Annuity on value of forest stock[c]	US$ billion/yr	3	7	10
Annuity per small farmer family[c]	US$ thousand/family/yr	2.7	5.3	8.0

Notes:
(a) Cartwright, 1985, for 'medium' value. Value presumed equal to cost.
(b) At 5%/yr discount.
(c) At 5%/yr interest.

163

(Fearnside 1989c, 1989d). The value of halting damages caused by the rich provides a potential key for solving social and environmental problems of the poor. While the value of avoided environmental impact achieved by halting clearing by large landholders might also be pocketed as a windfall, it also provides a basis for negotiating a middle ground between the 'Robin Hood' and 'windfall' extremes.

Value derived from the environmental damage avoided could be sufficient to offer sustainable livelihoods to a large number of people. As Table 11.2 makes evident, capturing the value of the stock of remaining forest has much greater potential than the value of avoided damage calculated based on the present rates of forest loss. This much larger value is currently not recognised in international conventions on climatic change and biodiversity, but it is important to keep this value in view. Whether the standing stock of forest has a value of zero or of hundreds of billions of dollars is obviously a tremendous point of uncertainty. As of now, only 'mutually agreed negotiated incremental costs' are recognised in the Framework Convention on Climate Change (FCCC), meaning that the value of standing forest is considered zero.

The value of avoided damages (changes in the flux) can also reach very high values when one considers not just the damage of one year of deforestation, but also the damage of continuing deforestation in future years. Here the damages in future years are calculated assuming that the annual rate of clearing remains fixed for 100 years at the level observed in 1990. This implies that population growth of the rural population in the region is stopped, which would be an improbable event in reality but which serves as an illustration of the magnitude of the values. Considering future years raises the value attributed to avoided damages approximately 20 fold (using a discount rate of 5 percent/year). That is, stopping deforestation forever has 20 times more value than suspending deforestation for one year (that is postponing all future deforestation by one year). Values based on stock maintenance are approximately 12 times higher than those based on avoided damages from stopping deforestation in 1990 (considering a discount rate of 5 percent/year).

Carbon
Maintaining carbon stocks also represents a valuable environmental service. Unlike biodiversity, carbon is completely interchangeable, an atom of carbon stocked in Amazonian forest has the same atmospheric effect as an atom of carbon stocked in a eucalyptus plantation or an atom of carbon stocked in the ground as fossil fuel that was not burned due to an energy conservation response option. What may vary is the time that the carbon may be held under different circumstances; but when comparisons are made on a carbon ton-year basis, they are completely equivalent (Fearnside, 1995).

Discounting is a matter of controversy regarding how the benefits should be calculated in programmes designed to combat global warming. Currently, the Global Environment Facility (GEF), which at present administers funds for combating global warming under the FCCC, does *not* apply discounting to physical quantities such as tons of carbon. However, there are strong reasons why discounting or some alternative form of time preference *should* be applied to carbon. The selfish interests of the current generation are not the only argument. Many people will die as impacts begin to appear from global warming. Global warming initiates a change in the probability of occurrence of droughts, floods and other unwanted events, rather than causing a one-time impact. If global warming impacts begin sooner rather than later, the number of lives that would be lost between the 'sooner' and the 'later' represents a net gain to be had from postponing global warming. Discounting is the mechanism by which a value for time is normally translated into economic decision-making. Postponing emissions from deforestation should be viewed as the same as postponing the emission of a ton of carbon by a given time. It therefore should be treated in a manner analogous to fossil fuel substitution, where a ton of carbon emission avoided this year is considered to have been avoided forever, even though that same carbon atom in the next year's stock of coal and oil will be released into the atmosphere just one year later.

The criterion that is used by the GEF in evaluating global warming projects is 'mutually agreed incremental costs'. This means that only the difference will be paid between what would happen under the 'project' scenario and what would happen under the 'no-project' scenario. If something is going to happen anyway then there is no need for the GEF to contribute funds, even though the event in question stores carbon. There is no 'benefit' from changing the course of events. Projects to avoid deforestation would therefore only be funded if the forest in question would have been cleared in the absence of the GEF project. Forests that are under immediate threat of clearing, such as those in Rondônia, would represent a gain if saved, whereas forests in remote areas of the state of Amazonas would represent no carbon benefit if protected as reserves. This sets up the potential for conflict between those whose primary interest is defending biodiversity and those interested mainly in global warming. To gain credit for carbon, only reserves near the deforestation front are rewarded, whereas for biodiversity, it may be (in the absence of discounting) much cheaper to set up large reserves in relatively unthreatened areas. The most threatened areas are also the areas with the greatest problems of conflicting land claims, population requiring resettlement or other measures, high land prices, and probable high costs of guards and other defensive measures to keep the threat of invasion at bay.

The question of how value is to be assigned to the damages of global warming is an extremely controversial one. This is in large part because not just financial losses are involved. The impacts of global warming are not restricted to damaging the economies of a few rich countries, even if this constitutes a major motivation behind the willingness of industrialised

Table 11.3: Carbon storage value

Type	Environmental value basis	Description	Units	Value		
				Low	Medium	High
Assumption		Value per ton of carbon permanently sequestered[a]	US$/t C	1.8	7.3	66.0
Constants		Net committed emission in 1990[b]	Million t CO_2 – equivalent C		267	
		Net committed emission/ha of deforestation in 1990[b]	t C/ha		194	
Calculated values	Damage per ha. of forest loss	Annual value[c]	US$/ha/yr	17.4	70.7	638.9
	Total damage in 1990	Damage[d]	US$/ha	349	1413	12,778
		Damage[d]	US$ million	481	1950	17,634
		Damage per small farmer family[d]	US$/family	378	1532	13,853
		Total annuity[e]	US$ million/yr	24	98	882
		Annuity per small farmer family[e]	US$/family/yr	19	77	693
	Damages in 1990 caused by small farmer population	Total damage in 1990[d]	US$ million	147	595	5378
		Damage in 1990 per small farmer family[d]	US$/family	115	467	4225

Table 11.3 continued

1990 and all future damage caused by total population				
NPV^f	US$ billion	9.6	39	352.7
NPV per small farmer family^f	US$ thousand/family	7.6	30.6	277.1
Total annuity^e	US$ million/yr	481	1950	17,634
Annuity per small farmer family^e	US$/family/yr	378	1532	13,853
1990 and all future damage of the 1990 small farmer population				
NPV^f	US$ billion	2.9	11.9	107.6
NPV per small farmer family^f	US$ thousand/family	2.3	9.3	84.5
Value of forest stock in 1990				
NPV^f	US$ billion	118	477	4316
NPV per small farmer family^f	US$ thousand/family	92.5	375	3,390.2
Annuity from value of forest stock^e	US$ billion/yr	6	24	216
Annuity per small farmer family^e	US$ thousand/family/yr	4.6	18.7	169.5

Notes:
(a) Nordhaus, 1991 (values used by Schneider, 1994).
(b) Updated from Fearnside (1997c) considering the impact of trace gases in the low trace gas scenario.
(c) Annualised at 5%/yr from value for permanent sequestration.
(d) Value of permanent sequestration (i.e. equivalent to NPV).
(e) At 5%/yr interest.
(f) At 5%/yr discount.

nations to invest in response options around the world, including maintaining tropical forests. The effects of global warming will also be felt each time a tropical storm hits the mudflats of Bangladesh or a drought hits already famine-prone areas of Africa. Millions of people are liable to die horrible deaths over the next century as a result of global warming (Daily and Ehrlich, 1990).

Considering the estimates of Fankhauser (1995) for doubling the pre-industrial concentration of CO_2, assuming that the world, including its population size, is fixed as it was in 1990, the result would be loss of 138,000 lives per year (115,000 of which would be in the poor countries). Since the world's population can be expected to increase substantially before pre-industrial CO_2 doubles, which would be in approximately 2070 under the IPCC reference scenario, the real cost in lost lives would be much greater than this (see Fankhauser and Tol, 1997). The annual monetary losses, without counting the value of human lives, would be US$221 billion, at 1990 prices (Pearce et al., 1996). It should be emphasised that these are *annual* losses (rather than one-time events), both in terms of human lives and money.

One common response to dealing with impacts on human life is to consider the value of human life as infinite, which ironically results in its being ignored in any form of cost/benefit calculation – in effect, loss of life being given a weight of zero. Formulations that are ultimately based on ability to pay to avoid risk impute greater monetary worth to lives lost in rich countries than in poor ones (for example, Fankhauser, 1992: 14). These are morally unacceptable to many, including this author (Fearnside, 1998).

Nevertheless, what the rich are willing to pay to avoid the impacts of global warming is perhaps a good measure of the volume of funds that could be tapped to maintain the carbon storage services of Amazonian forest. Since this reflects only impacts on the rich, it is grossly unfair as a measure of real damage that would be done by global warming, which would also fall on people who cannot afford to pay anything to avoid impacts. Nordhaus (1991) derived values based on willingness to pay, which, along with other indicators of this willingness, have been used by Schneider (1994) to estimate per-hectare values for carbon storage in Amazonian forests. Additional values per ton of carbon stored considered by Schneider (1994) are from enacted carbon taxes: US$6.10/t in Finland and US$45.00/t in the Netherlands and Sweden (Shah and Larson, 1992), and from a proposed penny-a-gallon (US$0.0027/l) gasoline tax in the United States equivalent to US$3.50/t of carbon. Recent calculations of how the United States might comply with the 1997 Kyoto Protocol indicate that carbon emission permit prices between US$25 and US$50/t of carbon would have to be paid (Romm et al., 1998). An illustration of the carbon storage value of forest, using low, medium and high values of US$1.80, US$7.30 and US$66.00/t from Nordhaus (1991), is given in Table 11.3. The table extends Schneider's (1994) analysis based on updated values for greenhouse gas emissions from deforestation (Fearnside, 1997c), and also includes interpretation of per-hectare values in terms of the total stock of forest, 1990 deforestation rate, and the portion of the rate attributable to small farmers.

It is important to distinguish between the true value of an environmental service like carbon storage versus the value as represented by willingness to pay. Willingness to pay is limited by the amount of money that individuals or countries have at their disposal, and, of course, by the other priorities that they may have for spending it. There is also a problem of scale: the world might be willing to pay, say, US$1 billion or US$10 billion on combating global warming, but not US$100 billion, even if the cost to the rich of global warming damages exceeded this value. The true value of the damages, of course, would always be much higher than the damages to the rich. The tremendous amount of environmental service that Brazil effectively has to offer means that the price obtained could decline, just as in any other kind of market. As Brazil well knows, if a country offers for sale a few sacks of a commodity like coffee or cacao the price may be 'X', but if the quantity offered is millions of sacks the price may no longer be 'X'. Considering prices without the effects of scale, however, provides a starting point for thinking about the problem of marketing environmental services. Willingness to pay may increase significantly in the future when the magnitude of potential damage from global warming becomes more apparent to decision-makers and the general public.

Water cycle
One consequence of massive conversion of forest to pasture would be a decrease in rainfall in Amazonia and in neighbouring regions. Half of Amazonia's rainfall is derived from water that recycles through forest as evapotranspiration, rather than from water vapour in clouds originating over the Atlantic Ocean. Four independent lines of evidence lead to this conclusion. First, water and energy balances derived from average charts of temperature and humidity indicate 56 percent of the precipitation as derived from evapotranspiration (Molion, 1975). Second, calculations of precipitable water and water vapour flux for a transect from Belém to Manaus indicate a contribution from evapotranspiration of 48 percent (Marques et al., 1977). Third, isotope ratioing of water vapour samples in the same area indicates up to 50 percent as recycled through the forest, depending on the month (Salati et al., 1978, 1979). Fourth, the volume of water flowing out of the Amazon River can be compared with the volume of water falling as rain in the catchment basin. River flow is 5.5×10^{12} m^3/year measured at the Amazon's narrow point at Óbidos, and rainfall is 12.0×10^{12} m^3/year estimated from pluviometers around the region (Villa Nova et al., 1976). The volume of water in the rain is slightly more than double the amount leaving through the

Table 11.4: Water cycling value

Type	Environmental value base	Description	Units	Low	Medium	High
Assumption		Percentage of harvest that depends on water from Amazonia	%	5	10	20
Constant		Gross value of Brazilian harvest	US$ billion		65	
Calculated values	Damage per ha. of forest loss	Annual value	US$/ha/yr	10	19	38
	Damages in 1990 caused by total population	NPV[a]	US$ million	266	531	1062
		NPV per small farmer family[a]	US$/family	209	417	835
		Total annuity[b]	US$ million/yr	13	27	53
		Annuity per small farmer family[b]	US$/family/yr	10	21	42
	1990 damage caused by small farmer population	NPV[a]	US$ million	81	161	323

Table 11.4 continued

1990 and all future damage caused by total population	NPV per small farmer family[a]	US$/family	63	127	254
	NPV[a]	US$ billion	5.3	10.7	21.3
	NPV per small farmer family[a]	US$ thousand/family	4.2	8.4	16.8
	Total annuity[b]	US$ million/yr	267	533	1067
	Annuity per small farmer family[b]	US$/family/yr	209	419	838
1990 and all future damage caused by small farmer population	NPV[a]	US$ billion	1.6	3.3	6.5
	NPV per small farmer family[a]	US$ thousand/family	1.3	2.6	5.1
Value of forest stock in 1990	NPV[a]	US$ billion	65	130	260
	NPV per small farmer family[a]	US$ thousand/family	51.1	102.1	204.2
	Annuity from value of forest stock[b]	US$ billion/yr	3	7	13
	Anuity per small farmer family[b]	US$ thousand/family/yr	2.6	5.1	10.2

Notes:
(a) At 5%/yr interest.
(b) At 5%/yr discount.

river, meaning that approximately half (54 percent) that does not drain out through the river has been returned to the atmosphere as evapotranspiration.

Only by seeing the Amazon River at flood season can one fully appreciate the immense volume of water involved: what one sees in the river is the same volume that is returning unseen to the atmosphere through the leaves of the forest. That the leaves of the forest are constantly giving off water is evident to anyone who has tied a plastic bag over a handful of leaves: in only a few minutes the inside of the bag is covered with water droplets condensed from evapotranspiration. Summed over the several hundred billion trees in Amazonia a vast amount of water is returned to the atmosphere. Since evapotranspiration is proportional to leaf area, the water recycled through the forest is much more than that recycled through the pasture, especially in the dry season when the pasture is dry while the forest remains evergreen. This is aggravated by the much higher runoff under pasture. Increases in runoff by one order of magnitude have been measured near Manaus (Amazonas), Altamira (Pará) and Ouro Preto do Oeste (Rondônia) (see Fearnside, 1989e). Soil under pasture quickly becomes highly compacted, inhibiting infiltration of rainwater into the soil (Dantas, 1979; Schubart et al., 1976). Rain falling on the compacted soil runs off quickly, becoming unavailable for later release to the atmosphere through transpiration.

An appreciable amount of the rain in Brazil's principal agricultural areas in the centre-south part of the country also derives from the Amazon forest (Salati and Vose, 1984). The rotation of the earth causes the predominant (trade) winds south of the equator to curve from an east–west to a north–south and then to a northwest–southeast direction. The movement of clouds in this direction is evident from images of the GOES meteorological satellite. A simulation using the global circulation model (GCM) of the Goddard Institute of Space Studies (GISS) in New York indicates that water that begins in Amazonia falls as rain in all Brazil, although it does not affect the climate of other continents (Eagleson, 1986).

No one knows how much the input of Amazonian rainfall is to agriculture in southern Brazil, nor how much the harvest would be affected by loss of this input. Brazil's harvest has a gross value of around US$65 billion annually, meaning that even a relatively small fraction of this lost to decreased water vapour supply would translate into a substantial financial impact. Merely as an illustration, if 10 percent were dependent on Amazonian water, the annual value is equivalent to US$19/ha of remaining forest in the Legal Amazon. An illustration of the water cycling value of forest is given in Table 11.4. Assuming 10 percent dependency (the 'medium' value) and that the effect continues indefinitely after deforestation, the net present value (NPV) of the forest loss calculated at a 5 percent/year discount is US$127/small farmer family if only clearing done by small farmers in 1990 is considered, or US$417/family if all of the 1990 annual deforestation rate is considered. Corresponding values, including future

Table 11.5: Summary of 'medium' estimates of forest value

Environmental value basis	Description	Units	Biodiversity	Carbon	Water	Total
Damage per ha. of forest loss						
	Annual value[a]	US$/ha/yr	20	71	19	110
	NPV[b]	US$/ha	400	1413	385	2198
Damage in 1990 caused by total population						
	NPV[b]	US$ million	552	1950	531	3034
	NPV/small farmer family[c]	US$/family	434	1532	417	2383
1990 and all future damage caused by total population						
	NPV[b, d]	US$ billion	11.1	39	10.7	60.8
	NPV/small farmer family[b, d]	US$ thousand/family	9	31	8	48
	Annual value[e]	US$ million/yr	554	1950	533	3098
	Value/yr/small farmer family[e]	US$/family/yr	435	1532	419	2387
Value of forest stock						
	Total NPV[b]	US$ billion	135	477	130	742
	Annual value[e]	US$ billion/yr	7	24	7	37
	Value/yr/small farmer family[e]	US$ thousand/family/yr	5	19	5	29

Notes:
(a) Value of carbon is for permanent sequestration annualised at 5%/yr.
(b) Biodiversity and water values are net present value (NPV).
(c) Carbon value same as NPV.
(d) Assuming no population growth either in total or in small farmer population, with deforestation remaining at 1990 rate for 100 years.
(e) At 5%/yr interest.

deforestation, are US$2600/family and US$8400/family, respectively. A much larger value lies in the stock of forest that remains uncleared: this stock has an NPV of US$130 billion if a 5 percent annual discount rate is considered, or over US$100,000/family. If considered at 5 percent/year interest, the value of the stock is equivalent to a total annuity of US$7 billion/year, or over US$5000/family/year.

The 'medium' estimates of value for the three categories of environmental services (biodiversity, carbon storage and water cycling) are summarised and totalled in Table 11.5. The great variety of values is evident depending on the measure adopted. Again, it should be remembered that the much higher values related to the value of the stock of remaining forest represent a form of value not recognised in current international conventions, which give no value to stocks or even to flows *per se*, but only to deliberately caused *changes* in flows.

How to Sustain the Forest

Involvement of local peoples

The involvement of local people represents the key to any plan to maintain areas of natural vegetation. Only grassroots organisations can exert social pressure on those who would invade and cut an area that has been agreed to remain as a reserve. The alternative approach, with functionaries of government agencies trying to enforce boundaries and regulations against the will of the surrounding population, has failed countless times.

Empowerment of local groups must be linked to the establishment and enforcement of limits – groups cannot be free to cut forest at will. The balance of responsibility and freedom in such relationships is a difficult area in which no set answers exist. Perhaps the best known example of the problem of local peoples (including Indians) not always acting in an environmentally benign way is the Navajo and Apache tribes in the United States, whose leaders have been negotiating for establishment of nuclear waste dumps on tribal land. The question remains unresolved of what means are necessary for protecting the environment when local peoples fail.

The question must be considered as to whether local peoples receiving funds derived from environmental services should have complete independence in deciding how the funds should be used, whether all or part of it should be used for maintaining the natural habitats that provide the services, or whether the funds should at least be restricted to uses that do not harm these habitats. For example, would it be acceptable if a community receiving funds for environmental services were to decide to use the money to buy chainsaws to cut down the rest of its forest? This example is not entirely hypothetical. In 1988 and 1989, the current governor of the state of Amazonas actually distributed free chainsaws to voters in the interior of the state (during a previous term in office).

Independent monitoring

One of the problems in achieving internationally negotiated agreements for forest protection is the question of how compliance would be monitored. Remote-sensing technology can greatly facilitate monitoring processes and increase the confidence that parties can place in agreements being carried out. Remote sensing can produce data by property, not just by state, as has been done so far. With proper priority, remote-sensing information can be obtained with a fast turnaround, but so far the motivation for such speed has been restricted to the 1989–92 period when international attention was focused on Amazonian deforestation. Although LANDSAT thematic mapper (TM) data have primarily been used for measurements of deforestation, logging scars too are visible on TM but disappear quickly (D. Nepstad, 1995, personal communication).

Monitoring the status of forest maintenance agreed to in any international negotiations would have to be done by a politically independent body (Fearnside, 1997d). Remote sensing alone is not sufficient, making free ground access essential. As in the case of nuclear disarmament negotiations, these questions are likely to be diplomatic stumbling blocks.

Economic viability for local peoples

Evaluating the economic viability of a proposal to maintain forest requires, among other things, defining the discount rates both of money and of environmental services such as biodiversity and carbon stock maintenance. In addition, mechanisms are needed by which the economic value of information can be captured, including genetic material and intellectual property rights (IPRs) (see Posey, Chapter 12 in this volume).

The value of a local community's role in conserving a resource cannot be calculated based on what the area of land involved would produce had it been instead a green revolution rice field. Local peoples rarely have land with soil or climate like that in green revolution areas, and their lack of capital means that even if they had such land no green revolution profits would have materialised (that is, it is not really an 'opportunity cost').

Establishing values for environmental services requires several steps. First, research to quantify the amount of the services, such as tons of carbon, numbers of species or cubic metres of water. These quantities then must be translated into prices, or in to subsidies. The values in question would be negotiated values, which are distinct from (and inevitably lower than) the true values of environmental services. The definition of ground rules is essential if biodiversity and carbon are to attain values. A key question is whether this kind of valuation is restricted to 'incremental costs', implying that resources are valuable only if they are doomed.

'Economic viability for whom?' is a recurrent question regarding evaluation of this and whether it refers to local people or only to the government and intermediaries is essential to whether this option constitutes a form of sustainable development.

One problem has been aptly summed up by Michael Dove (1993) by analogy to John Steinbeck's (1945) short story 'The Pearl' (and its Indonesian analogue: 'little man and the big stone'). In Steinbeck's story a poor Indian named Kino in an unnamed Latin American country lives by the ocean and makes a meagre living diving for pearls. One day he finds a huge pearl and imagines that his son will be able to gain an education and leave the cycle of poverty. Instead, the wealthy of the village try every possible artifice to trick Kino into giving up the pearl. Finally, he throws the pearl back into the ocean, ending the story. In the case of tropical forests, the same might be expected to happen were any marvellous new source of money discovered. Were a poor forest dweller to find a tree with a cure for AIDS, for example, it is highly unlikely that any of the great value of the discovery would return to the poor person or community that found it. In the same way, if large sums of money were to materialise for environmental services of standing forest, the rich would enter into action to capture the benefits for themselves. As in the story, the surrounding society can be expected to employ all imaginable means to take the pearl away, almost as if it were a moral duty not to allow a poor person to keep the benefits of such a find. A major challenge in defining strategies for sustainable development, then, is to find ways to ensure that forest dwellers get to keep the pearl of environmental services.

The government's percentage of returns from biodiversity use is less fundamental than the mechanism by which returns will be transferred to local peoples. Governments (for example, Brazil) are anxious to avoid allowing funds to pass directly from abroad to local peoples. However, if funds are given to government for redistribution to local peoples, the practical consequence is likely to be that local peoples will never receive anything. Aside from funds siphoned off in illicit ways, the normal delays of months (or sometimes years), with inflation at its usual high rate, means that the value of any funds evaporates before the money ever reaches its intended beneficiaries.

Identification of which local partners within a community should receive benefits or enter into agreements is more difficult than it appears, and can have divisive effects. An example is provided by the destructive results in distribution of proceeds from rights for a film on Chico Mendes, which led to ugly infighting between factions of rubber-tappers, an aspect that did not exist before the possibility of significant monetary flows became apparent. This would be a natural human reaction if a large amount of money were dropped on any community in interior Amazonia. The problem of factions within local communities can impede return of funds from biodiversity or other sources.

Responsibility of local people to maintain natural habitats that provide environmental services needs to be made clear. Linkage of this responsibility to revenue from forest, for example from the economic use of biodiversity, would be a useful way of making this operational.

How to Make Services into Development

What needs to be done to transform environmental services into sustainable development? One obvious need is to quantify basic costs. This is especially true for avoidance of deforestation. How much does it really cost to avoid a hectare of deforestation in Rondônia? No one has an adequate answer to such a question today. Costs of silvicultural plantations, in contrast, are relatively well known, due to years of experience in planting them and due to the relatively few uncertainties in foreseeing their future if specified investments are made. Deforestation, on the other hand, is strongly influenced by government policy decisions that have little direct connection with financial costs. For example, tax policies that allow land speculation to continue as a highly profitable activity, and policies that to this day allow deforestation to justify land titling as an 'improvement', could be changed at no financial cost, although there would clearly be political costs for making the change.

Significant difficulties exist in financing the conservation of tropical forests (see, for example, Dobson and Absher, 1991; Goodland, 1992). In addition to international agencies such as the GEF, private and public deals for carbon offset already exist on a limited scale, and these may potentially be applied to other environmental services. Carbon offsets do not imply conservation in perpetuity, although similar projects for biodiversity might well make this a requirement. In the case of carbon, benefits need to be viewed in terms of ton-years of carbon storage with appropriate adjustments for time preference (Fearnside, 1995, 1997e). Political feasibility, especially perceived infringement of sovereignty, has been a major barrier to carbon offsets (see, for example, Brown and Adger, 1994). Under the 1997 Kyoto Protocol of the Framework Convention on Climate Change, for example, actions implemented jointly are currently limited to projects in industrialised countries (that is, mainly related to reduced energy emissions in eastern Europe). Future protocols may someday include the potential of tropical forests in global warming mitigation. Such projects have substantial potential (Sathaye and Makundi, 1995; Sathaye et al., 1995).

Another area of great doubt in translating environmental services into a means of support is the mechanism by which funds received on the basis of services would be distributed. Would this be done, for example, by a successor to the recently disbanded Brazilian Legion for Assistance (LBA), which became a symbol of corruption in Brazil after a long series of scandals involving the wife of former President Collor? What is the Brazilian proposal for using funds received? If the nations of the world miraculously agreed to pay handsomely for the environmental services of Amazon rainforest and sent the government a cheque, how much of this money would actually go to the two principal objectives: maintaining the forest and supporting the region's population?

The channel that would be used for transferring funds to Brazil and to the individual activities needing support is another area of doubt. The Pilot Programme to Conserve the Brazilian Rainforest, administered by the World Bank and funded by G-7 countries as a result of a commitment made in Houston in 1990, encountered frustrating impediments to getting its programme under way. While a number of these problems have been solved, and several parts of the programme are finally under way, the four-year delay made clear that transferring much larger sums would not be an easy task. It is hoped that the experience of the pilot programme will serve to unplug some of the pipelines through which such larger inflows might one day pass. Although some progress has been made, much more needs to be done.

Employment is often raised as a key question in discussions of forest preservation in protected areas. What will Brazil or the Amazonian states gain from reserves in terms of employment? Would it not be better to hand out land as agricultural lots to support part of the unemployed population? The answer to employment depends very much on what is to be done with money that is brought in by environmental services of the forest. If the sums involved are large, as the true importance of the services implies they should be, then there is substantial scope for creating employment. One form of employment is guarding the reserves themselves. It is important to realise that this form of employment can only occupy a limited number of people, and that these are not the same people who would receive lots if the land were to be handed out for agricultural settlement instead of being made into reserves. However, this is an important option for the true 'local' inhabitants (rubber-tappers, and so on), already in the interior. Often these people would not have other opportunities for employment. Rural employment could also be generated in scientific research in the reserves, for example, in botanically collecting, mapping, and measuring trees in large areas of reserves, and monitoring tree mortality, regeneration and phenology. Unfortunately, these options are severely limited in their potential scale by the number of taxonomists and other scientists available to process material and information gathered by field personnel employed in such projects.

It must be recognised that Amazonia's population is rapidly becoming urban. Employment in urban centres is, in some ways, easier to create than rural employment. Activities somehow linked to forest maintenance would be preferable. For example, laboratories could be set up in Amazonian cities to analyse plant secondary compounds obtained from the reserves.

A certain danger exists of pernicious effects arising from any form of welfare or give-away of money coming from payments for environmental services. For example, cash payments made to individual members of a tribe in the south-western United States as compensation for damages caused by a copper mine on tribal lands led to disintegration of much of the tribe's culture, severe problems with alcoholism and high mortality from automobile accidents (G. Nabhan, 1994, personal communication). In addition, most 'made-work' has a tendency to be relatively unproductive. A good example is the case of Trinidad and Tobago, a small Caribbean country (population 1.2 million) that has the good fortune to have oil. Public works, such as endless repair of roads with mostly idle crews, are the means of transferring government wealth to the people. It must be remembered that potential for political abuse is very high. If Amazonian state governments are given the opportunity of handing out a significant number of make-work jobs using money received from payments for environmental services, it is likely that this would be used primarily to assure electoral benefits to whoever is in power. Safeguards are therefore needed in any way that the employment question is addressed.

One of the dilemmas of sustainable development proposals is that success can attract the destruction of the very features that made a given activity sustainable. For example, if an agroforestry system proves to be sustainable and a financial success, it can attract a migration of population eager to share in the success, leading to increased deforestation to expand the system. This has occurred on the island of Sumatra, Indonesia, where areas with financially successful tree crops have experienced an increase rather than a decrease of deforestation (Alternatives to Slash-and-Burn, 1995: 131). One is placed in a situation of being 'damned if you do and damned if you don't': if a settlement project is an agronomic failure then people will invade surrounding forest and cut for slash-and-burn agriculture, whereas if it is a success, then others will be drawn to the area and will cut the forest just the same.

The tremendous pool of people in non-Amazonian parts of Brazil who would be drawn to any source of easy money is a problem that must be faced effectively. The great value of the forest means that, in theory, one could even contemplate pensioning off the current residents in luxurious circumstances – the 'Copacabana solution'. Many Brazilians regard living in an apartment near Copacabana Beach in Rio de Janeiro as the pinnacle of material achievement. But for the limitations of space (the rural population of the Legal Amazon is about the same as the city of Rio de Janeiro), the annuities from forest standing stock are of an order of magnitude sufficient to support such an expense. If they could be collected (note that the limits of available funds make 'willingness to pay' figures based on linear extrapolation to large scales unrealistic, as noted earlier), annuities at 5 percent/year would yield US$7 billion/year from biodiversity, US$24 billion/year from carbon storage and US$7 billion/year from water cycling, or US$37 billion/year total, equivalent to almost US$29,000/family of small farmers (Table 11.5). The gravest problem with such a hypothetical scenario, of course, is that if one ever tried to transport Amazonia's rural population to

Copacabana or any equivalent place, others would soon occupy the deforestation frontier and clearing would continue.

In order for any form of development to be sustainable, population growth in the area, both from reproduction and from migration effects, must remain within the limits of carrying capacity, which, while not fixed, is also not free to increase at will (see, for example, Fearnside, 1986, 1997f; Cohen, 1995). There is no such thing as 'sustainable development' for an infinite number of people.

4. CONCLUSIONS

A strategy for achieving sustainable development in rural Amazonia requires both short-term and long-term measures. While immediate steps to maintain the population and to prevent further loss of forest are needed, progress also must be made on long-term goals that will provide a stable basis for maintaining both the forest and the population. This should focus on the environmental services of standing forest. The biodiversity maintenance, carbon storage and water cycling functions of rainforest are worth more to rich countries than the value of land in Amazonia, which reflects the potential profitability of selling timber and replacing forest with agriculture or ranching. How to convert environmental services of forest into an income stream, and how to convert this stream into a foundation for sustainable development in rural Amazonia is a great challenge.

ACKNOWLEDGEMENTS

Earlier versions of this paper were presented at the conference on 'The Development Enterprise: Economic, Environmental and Sociological Perspectives on Sustainability', Chicago, IL, 26–29 October 1995, and at the Workshop 'Meio Ambiente, Desenvolvimento e Política do Governo', Fundação Joaquim Nabuco, Recife, Pernambuco, 22–25 April 1996. The calculations presented here have been updated from previous versions of this proposal (Fearnside, 1997g, 1997h). I thank Elsevier Science-NL, Sara Burgerhartstraat 25, 1055 KV Amsterdam, The Netherlands, for kind permission to publish parts of my article appearing in *Ecological Economics* **20** (1): 53–70 (1997). The Conselho Nacional de Desenvolvimento Científico e Tecnológico – CNPq (BPP 350230/97–98), the Instituto Nacional de Pesquisas da Amazônia – INPA (PPI 5-3150), and the Pew Scholars Program in Conservation and the Environment provided financial support. R.I. Barbosa, C. Cavalcanti, P.M.L.A. Graça, S.V. Wilson and two anonymous reviewers commented on the manuscript.

REFERENCES

Adger, W.N., Brown, K., Cervigni, R. and Moran, D. (1995), 'Total economic value of forests in Mexico', *Ambio*, **24** (5): 286–296.

Alternatives to Slash-and-Burn (ASB) (1995), *Alternatives to slash-and-burn in Indonesia. Phase I Report*, Bogor, Indonesia: ASB/International Centre for Agroforestry-Southeast Asia.

Brazil, Instituto Brasileiro de Geografia e Estatística (IBGE) (1989), *Anuário estatístico do Brasil 1989*, Vol. 49, Rio de Janeiro, Brazil: IBGE.

Brazil, Instituto Brasileiro de Geografia e Estatística (IBGE) (1992), *Anuário estatístico do Brasil 1992*, Vol. 52, Rio de Janeiro, Brazil: IBGE (electronic version).

Brazil, Instituto Nacional de Pesquisas Espaciais (INPE) (1998), 'Amazônia: desflorestamento 1995–1997', INPE, São José dos Campos, São Paulo, Brazil (document released via internet (http://www.inpe.br)).

Brown, K. and Adger, W.N. (1994), 'Economic and political feasibility of international carbon offsets', *Forest Ecology and Management*, 68: 217–229.

Cartwright, J. (1985), 'The politics of preserving natural areas in Third World States', *The Environmentalist*, **5** (3): 179–186.

Cohen, J. (1995), 'Population growth and earth's human carrying capacity', *Science*, 269: 341–346.

Cordell, G.A. (1995), 'Natural products as medicinal and biological agents: potentiating the resources of the rain forest', in P.R. Seidl, O.R. Gottlieb and M.A.C. Kaplan (eds), *Chemistry of the Amazon: biodiversity, natural products and environmental issues*, Washington, DC: American Chemical Society, pp. 8–18.

Costanza, R., d'Arge, R., de Groot, R., Farber, S., Grasso, M., Hannon, B., Limburg, K., Naeem, S., O'Neill, R.V., Paruelo, J., Raskin, R.G., Sutton, P. and van den Belt, M. (1997), 'The value of the world's ecosystem services and natural capital', *Nature*, 387: 253–260.

Daily, G.C. and Ehrlich, P.R. (1990), 'An exploratory model of the impact of rapid climate change on the world food situation', *Proceedings of the Royal Society of London*, B 241: 232–244.

Dantas, M. (1979), 'Pastagens da Amazônia Central: ecologia e fauna do solo', *Acta Amazonica*, 9 (2) suplemento: 1–54.

Dobson, A. and Absher, R. (1991), 'How to pay for tropical rain forests', *Trends in Ecology and Evolution*, **6** (11): 348–351.

Dove, M. (1993), 'A revisionist view of tropical deforestation and development', *Environmental Conservation*, **20** (1): 17–24, 56.

Eagleson, P.S. (1986), 'The emergence of global-scale hydrology', *Water Resources Research*, **22** (9): 6s–14s.

Elisabetsky, E. and Shanley, P. (1994), 'Ethnopharmacology in the Brazilian Amazon', *Pharmacology and Therapeutics.*, 64: 201–214.

Fankhauser, S. (1992), 'Global warming damage costs: some monetary estimates', Centre for Social and Economic Research on the Global Environment (CSERG) Working Paper GEC 92-29, University College, London and University of East Anglia, Norwich, UK.

Fankhauser, S. (1995), *Valuing climate change – the economics of the greenhouse*, London: Earthscan.

Fankhauser, S. and Tol, R.S.J. (1997), 'The social costs of climate change: the IPCC Second Assessment Report and beyond', *Mitigation and Adaptation Strategies for Global Change*, **1** (4): 385–403.

Fearnside, P.M. (1980), 'Land use allocation of the Transamazon Highway colonists of Brazil and its relation to human carrying capacity', in F. Barbira-Scazzocchio (ed.), *Land, people and planning in contemporary Amazonia*, University of Cambridge Centre of Latin American Studies Occasional Paper No. 3, Cambridge, UK: University of Cambridge, pp. 114–138.

Fearnside, P.M. (1984), 'Land clearing behaviour in small farmer settlement schemes in the Brazilian Amazon and its relation to human carrying capacity', in A.C. Chadwick and S.L. Sutton (eds), *Tropical rain forest: the Leeds Symposium*, Leeds: Leeds Philosophical and Literary Society, pp. 255–271.

Fearnside, P.M. (1986), *Human carrying capacity of the Brazilian rainforest*, New York: Columbia University Press.

Fearnside, P.M. (1989a), 'Brazil's Balbina Dam: environment versus the legacy of the pharaohs in Amazonia', *Environmental Management*, **13** (4): 401–423.

Fearnside, P.M. (1989b), 'Extractive reserves in Brazilian Amazonia: an opportunity to maintain tropical rain forest under sustainable use', *BioScience* **39** (6): 387–393.

Fearnside, P.M. (1989c), 'A prescription for slowing deforestation in Brazilian Amazonia', *Environment*, **31** (4): 16–20, 39–40.

Fearnside, P.M. (1989d), 'Deforestation in the Amazon', *Environment*, **31** (7): 4–5.

Fearnside, P.M. (1989e), *A ocupação humana de Rondônia: impactos, limites e planejamento*, CNPq Relatórios de Pesquisa No. 5, Brasília: Conselho Nacional de Desenvolvimento Científico e Tecnológico (CNPq).

Fearnside, P.M. (1993a), 'Forests or fields: a response to the theory that tropical forest conservation poses a threat to the poor', *Land Use Policy*, **10** (2): 108–121.

Fearnside, P.M. (1993b), 'Deforestation in Brazilian Amazonia: the effect of population and land tenure', *Ambio*, **22** (8): 537–545.

Fearnside, P.M. (1995), 'Global warming response options in Brazil's forest sector: comparison of project-level costs and benefits', *Biomass and Bioenergy*, **8** (5): 309–322.

Fearnside, P.M. (1997a), 'Limiting factors for development of agriculture and ranching in Brazilian Amazonia', *Revista Brasileira de Biologia*, **57** (4): 531–549.

Fearnside, P.M. (1997b), 'Protection of mahogany: a catalytic species in the destruction of rain forests in the American tropics', *Environmental Conservation*, **24** (4): 303–306.

Fearnside, P.M. (1997c), 'Greenhouse gases from deforestation in Brazilian Amazonia: net committed emissions', *Climatic Change*, **35** (3): 285–302.

Fearnside, P.M. (1997d), 'Monitoring needs to transform Amazonian forest maintenance into a global warming mitigation option', *Mitigation and Adaptation Strategies for Global Change*, **2** (2–3): 285–302.

Fearnside, P.M. (1997e), 'Greenhouse-gas emissions from Amazonian hydroelectric reservoirs: the example of Brazil's Tucuruí Dam as compared to fossil fuel alternatives', *Environmental Conservation*, **24** (1): 64–75.

Fearnside, P.M. (1997f), 'Human carrying capacity estimation in Brazilian Amazonia as a basis for sustainable development', *Environmental Conservation*, **24** (3): 271–282.

Fearnside, P.M. (1997g), 'Environmental services as a strategy for sustainable development in rural Amazonia', *Ecological Economics*, **20** (1): 53–70.

Fearnside, P.M. (1997h), 'Serviços ambientais como estratégia para o desenvolvimento sustentável na Amazônia rural', in C. Cavalcanti (ed.), *Meio ambiente, desenvolvimento sustentável e políticas públicas*, São Paulo, Brazil: Cortez Editora, pp. 314–344.

Fearnside, P.M. (1998), 'The value of human life in global warming impacts', *Mitigation and Adaptation Strategies for Global Change*, 3 (1):83-85.

Goodland, R. (1992), 'Neotropical moist forests: priorities for the next two decades, in K.H. Redford and C. Padoch (eds), *Conservation of neotropical forests: working from traditional resource use*, New York: Columbia University Press, pp. 416–433.

Goodland, R. and Ledec, G. (1987), 'Neoclassical economics and principles of sustainable development', *Ecological Modelling*, 38: 19–46.

Grimes, A., Loomis, S., Jahnige, P., Burnham, M., Onthank, K., Alcarón, R., Cuenca, W.P., Martinez, C.C., Neill, D., Balick, M., Bennett, B. and Mendelsohn, R. (1994), 'Valuing the rain forest: the economic value of nontimber forest products in Ecuador', *Ambio*, 23 (7): 405–410.

Hecht, S.B. (1992), 'Valuing land uses in Amazonia: colonist agriculture, cattle, and petty extraction in comparative perspective', in K.H. Redford and C. Padoch (eds), *Conservation of neotropical forests: working from traditional resource use*, New York: Columbia University Press, pp. 379–399.

Kaplan, M.A.C. and Gottlieb, O.R. (1990), 'Busca racional de princípios ativos em plantas', *Interciencia*, 15 (1): 26–29.

Marques, J., dos Santos, J.M., Villa Nova, N.A. and Salati. E. (1977), 'Precipitable water and water vapor flux between Belém and Manaus', *Acta Amazonica*, 7 (3): 355–362.

Molion, L.C.B. (1975), 'A climatonomic study of the energy and moisture fluxes of the Amazonas Basin with considerations of deforestation effects', PhD dissertation in meteorology, University of Wisconsin, Madison, Ann Arbor, MI: University Microfilms International.

Myers, N. (1989), 'Loss of biological diversity and its potential impact on agriculture and food production', in D. Pimentel and C.W. Hall (eds), *Food and natural resources*, San Diego, CA: Academic Press, pp. 49–68.

Nordhaus, W. (1991), 'A sketch of the economics of the greenhouse effect', *American Economic Review*, 81 (2): 146–150.

Norton, B. (1988), 'Commodity, amenity and morality: the limits of quantification in valuing biodiversity', in E.O. Wilson (ed.), *Biodiversity*, Washington, DC: National Academy Press, pp. 200–205.

Noss, R. (1990), 'Indicators for monitoring biodiversity: a hierarchical approach', *Conservation Biology*, 4: 355–364.

Pachauski, F. (1994), 'Trabalha, escravo', *Isto É* (Brasília), 4 May 1994, pp. 32–35.

Pamplona, G. and Rodrigues, A. (1995), 'História sem fim: Um ano depois da denúncia de ISTOÉ, carvoeiros ainda trabalham como escravos no norte de Minas', *Isto É* (Brasilia), 21 June 1995, pp. 46–47.

Pearce, D.W., Cline, W.R., Achanta, A.N., Fankhauser, S., Pachauri, R.K., Tol, R.S.J. and Velinga, P. (1996), 'The social costs of climate change: greenhouse damage and the benefits of control', in J.P. Bruce, H. Lee and E.F. Haites (eds), *Climate change 1995: economic and social dimensions – contributions of Working Group III to the Second Assessment Report of the Intergovernmental Panel on Climate Change*, Cambridge, UK: Cambridge University Press, pp. 179–224.

Peters, C.M., Gentry, A.H. and Mendelsohn, R.O. (1989), 'Valuation of an Amazonian rainforest', *Nature*, 339: 655–656.

Pimentel, D., Wilson, C., McCullum, C., Huang, R., Dwen, P., Flack, J., Tran, Q., Saltman, T. and Cliff, B. (1997a), 'Economic and environmental benefits of biodiversity', *BioScience*, 47 (11): 747–757.

Pimentel, D., McNair, M., Buck, L., Pimentel, M. and Kamil, J. (1997b), 'The value of forests to world food security', *Human Ecology*, 25 (1): 91–120.

Ribeiro Jr, A. (1994), 'Carvoeiros são "escravos" em MG', *A Folha de São Paulo*, 31 July 1994, pp. 1–12.

Richards, M. (1993), 'The potential of non-timber forest products in sustainable forest management in Amazonia', *Commonwealth Forestry Review*, 72 (1): 21–27.

Romm, J., Levine, M., Brown, M. and Peterson, E. (1998), 'A road map for U.S. carbon reductions', *Science*, 279: 669–670.

Salati, E., Marques, J. and Molion, L.C.B. (1978), 'Origem e distribuição das chuvas na Amazônia', *Interciencia*, 3 (4): 200–206.

Salati, E., Dall'Olio, A., Matusi, E. and Gat, J.R. (1979), 'Recycling of water in the Brazilian Amazon Basin: An isotopic study', *Water Resources Research*, 15: 1250–1258.

Salati, E. and Vose, P.B. (1984), 'Amazon Basin: a system in equilibrium', *Science*, 225: 129–138.

Sathaye, J. and Makundi, W.R. (eds) (1995), 'Forestry and climate change', Special issue of *Biomass and Bioenergy*, 8 (5): 279–393.

Sathaye, J., Myers, S., Allen-Diaz, B., Cirillo, R., Gibbs, M., Hillsman, E., Ohi, J., Conzelmann, G., Corbus, D., Gadgil, A., Heaps, C., Koomey, J., Lazarus, M., Mark, J., Ojima, D., Ross, M., Sanstad, A., Unander, F. and Weyant, J. (1995), *Greenhouse gas mitigation assessment: a guidebook*, Dordrecht, The Netherlands: Kluwer Academic Publishers.

Schneider, R.R. (1994), *Government and the economy on the Amazon frontier*, Latin America and the Caribbean Technical Department Regional Studies Program Report No. 34, Washington, DC: The World Bank.

Schubart, H.O.R., Junk, W.J. and Petrere Jr, M. (1976), 'Sumário de ecologia Amazônica', *Ciência e Cultura*, 28 (5): 507–509.

Shah, A. and Larson, B. (1992), 'Carbon taxes, the greenhouse effect and developing countries', in *World Development Report 1992*, Washington, DC: The World Bank and New York: Oxford University Press.

Steinbeck, J. (1945 [1974]), *The Pearl*, New York: Bantam Books.

Stirling, A. (1993), 'Environmental valuation: How much is the emperor wearing?', *The Ecologist*, 23 (3): 97–103.

Sutton, A. (1994), *Slavery in Brazil – A link in the chain of modernization*, Oxford: Oxford University Press.

Traumann, T. (1998), 'Os novos vilões: Ação dos sem-terra e de pequenos agricultores contrubui para o desmatamento da Amazônia', *Veja* [São Paulo] (4 Feb. 1998), 31 (5): 34–35.

Vásquez, R. and Gentry, A.H. (1989), 'Use and misuse of forest-harvested fruits in the Iquitos area', *Conservation Biology*, 3 (4): 350–361.

Villa Nova, N.A., Salati, E. and Matusi, E. (1976), 'Estimativa da evapotranspiração na Bacia Amazônia', *Acta Amazonica*, 6 (2): 215–228.

Whitehead, B.W. and Godoy, R. (1991), 'The extraction of rattan-like lianas in the new world tropics: A possible prototype for sustainable forest management', *Agroforestry Systems*, 16: 247–255.

Willers, B. (1994), 'Sustainable development: a new world deception', *Conservation Biology*, **8** (4): 1146–1148.

12. Exploitation of Biodiversity and Indigenous Knowledge in Latin America: Challenges to Sovereignty and the Old Order

Darrell A. Posey

Since colonisation began, Brazil has provided cheap labour and natural resources for economically dominant countries out of the region. Indeed, the country's existing class and political systems are built upon those who provide these resources. Easy access and virtually uncontrolled exploitation of flora, fauna, mineral and water resources have remained critical to the perceived economic interests of Brazil and other Latin American countries.

During the last decade, however, a biodiversity conservation movement has swept Latin America – and the rest of the world. Increasingly, countries like Brazil, Costa Rica, Colombia and Mexico have become aware of the economic interests Northern countries have in their biodiversity. Some countries, like Bolivia, Ecuador and Peru have already benefited from debt-for-nature swaps, but the 'green funds' that were being transferred from non-governmental organisations (NGOs) in the First World to NGOs within their borders defied governmental controls and led to suspicions – as in Brazil – that environmentalism was only a cover for foreign takeover of national lands and resources. Biodiversity, then, if anything, was considered a subversive threat to national sovereignty and remains a 'bad word' (*palavrão*) to many in power.

Meanwhile, corporate interest in new products and genetic materials found in the components of biological diversity led to a frenzy of 'biodiversity prospecting'. Frequently cited market potential figures, like an annual production of US$ 43 billion per annum for pharmaceuticals,[1] US$54 billion per annum for seeds and agricultural products,[2] and similar figures for other natural compounds, led Brazil and other Latin American countries to re-evaluate attitudes toward the value of their flora, fauna and natural resources. It seemed that the traditional governmental policies that provoked the unbridled environmental devastation of tropical ecosystems – and the peoples who live in them – might, after all, be contrary to national interests for long-term economic growth built upon biotechnology.

Furthermore, industry was not only interested in the biogenetic resources, but also the traditional knowledge that local communities have about the utilisation of flora and fauna. Companies like Shaman Pharmaceuticals and The Body Shop found that research and development costs could be cut by as much as 40 percent, which – given that a single new medicine can cost US$150 million to develop – represents no inconsiderable saving. So, biodiversity prospectors are not just after genes, they are also after the information of indigenous and local communities.

Throughout the history of Latin America, indigenous and traditional peoples (*camponeses, caboclos, seringueiros, peões, colonos, caiçaras,* and so on) have been treated – at best – with disdain by the ruling elite. It was not until the 17th century, for example, that *índios* (Amerindians) were considered to be humans with souls; and western scientists still by and large believe traditional knowledge is only folklore and in no way scientific. In short, these 'backward and primitive' peoples are barriers to development, learning and civilisation.

Armed with those assumptions, governments – and even environmentalists – have found it easy to justify the dispossession of indians and peasants of their land and resources in the name of development, conservation and progress. Unfortunately, with loss of land and erosion of culture goes loss of knowledge about and degradation of the ecosystems managed, defended and moulded by the local peoples.

Given this scenario, it is not surprising that Latin American countries are finding it difficult to deal with the political and economic problems raised by the global biodiversity debate. In short, how can 500 years of systematic ecological exploitation and political marginalisation (or annihilation) of indigenous and traditional communities be reversed to protect flora, fauna and the people who know the 'secrets' to this new source of national wealth? Or perhaps the better question: how can the concept of biodiversity – until recently considered subversive – now be embraced without undermining the power bases for the old land-based oligarchies and extractive industries whose survival depends on cheap natural and human resources?

As Brazil and other Latin American countries struggle with these questions, biodiversity prospectors are swarming in the most remote corners of jungles, mountains and coastal reefs – gleaning from the 'public domain' everything they can before regulations on access are enacted. By the time most Latin American countries do get around to legislating on biogenetic resources and traditional knowledge, the more aspirant and persistent corporations may feel they will have all they need for the development of new products for a long time to come. 'What's a "poor" country rich in bio-cultural diversity to do?'

If Brazil is any example, the answer is to continue alienating, marginalising and eroding the indigenous and local peoples upon which its new wealth depends. This is seen nowhere more clearly than in Decree 1.775 (issued in Jan. 1996) to contest all of the demarcated or proposed lands of indigenous and *remanescentes* in the Nation. The indisputable effects of this Decree would be to weaken local communities, thereby destroying the biodiversity and traditional knowledge that is inextricably linked to them. Who might be behind such a move? The prime 'movers and shakers' are (no surprise) representatives of the oligarchies who refuse to see that the future economies of their regions are based on biogenetic resources and principles of sustainability of traditional peoples.

1. INDIGENOUS AND TRADITIONAL PEOPLES AND SUSTAINABILITY

The concept of sustainability is embodied in indigenous and traditional livelihood systems. Historical evidence exists which demonstrates the sustained productivity of indigenous systems, in some cases, for thousands of years on the same land.[3] Indigenous and traditional communities possess an 'environmental ethic' developed from living in particular ecosystems. This ethic cannot be regarded as universal, but indigenous systems do tend to emphasise the following specific values and features:

- co-operation;
- family bonding and cross-generational communication, including links with ancestors;
- concern for the well-being of future generations;
- local-scale, self-sufficiency and reliance on locally available natural resources;
- restraint in resource exploitation and respect for nature, especially for sacred sites.

The 'traditional knowledge, innovations and practices' of 'local communities embodying traditional lifestyles' are often referred to by scientists as Traditional Ecological Knowledge (TEK).[4] TEK is far more than a simple compilation of facts. It is the basis for local-level decision-making in areas of contemporary life, including natural resource management, nutrition, food preparation, health, education, and community and social organisation. TEK is holistic, inherently dynamic, constantly evolving through experimentation and innovation, fresh insight, and external stimuli. Scientists are becoming increasingly aware of the sophistication of TEK among many forest communities. For example, the Shuar people of Ecuador's Amazonian lowlands use 800 species of plants for medicine, food, animal fodder, fuel, construction, fishing and hunting supplies. Traditional healers in Southeast Asia rely on as many as 6,500 medicinal plants, and shifting cultivators throughout the tropics frequently sow more than 100 crops in their forest farms.[5]

A failure to understand the human-modified nature of 'wild' landscapes, including those which are sparsely populated at the present time, has blinded outsiders to the management practices of indigenous peoples and local communities. Many so-called 'pristine' landscapes are in fact *cultural landscapes*, either created by humans or modified by human activity (such as natural forest management, cultivation and the use of fire). Indigenous peoples and a growing number of scientists believe that it is no longer acceptable simply to assume that just because landscapes and species appear to outsiders to be 'natural', they are therefore 'wild'. According to a Resolution from the 1995 Ecopolitics IX Conference in Darwin, Australia:

> The term 'wilderness' as it is popularly used, and related concepts as 'wild resources', 'wild foods', etc., [are unacceptable]. These terms have connotations of *terra nullius* [empty or unowned land and resources] and, as such, all concerned people and organisations should look for alternative terminology which does not exclude Indigenous history and meaning.

For indigenous peoples, for example, forests are far more than just a source of timber. Most traditional peoples who inhabit forests or areas close to forests rely extensively upon hunted, collected, or gathered foods and resources, a significant portion of which are influenced by humans to meet their needs. These species, sometimes called 'semi-domesticates' or 'human modified species',[6] form the basis for a vast treasury of useful species that have systematically been undervalued and overlooked by science, yet provide the food and medicinal securities for local communities around the world.[7]

Indigenous peoples plant forest gardens and manage regeneration of bush fallows in ways which take advantage of natural processes and mimic the biodiversity of natural forests. Much of the world's crop diversity is in the custody of farmers who follow age-old farming and land use practices that conserve biodiversity and provide other local benefits. Among such benefits are the promotion of indigenous diet diversity, income generation, production stability, minimisation of risk, reduced insect and disease incidence, efficient use of labour, intensification of production with limited resources, and maximisation of returns under low levels of technology. These ecologically complex agricultural systems associated with centres of crop genetic diversity include traditional cultivars or 'landraces' that constitute an essential part of our world crop genetic heritage, and undomesticated plant and animal species that serve humanity as biological resources. There are numerous categories of traditional knowledge among indigenous peoples, which clearly have great potential for application in a wide range of sustainability strategies. Indigenous peoples conserve biological diversity, and in some cases provide other environmental benefits through, for example, soil and water conservation, soil fertility enhancement, and management of game and fisheries, and forest management.

Let us take the Kayapó Indian example from Amazonia. The principal elements of Kayapó management have been previously described in some detail,[8] and include:

1. overlapping and interrelated ecological categories;
2. emphasis on ecotone utilisation;
3. modification of 'natural ecosystems' to create ecotones;
4. extensive utilisation of 'semi-domesticates';
5. transfer of biogenetic materials between similar ecozones;
6. integration of agricultural with forest management cycles.

These principles are permeated by diachronic processes and historical developments that depend upon interactions within and between ecological zones.

Several options are possible to represent indigenous resource management models. The most inclusive and descriptive representation of the Kayapó system places savannah or grasslands at one end of a continuum (with *kapot* as the focal type, or the ecozone that most typifies the category) and forests at the other (with *ba* as the focal type). Those *kapot* types with more forest elements would be represented towards the forest pole, while *ba* types that are more open and with grassy elements would lie on the savannah end of the continuum. This would put *apete* at the conceptual centre, or cognitive interface, since these ecozones introduce forest elements into the savannah. However, agricultural plots (*puru*) also lie conceptually at the same place on the continuum since these bring sun-tolerant vegetation into forest niches. On this basis, I have also suggested that *apete* are conceptual inverses of *puru*, but function in similar ways since they both serve as 'resource islands' where useful plants can be concentrated in known, managed areas.

Ecological types like high forest (*ba tyk*) or transitional forest (*ba kamrek*) are not, however, uniform. All forests have edges (*ka*), or openings caused by fallen trees (*ba kre ti*). These provide zonal variations within the conceptual type and provide transitions between different types. Thus, a plant that likes the margins of a high forest might also grow well at the margin of a field or an *apete*. A plant that likes light gaps provided by forest openings might also like forest edges or old fields. Plants from open forest types or forest edges could also be predicted to do well along edges of trails (*pry*) or thicker zones of *apete*. Using the same logic, the Kayapó would transfer biogenetic materials between matching microzones so that ecological types are interrelated by their similarities rather than isolated by their differences.

Ecotone recognition and management are, therefore, the uniting elements of the overall system.

In contrast, another interesting dimension to the model emerges when looking diachronically across the system. Agricultural clearings are essentially planted with rapidly growing domesticates, but almost immediately thereafter are managed for secondary forest species. This management depends upon a variety of strategies, including introduction of some varieties (planting and transplanting), removal of some elements, allowing others to grow, encouraging some with fertiliser and ash and preparing or working the soils to favour certain species.[9] The introductions are to provide long-term supplies of medicinals and other useful products, as well as food for humans and animals. The old fields (*puru tum*), sometimes erroneously considered inactive 'fallows', are as useful to the Kayapó as agricultural plots or mature forest.

A high percentage (I have estimated 85 percent, although it is only an estimate based upon surveys of sample plots; elsewhere I have argued that fundamentally the Kayapó believe EACH and EVERY plant has a use or potential use) of plants in this transition have single or multiple uses. When the secondary forest grows too high to provide undergrowth as food for animals (and hunting becomes difficult), then the forest is cut again for use as an agricultural plot.

So what does this Kayapó system have to do with Brazil and sustainability? After all, none of us is going to go live like the Kayapó!

But there are invaluable lessons to be learned from the Kayapó. Their system is focused on the management of transitional forests (*chronological ecotones*), in which agriculture is only a useful phase, not the central focus. The system depends more on semi-domesticates (varieties that have been managed, but not brought into domestication) than cultivars, and there is flexibility and adaptability built into all aspects of the overall system.

Imagine what Amazonia would be like if every plant had economic value and soil fertility were maintained by carefully managing agricultural plots to become productive forests. Think of the consequences if, worldwide, we began to focus our exploitation of nature on maintenance – or even creation – of diverse landscapes and ecological systems. And think of what would happen if our yards, roadsides and parks became 'resource islands' for medicines, foods, oils, essences, dyes, colourings, building supplies and game sources.

This 'vision' is not so far from even the international eye. The Convention on Biological Diversity (CBD), for example, recognises the central role of indigenous, traditional and local communities in the sustainable conservation and use of biological resources. A specific call is made for the wider application of traditional knowledge, innovations and practices, which are also considered to be traditional technologies. Certainly an international Convention signed by 154 countries should be enough to convince Brazil that its indigenous and traditional peoples – and the biogenetic resources they utilise and manage – are critical to sustainable practices and economic growth.

2. RECOGNISING INDIGENOUS AND TRADITIONAL PEOPLES IN THE CBD

The CBD was signed during the United Nations Conference on the Environment and Development (UNCED) in Rio de Janeiro in 1992. It is essentially a Nation State sovereignty grab to extend Nation States' rights over all biological and ecological resources. This desperate grasp, hotly abetted by the Group of 77 (that has the active participation of Brazil), stretches to control not only flora and fauna, but also relevant technologies – which may even include human genetic materials and peoples' knowledge systems!

These intentions are masked by the grandiose words of Article 1 of the Biodiversity Convention that call for:

> ... the conservation of biological diversity, the sustainable use of its components and the fair and equitable sharing of the benefits arising out of the utilisation of genetic resources, including by appropriate access to genetic resources and by appropriate transfer of relevant technologies, taking into account all rights over those resources and technologies, and by appropriate funding.

Rights refers to the sovereign rights of states, just as equitable sharing refers to the Parties (short for 'Contracting Parties', which are Nation State 'Signatories' or 'Signers' of the CBD) of the Convention, not to individuals or communities. It is important to note, however, that 'relevant technologies' can be interpreted to mean 'indigenous and traditional technologies' (in reference to the language of Article 18.4 in the 'Access to and Transfer of Technology' Section), or those based upon 'knowledge, innovations and practices of indigenous and local communities embodying traditional lifestyles relevant for the conservation and sustainable use of biological diversity' (in reference to language used in Article 8.j).

Appendix 1 provides a summary of principles in the CBD and Rio Declaration which affect the rights of indigenous peoples and local communities. Appendix 2 shows mechanisms provided in the CBD to implement the Convention which require the effective participation of these peoples and communities.

Article 8.j states that each Contracting Party must:

> Subject to its national legislation, respect, preserve and maintain knowledge, innovations and practices of indigenous and local communities embodying

traditional lifestyles relevant for the conservation and sustainable use of biological diversity and promote the wider application with the approval and involvement of the holders of such knowledge, innovations and practices and encourage the equitable sharing of the benefits arising from the utilisation of such knowledge, innovations and practices.

While indigenous peoples might be flattered with the recognition of their relevance to *in situ* conservation, they are hardly convinced that the governments that have tried so hard to destroy them and their habitats are now suddenly going to zealously defend their rights. They are also not satisfied that any 'equitable sharing' will ever trickle down to the source of both the knowledge and resource, that is their communities. Indigenous leaders are both frustrated and angry that, while Nation States do little to protect their interests or guarantee even their most basic rights, they are now anxious to claim sovereignty over even local knowledge systems.

As a 1994 COICA (The Co-ordinating Group of the Indigenous Peoples of the Amazon Basin) statement puts it:

> For members of Indigenous peoples, knowledge and determination of the use of resources are collective and inter-generational. No Indigenous population, whether of individuals or communities, nor the government, can sell or transfer ownership of resources which are the property of the people and which each generation has an obligation to safeguard for the next.

3. UNINTENTIONS OR MISINTENTIONS?

The problems go beyond a question of intentions of governments. Even scientists and researchers with the best of intentions find themselves with few legal guidelines and confronted with intellectual and moral quagmires. Take for example, the famous case of *tiki uba*.

In a 1988 issue of *National Geographic* magazine,[10] Loren McIntyre describes the 'Last days of Eden' for the 350 members of the Amazonian Urueu-Wau-Wau tribe. They are portrayed as being vulnerable to diseases carried by outsiders and trying to resist the encroachments of settlers on their lands. Three photos on one of the pages, one of which shows a tapir bleeding from an arrow wound, are accompanied by the following caption:

> Secrets of rain forest chemistry provide a feast for the Urueu-Wau-Wau. Using poison arrows, they down a young tapir that bubbled into their village at night. Wooden arrow points are coated with sap squeezed from the stringy red bark of tiki uba trees and hardened by fire. An anticoagulant, tiki uba causes victims to bleed to death. In addition to such deadly jungle lore, knowledge of potentially useful foods and drugs, accumulated over thousands of years, may be lost forever if the forest and its inhabitants disappear.

Jesco von Puttkamer, who took photographs which accompanied the article, was quoted as saying in reference to the plant: 'I think it may be a great pharmaceutical find'.

This article attracted the attention of researchers working for the US pharmaceutical company Merck, and von Puttkamer agreed to send them bark and sap specimens in order for them to carry out tests. These tests confirmed that the bark contained at least one compound that inhibited enzymes that cause blood clotting and efforts immediately began to commercialise a product useful in heart surgery.

McIntyre and von Puttkamer felt they were acting in the best interests of humankind when they described the *tiki uba* in their article. However, by doing so they made it possible for a drug company to appropriate their knowledge without any obligations to compensate the Urueu-Wau-Wau, who, in their present situation, could well find compensation highly beneficial.

Another example is illustrated by the exploitation of a plant called *Pilocarpus jaborandi* to treat glaucoma. Although Brazil now earns US$25 million a year from exporting the plant, the Guajajara indians who originally provided the 'lead' that led to the 'discovery' of the plant by ethnobotanists now suffer from debt peonage and slavery at the hands of agents of the company involved in the trade. Furthermore, the species itself is being rapidly exhausted by unsustainable collecting practices.

Yet another example of commercial exploitation of indigenous resources is the case of patents on indigenous cell lines. Indigenous peoples are particularly disturbed about the 'discoveries' made from blood samples. Under the guise of 'good science', the Human Genome Organisation (HUGO) and one of its subsidiary projects (the Human Genome Diversity Project), co-ordinate the collection of blood samples from isolated communities 'threatened with extinction'. The results will supposedly reveal evolutionary links and identify genetic sequences for gene therapy to improve human health.[11]

The 'Vampire Project', as it is known by indigenous peoples, has brought much discredit to scientific research because, once collected, data and cells are available for commercial exploitation. Collections are also made without the prior informed consent of the sample groups.

At least three patent applications have been made for cell lines developed from blood 'donated' by indigenous peoples, including one from a member of a recently-contacted group of 260 hunter-cultivators in New Guinea, another from the Solomon Islands, and a third from the Guaymi Indians of Panama. The patent holder is the US National Institutes of Health with the US government scientists involved in the project named on the patent as 'inventors'.

These examples illustrate why indigenous communities are less than enthusiastic about or trustful of scientists. In a now famous declaration from

Fiji earlier in 1996, indigenous leaders of the Pacific declared a moratorium on all research and bioprospecting '*until appropriate protection measures are in place*'.

The threat of a moratorium sends shivers up scientific spines. Increasingly, scientists and research institutions are dependent upon the private sector for their livelihoods. This means the fruits of their labours – good old data – are subject to commercial exploitation, or indeed, are now designed for that purpose.[12]

It is often hard for scientists themselves to know when they must wear the hat of their patrons versus the mantle of their scientific discipline. From the indigenous perspective, they (we) are all the same. This means that negotiating access by scientists to indigenous and local communities – whether for bioprospecting or scientific purposes – may take considerable time and energy and has become a profoundly political act.

The private sector and scientific interests are eager that the CBD resolve these dilemmas to become an international vehicle for clarification of the terms of access for and transfer of biogenetic resources and appropriate technologies. Developing countries, especially the Group of 77, also see the CBD as a much more favourable forum for developing mutually beneficial terms than, say, GATT/WTO (the famous Uruguay Round of the General Agreement on Tariffs and Trade, now under the authority of the World Trade Organisation).

A substantial barrier to this process, however, is the assumption within GATT and the CBD that IPRs (Intellectual Property Rights) are adequate mechanisms to effect the equitable access and transfer agreements and terms. Yet, IPRs have become a *cause célèbre* of groups attacking Northern economic exploitation and globalisation of trade.

4. INTELLECTUAL PROPERTY RIGHTS AND INDIGENOUS PEOPLES

Intellectual Property Rights (IPRs) are assumed by the CBD to be the principal mechanisms to provide 'equitable sharing', but IPRs are problematic for developing countries in general – and indigenous, traditional and local communities in particular – for the following reasons:

(i) they are intended to benefit society through the granting of exclusive rights to 'natural' and 'juridical' persons or 'creative individuals', not collective entities such as indigenous peoples;

(ii) they cannot protect information that does not result from a specific historic act of 'discovery'. Indigenous knowledge is transgenerational and communally shared. Knowledge may come from ancestor spirits, vision quests, or orally-transmitted lineage groups. It is considered to be in the 'public domain' and, therefore, unprotectable;

(iii) they cannot accommodate complex non-Western systems of ownership, tenure and access. IPR law assigns authorship of a song to a writer or publishing company that can record or publish as it sees fit. Indigenous singers, however, may attribute songs to the creator spirit and elders may reserve the right to prohibit its performance, or to limit it to certain occasions and to restricted audiences;

(iv) they serve to stimulate commercialisation and distribution, whereas indigenous concerns may be primarily to prohibit commercialisation and to restrict use and distribution;

(v) they recognise only market economic values, failing to consider spiritual, aesthetic or cultural – or even local economic – values. Information or objects may have their greatest value to indigenous peoples because of their ties with cultural identity and symbolic unity;

(vi) they are subject to manipulation to economic interests that wield political power. *Sui generis* protection has been obtained for semi-conductor chips and 'literary works' generated by computers, whereas indigenous peoples have insufficient power to protect even their most sacred plants, places or artefacts;

(vii) they are expensive, complicated, and time-consuming to obtain, and even more difficult to defend.

A number of initiatives are under way in Latin America to find alternative systems of access and transfer that employ more appropriate IPR systems. The overall goal is to find legal ways of sustainably exploiting biodiversity in a commercial, yet equitable manner. Perhaps the most well known of these is the Merck-INBio Agreement in Costa Rica.

1. The National Biodiversity Institute of Costa Rica

In Costa Rica, the National Biodiversity Institute (INBio), an NGO closely linked with the government, was established to carry out a species inventory of the country and to explore the commercial potential of biological resources with corporations through Material Transfer Agreements (MTAs). According to Costa Rican law, the biological diversity of the country on public and private lands is national patrimony and the state has the exclusive right to grant permits to organisations such as INBio to investigate, collect and exploit the country's biological resources within its Conservation Areas. The agreement between Merck and INBio provides the latter with an advanced payment of $1 million and royalties in case a product is derived from any of the extracts which INBio will transfer to Merck. 50 percent of the royalties are to be forwarded to the government's National Parks Fund.

There are several problems with this approach:

(i) The government claims sovereignty over the country's biodiversity and does not recognise the territorial and resources rights of indigenous peoples and local communities.
(ii) INBio has secured prospecting rights to lands which according to national laws are under state ownership, permitting very little in the way of local control. In fact, the Director of INBio was unaware that there were indigenous peoples in the country – although the agreement was for collecting on national lands, including those of eight indigenous peoples.
(iii) Although the agreement with Merck provides benefits for the government and for INBio, no benefits will go to local communities except for the training of a small group of 'parataxonomists'. Furthermore, INBio will not contribute at all to revitalising local knowledge traditions because it professes to have no interest at all in such knowledge.
(iv) Although the advance payment by Merck seems substantial, it is hardly generous (neither is the agreed royalty percentage of between 3–4 percent).
(v) There is no provision in the agreement for co-patenting. Therefore, Merck will have exclusive intellectual property rights.

2. The Andean Pact

Some countries, for example the Andean Pact countries, are responding through discussions on appropriate legislation intended to establish equitable terms for granting access to biogenetic resources and sharing benefits with indigenous peoples. The Andean Pact countries (Bolivia, Colombia, Ecuador, Peru and Venezuela), aided by IUCN, have developed guidelines for legislation to set terms for access to their biological resources. These terms include:

(i) sharing of benefits between receivers of biological resources, member states and providers, which may be legal entities, private individuals, or indigenous or local communities;
(ii) restrictions on transfer to third parties;
(iii) reporting on obligations on future uses;
(iv) obligations related to intellectual property;
(v) exclusivity and confidentiality;
(vi) recognition of the member states or provider in the publication of research results.

Member states would recognise the rights of indigenous and local communities over their knowledge, innovations and practices, and would concede to local communities the 'authority to decide whether and how to share such knowledge, innovations and practices'.

Andean Pact countries, as well as Brazil, ascribe biodiversity to the national patrimony. However, it is unclear if states (governments) have the exclusive rights to determine access and set terms for transfer and benefit-sharing. It is equally unclear what authority local, state and regional governments have *vis-à-vis* national or federal governments. In the absence of clear laws on biogenetic resources, most countries find they are incapable of limiting access or even monitoring activities within their borders.

In the Brazilian State of Amazonas, for example, the governor has established his own bioprospecting institution, legally constituted under state law. The purpose of the institution is to commercialise biotechnology and the products of biodiversity. This flies in the face of the federal government, which is unable to act because of lack of legislative authority. Thus, the patrimony of the Union is being exported for profit by a legally incorporated state institution. Furthermore, in the absence of state or national legislation, bioprospectors are not legally obliged to collaborate with governments whatsoever.

3. The Brazilian Indigenous Societies Act

Proposed law (PL 2057/91) was approved in 1994 by the Chamber of Deputies of the national legislature. It has never passed into the Senate and is still under consideration for its legality. The proposed law is intended to protect and assure respect for indigenous peoples' social organisation, customs, languages, beliefs and traditions, and rights over their territories and possessions.

Articles 18–29 deal with the intellectual property of indigenous peoples. Among the important provisions of potential benefit to indigenous peoples are the following:

- the right to maintain the secrecy of traditional knowledge;
- the right to refuse access to traditional knowledge;
- the right to apply for IPR protection, which, in the case of collective knowledge, will be granted in the name of the community or society;
- the right of prior informed consent (to be given in writing) for access to, use of and application of traditional knowledge;
- the right to co-ownership of research data, patents and products derived from the research but without the community having to pay patent fees;

- and the right of communities to nullify patents illegally derived from their knowledge.

The Act would redefine patents and copyright by allowing community IPR to continue without time limit.

4. Other Initiatives: Traditional Resource Rights

Traditional Resource Rights (*TRR*) has emerged as a unifying concept that more accurately reflects indigenous peoples' views and concerns than narrower systems of rights such as IPR. The term TRR has been coined to reflect the necessity of reconceptualising the limited and limiting concept of IPR, while emphasising that a wide range of relevant international agreements exist to form the basis for a *sui generis* system of protection for traditional and indigenous peoples and their resources. Some of these rights and the international agreements which support them are identified in Appendix 3.

Specifically, a number of overlapping areas of international law and practice can be identified to provide the synthesis for an ideological basis for newly designed TRR-type systems at national and international levels.[13] Appendix 3 sets out these rights and others with the international agreements which support them. A highly significant feature of these rights is that they are overlapping and therefore mutually supportive or 'synergistic'.

TRR is an integrated rights concept which recognises the inextricable link between cultural and biological diversity, and sees no contradiction between the human rights of indigenous peoples, including the right to development and environmental conservation. Indeed, they are mutually supportive since the destiny of indigenous peoples largely determines and is determined by, the state of the world's biological diversity.

Traditional Resource Rights can be implemented locally, nationally and internationally as a set of principles to guide the *process of dialogue* between indigenous and local communities and governmental and non-governmental institutions. For example, TRR can guide the development of innovative contracts providing benefits from the transfer of traditional resources, new codes of ethics and standards of professional conduct, socially and ecologically responsible business practices, and holistic approaches to sustainability.

The Second Convention of the Parties (COPII) of the CBD has called for the development of a *sui generis* alternative to IPRs following the lines of TRR. It is anticipated that these principles will also guide discussions in GATT/WTO – and even the revision of the International Undertaking on Plant Genetic Resources (IUPGR) that must be harmonised with the CBD as well.

5. CONCLUSIONS AND RECOMMENDATIONS

The political legacy of ruthless exploitation of natural resources leading to ecological destruction – and the systematic annihilation and marginalisation of indigenous, traditional and local communities – leaves countries like Brazil unprepared to deal with the economic and political issues raised by global biodiversity developments. Although the country has acted to declare sovereign rights over flora, fauna and appropriate technologies for sustainable development and biodiversity conservation, legal structures and political institutions are inadequate or non-existent to protect, monitor or control access and transfer.

Some recent efforts attempt to establish alternative IPR regimes that will protect traditional resources while facilitating access. These proposals are fundamentally radical in that they recognise the collective and community-based nature of *in situ* biodiversity conservation, which implies recognition of indigenous land, territorial and resource rights. These rights are sometimes subsumed under the rubric of 'self-determination', historically seen as a threat to national sovereignty. However, with the rampant loss of biogenetic resources and traditional knowledge through biodiversity prospecting – by national, international and multinational interests – Brazil will have to forge equitable partnerships with indigenous peoples in order to attain local access to knowledge, flora and fauna.

The growing political awareness and effective international organisation of indigenous groups – combined with the ethical, moral and legal concerns of scientists co-opted by commercial concerns – means that actions to develop principles and guidelines for access, transfer and benefit-sharing will no longer await government paralysis. By the time Latin American governments actually do act to protect traditional resources, they may find their sovereign rights undermined by research moratoria, private corporations, government entrepreneurs, and extensive data banks of 'national patrimony' being beamed around the planet on the Internet.

It is unclear if biodiversity and biotechnology will dominate the future Brazilian economy, but it is certain that 'business as usual' will only lead to increased undermining of national sovereignty over traditional resources, as well as loss of local knowledge and the biodiversity that is inextricably linked to it.

To ensure that Brazil conserves and sustainably utilises its cultural and biogenetic resources in an equitable and sustainable manner, it is recommended that the following actions be taken.

1. Immediate enactment of *The Brazilian Indigenous Societies Act* (PL 2057/91) to protect the collective knowledge and biogenetic resources of indigenous and traditional peoples.

2. Urgent action to overturn *Decreto* 1.775 and similar decrees, laws or declarations that weaken indigenous and traditional peoples' land and territorial claims.

3. Vigorously uphold indigenous and *remanescente* communities' claims to their lands and territories, providing the political and economic backing necessary to effect all claims with the utmost expediency.

4. Development and expansion of national and regional centres to look at the wider use and application of indigenous and traditional 'knowledge, innovations and practices'.

5. Establishment of Resource and Advisory Centres for local communities on Traditional Resource Rights, Intellectual Property Rights, and general ways of protecting knowledge and biogenetic resources, while ensuring equitable benefit-sharing from authorised use.

6. Development of national laws that harmonise CBD agreements with human rights accords to ensure that healthy economic growth is balanced with concerns for conservation of biological and cultural diversity.

7. Assist indigenous and traditional communities to fund their own projects for conservation and self-development that include their own criteria for success and sustainability.

8. Strengthen the *Centro Nacional de Populações Traditionais*, including the extension of its mandate to include: (a) research into traditional knowledge and its application; (b) development of alternative and additional markets and necessary infrastructure to develop community-based product production; (c) provision of a legal service to advise and represent indigenous and local communities in disputes over unauthorised or inequitable use and exploitation of traditional knowledge, as well as floral and faunal resources.

9. Establish a *CNPq* (National Council for the Development of Science and Technology) *Special Programme for Ethnobiology and Ethnoecology*. This Programme would: (a) encourage the scientific investigation of indigenous and traditional knowledge, innovations, and practices that relate to use and management of forests, agriculture, savannahs, soils, ecosystems, watersheds, and so on; (b) stimulate and develop co-directed research projects and community-controlled natural resource inventories; (c) sponsor and catalyse land, territorial, and resource mapping; (d) provide fellowships and scholarships for students of ethnoecology; (e) develop a national plan for the equitable and effective use of traditional knowledge and biogenetic resources; (f) provide funding for such activities that stimulate, support and implement the national plan for ethnoecology and ethnobiology.

10. Provide to the Ministry of Justice, together with FUNAI (the National Foundation for the Indians) a mandate to develop a *special (sui generis) system for the protection* of the millennial, collective, diverse and inextricably cultural nature of indigenous and traditional knowledge,

including the extension of that knowledge in a way that respects local languages, societies and cultures. This would necessarily become a human rights-based system that would also provide guarantees of local control of access, self-determination, and equitable benefit sharing.

11. Develop a *Traditional Resource Rights process* that would: (a) identify international laws and agreements that Brazil has signed and/or ratified in order to identify areas of harmonisation, overlap or conflict; (b) establish a national strategy to synergise (and harmonise) all human rights, trade, sustainable development and environmental commitments.

APPENDIX 1: PRINCIPLES AFFECTING RIGHTS OF LOCAL COMMUNITIES

Key: *A = Article (CBD); P = Principle (RD); Pre = Preamble* (see spelling of acronyms at the end of Appendix 3)

I. Vital Role of Communities

- vital role of indigenous communities *(P22)*
- recognise and support Indigenous Peoples *(P22)*
- special protection for oppressed *(P23)*
- support of local populations *(A10d;P22)*
- local communities embodying traditional lifestyles *(Pre12;A8j)*
- local communities and *in situ* conservation *(A8j)*

II. Communities and the Precautionary Principle

- precautionary approach (principle) *(Pre9;P15)*
- restoration and compensation *(A14.2)*
- control of alien species/modified organisms *(A8g,h)*

III. Participation and Consent (Prior Informed Consent)

- effective citizen participation *(P10)*
- public awareness/decision-making/approval *(A8j;A13b;P10)*
- access to information/approval *(A15.5;A19.3,.4;P10)*

IV. Traditional Resource Rights

- traditional knowledge, innovation and practices *(A8j;P22)*
- wider application of knowledge, innovation and practices *(A8j)*
- protect and encourage customary use *(A10c)*
- indigenous and traditional technologies *(A18.4)*
- intellectual protection of technologies/IPR *(A16.2,.3,.5)*

V. Equity and Access

- fair and equitable sharing of benefits *(Pre12;A1;A8j;A15.7)*
- intergenerational sharing *(Pre23;P3)*
- access to information *(A14c;P10)*
- appropriate access to genetic resources *(A1;A15.2)*
- appropriate transfer of relevant technologies *(Pre15,16;A1;A16)*

VI. Special Actions

- remedial action *(A8f;A10d)*
- redress and remedy *(A14.2;P10)*
- appropriate funding *(Pre15,16;A1;A16.1;A20;A21)*

APPENDIX 2: MECHANISMS REQUIRING EFFECTIVE PARTICIPATION OF INDIGENOUS, TRADITIONAL AND LOCAL COMMUNITIES

I. CBD Institutional Participation

- Secretariat
- Subsidiary Bodies:
  - Scientific, Technical and Technological
  - (proposed) Traditional, Technical and Technological
- Clearing House Mechanism
  - (proposed) Traditional Knowledge, Innovations and Practices

II. National and Regional

- Environmental Impact Assessments (A14;P17)
- Country Studies (A6)
- National Surveys and Inventories (A7)
- Identification and Monitoring (A7)

III. Financial

- Incentive Measures (A11)
- Funding Mechanisms (GEF) (A21;A39)

IV. Human Resources

- Research, training and education
- Scientific and technical co-operation
- Exchange of information
- Repatriation of information

V. Protocols/Guidelines

- (proposed) Biosafety
- (proposed) Local Communities Embodying Traditional Lifestyles

APPENDIX 3: TRADITIONAL RESOURCE RIGHTS

TRR is based on the following bundles of rights:

RIGHT (bundle)	SUPPORTING AGREEMENTS: legally binding	SUPPORTING AGREEMENTS: non-legally binding
Human rights	ICESCR, ICCPR, CDW, CERD, CG, CRC, NLs	UDHR, DDRIP, VDPA
Right to self-determination	ICESCR, ICCPR	DDRIP, VDPA
Collective rights	ILO169, ICESCR, ICCPR	DDRIP, VDPA
Land and territorial rights	ILO169, NLs	DDRIP
Right to religious freedom	ICCPR, NLs	UDHR
Right to development	ICESCR, ICCPR, ILO169	DDHRE, DDRIP, DHRD, VDPA
Right to privacy	ICCPR, NLs	UDHR
Prior informed consent	CBD, NLs	DDRIP
Environmental integrity	CBD	RD, DDHRE
Intellectual property rights	CBD, WIPO, GATT, UPOV, NLs	
Neighbouring rights	RC, NLs	
Right to enter into legal agreements, such as contracts and covenants	NLs	
Cultural property rights	UNESCO-CCP, NLs	
Right to protection of folklore	NLs	UNESCO-WIPO, UNESCO-F
Right to protection of cultural heritage	UNESCO-WHC, NLs	UNESCO-PICC
Recognition of cultural landscapes	UNESCO-WHC	
Recognition of customary law and practice	ILO169, NLs	DDRIP
Farmers' rights		FAO-IUPGR

International Agreements Supporting the TRR Concept

Legally binding agreements in force (with number of States Parties):

CBD   =   Convention on Biological Diversity (1992), *States Parties*: 108 as at 31 Dec. 1994

CDW   =   Convention on the Elimination of all Forms of Discrimination Against Women (1979), *States Parties*: 138 as at 31 Dec. 1994

CERD   =   Convention on the Elimination of all Forms of Racial Discrimination (1966), *States Parties*: 142 as at 31 Dec. 1994

CG   =   Convention on the Prevention and Punishment of the Crime of Genocide (1948), *States Parties*: 116 as at 31 Dec. 1994

CRC   =   Convention on the Rights of the Child, *States Parties*: 168 as at 31 Dec. 1994

GATT   =   Final Act Embodying the Results of the Uruguay Round of Multilateral Trade Negotiations (1994)

ICESCR   =   UN International Covenant on Economic, Social and Cultural Rights (1966), *States Parties*: 131 as at 31 Dec. 1994

ICCPR   =   UN International Covenant on Civil and Political Rights (1966), *States Parties*: 129 as at 31 Dec. 1994

ILO169   =   International Labour Organisation Convention 169: Convention Concerning Indigenous and Tribal Peoples in Independent Countries (1989), *States Parties*: 7

NLs   =   National Laws

RC   =   Rome Convention for the Protection of Performers, Producers of Phonograms and Broadcasting Organisations (1961), *States Parties*: 47 as at 31 December 1994

UNESCO-WHC =   UNESCO Convention Concerning the Protection of the World Cultural and Natural Heritage (1972), *States Parties*: 135 AS AT 1 Jan. 1994

UNESCO-CCP   =   UNESCO Convention on the Means of Prohibiting and CCP Preventing the Illicit Import, Export and Transfer of Ownership of Cultural Property (1970), *States Parties*: 79 as at 1 Jan. 1994

UPOV   =   International Union for the Protection of New Varieties of Plants (1961, revised in 1972, 1978 and 1991), *States Parties*: 27 as at 31 Dec. 1994

WIPO   = The World Intellectual Property Organisation, which
                   administers international IPR agreements, such as:
                   – The Convention of Paris for the Protection of
                      Industrial Property (1883, revised most recently in
                      1967), *States Parties*: 129 as at 31 Dec. 1994
                   – The Berne Convention for the Protection of Literary
                      and Artistic Works (1886, revised most recently in
                      1971), *States Parties*: 111 as at 31 Dec. 1994
                   – The Madrid Agreement Concerning the International
                      Registration of Trademarks (1891, revised most
                      recently in 1967), *State Parties*: 43 as at 31 Dec.
                      1994
                   – The Lisbon Agreement for the Protection of
                      Appellations of Origin and their International
                      Registration (1958, revised most recently in 1967),
                      State Parties: 17 as at 31 Dec. 1994
                   – The Patent Cooperation Treaty (1970), *States
                      Parties*: 77 as at 31 Dec. 1994

Non-legal agreements:

DDHRE   = UN Draft Declaration of Principles on Human Rights
                   and the Environment (1994)
DDRIP   = UN Draft Declaration on the Rights of Indigenous
                   Peoples (formally adopted by the UN Working Group
                   on Indigenous Populations in July 1994)
DHRD   = UN Declaration on the Human Right to Development
                   (1986)
FAO-IUPGR   = FAO International Undertaking on Plant Genetic
                   Resources (1987 version)
RD   = Rio Declaration (1992)
UDHR   = Universal Declaration of Human Rights (1948)
UNESCO-F   = UNESCO Recommendations on the Safeguarding of
                   Traditional Culture and Folklore (1989)
UNESCO-PICC = UNESCO Declaration on the Principles of International
                   Cultural Cooperation (1966)
UNESCO-WIPO = UNESCO Model Provisions for National Laws on
                   Protection of Expressions of Folklore Against Illicit
                   Exploitation and Other Prejudicial Actions (1985)
VDPA   = UN Vienna Declaration and Programme of Action
                   (1993)

NOTES

1. P. P. Principe, The economic significance of plants and their constituents as drugs, in H. Wagner, H. Hikino and N. R. Farnsworth (eds), *Economic and medicinal plants research*, Volume 3, London and San Diego: Academic Press, 1989.
2. United Nations Development Programme, *Conserving indigenous knowledge: integrating two systems of innovation*, an independent study by Rural Advancement Foundation International, Commissioned by the United Nations Development Programme, New York: UN, 1994, p. 19.
3. See D. M. Warren, L. J. Slikkerveer and D. Brokensha (eds), *The cultural dimension of development: indigenous knowledge systems*, London: Intermediate Technology, 1995.
4. Defined by Gadgil et al. (p. 151) as 'A cumulative body of knowledge and beliefs handed down through generations by cultural transmission about the relationship of living beings (including humans) with one another and with their environment.' M. Gadgil, F. Berkes, and C. Folke, 'Indigenous knowledge for biodiversity conservation', *Ambio*, **22** (2–3) (1993): 151–156.
5. A.T. Durning, *Guardians of the land: indigenous peoples and the health of the Earth*, Worldwatch Paper 112, Washington, DC, 1992.
6. See D.A. Posey, 'International agreements and intellectual property rights for indigenous peoples', in T. Greaves (ed.), *Intellectual property rights for indigenous peoples: a sourcebook*, Oklahoma City: Society for Applied Anthropology, 1994, pp. 223–251.
7. Such useful species provide most of the foods, medicines, oils, essences, dyes, colours, repellents, insecticides, building materials and clothes needed by a local community.
8. See D.A. Posey, 'Indigenous management of tropical forest ecosystems: the case of the Kayapó Indians of Brazil', *Agroforestry Systems*, 3: 139.
9. S.B. Hecht and D.A. Posey, 'Management and classification of soils by the Kayapó Indians of Amazonia', in D.A. Posey and W. Balee (eds), *Resource management by Caboclos and Indians in Amazonia*, New York: New York Botanical Garden, 1988.
10. L. McIntyre, 'Last days of Eden', *National Geographic*, **174** (6) (1988): 800–817. See also D.A. Posey, G. Dutfield and K. Plenderleith, 'Collaborative research and intellectual property rights', *Biodiversity and Conservation*, **4** (8): 892–902.
11. See D.A. Posey and G. Dutfield, *Beyond intellectual property rights: towards traditional resource rights for indigenous peoples and local communities*, Ottawa: International Development Research Center, 1996, Appendix 1.
12. D.A. Posey, *Indigenous peoples and traditional resource rights: a basis for equitable relationships?*, Oxford: Green College Centre for Environmental Policy and Understanding, 1995.
13. See D.A. Posey, 'International agreements and intellectual property rights for indigenous peoples', in T. Greaves (ed.), *Intellectual property rights for indigenous peoples: a sourcebook*, Oklahoma City: Society for Applied Anthropology, 1994, pp. 223–251; D.A. Posey, 'Traditional resource rights (TRR): de facto self-determination for indigenous peoples', in L. van der Vlist (ed.), *Voices of the Earth: indigenous peoples, new partners & the right to self-determination in practice*, Amsterdam: Dutch Centre for Indigenous Peoples – NCIV – & International Books, 1994, pp. 217–235; D.A. Posey and G. Dutfield, *Beyond intellectual property rights: towards traditional resource rights for indigenous peoples and local communities*, Ottawa: IDRC, 1996.

Index